Sentinels of
Empire

Sentinels of Empire

THE UNITED STATES AND LATIN AMERICAN MILITARISM

Jan Knippers Black

CONTRIBUTIONS IN POLITICAL SCIENCE,
NUMBER 144

GREENWOOD PRESS
New York · Westport, Connecticut · London

Library of Congress Cataloging-in-Publication Data

Black, Jan Knippers, 1940–
   Sentinels of empire.

   (Contributions in political science, ISSN 0147-1066 ;
no. 144)
   Bibliography: p.
   Includes index.
    1. Civil-military relations—Latin America.
2. Latin America—Armed Forces—Political activity.
3. United States—Military relations—Latin America.
4. Latin America—Military relations—United States.
5. United States—Foreign relations—Latin America.
6. Latin America—Foreign relations—United States.
I. Title. II. Series.
JL956.C58B43   1986   322'.5'098   85-21850

ISBN 0-313-25155-X (lib. bdg. : alk. paper)

Library of Congress Catalog Card Number: 85-21850
ISBN: 0-313-25155-X
ISSN: 0147-1066

First published in 1986

Greenwood Press, Inc.
88 Post Road West
Westport, Connecticut 06881

Printed in the United States of America

The paper used in this book complies with the
Permanent Paper Standard issued by the National
Information Standards Organization (Z39.48-1984).

10 9 8 7 6 5 4 3 2 1

To my husband, Martin C. Needler

Contents

Acknowledgments

The author acknowledges with gratitude the assistance of the Inter-University Seminar on the Armed Forces and Society and the Stockholm International Peace Research Institute in funding portions of the research for this book. Special thanks are due also to Jorge Nef and Martin C. Needler for their critical comments on the manuscript, to Susan Hunter-Mullen for a careful proofreading, and to my typist, Ronna Kalish.

Some of those who very graciously provided information or insights, or who otherwise influenced my thinking in the preparation of this book, are listed in the bibliography. Many others who were helpful and influential will not be listed, as such notice might jeopardize their positions or their safety.

Prologue: Chile Revisited

The willows weep. But the poplars grow defiantly straight and tall, and the mountains still go wading in the sea. There is a haunting, deceptive sameness to the Chile I left in 1964. The streets still bustle with activity, at least in the daytime. But there is no music and no laughter. And no illusion.

There had been a building boom of sorts in the *barrio alto*, the upper-class residential district; but except for a short stretch of subway and a funny-looking tower, the inanimate structures of downtown Santiago are unchanged. Only the patched-up artillery holes in the presidential palace bear witness to the nightmare that has engulfed the Chilean people since I lived among them as an idealistic and hopelessly naive Peace Corps Volunteer.

The counterrevolution of September 11, 1973, that killed Chile's president, Salvador Allende, and replaced his democratically elected, socialist government with a Rightist military regime resulted in the massacre of thousands, the detention and torture

Note: For the protection of the author's friends and sources of information, their names have been changed.

of untold thousands more, the smothering of free expression and association, searches and seizures and burning of books and electoral rolls, and a precipitous drop in the standard of living of the majority.

One of the first things that had caught my eye upon my arrival in Chile in 1962 had been the legends scrawled on the walls that lined our route from the airport: "Cuba si, Yanqui no" and "Yanqui go home." I kidded later with my Chilean friends about those slogans, assuring them that I would feel at home in Chile because Yankees hadn't been very welcome where I came from in Tennessee either.

In fact, I had felt very much at home in Chile. In spite of a general resentment of the traditional U.S. role in the hemisphere, and of the more immediate irritant of the Bay of Pigs invasion of Cuba, I had arrived during an era of good feeling. Fondness for JFK was extraordinarily broadly based, and the volunteers tended to be viewed as an extension of Kennedy himself rather than of the traditional tentacles of U.S. interests. Even those at Right and Left extremes of the political spectrum had generally taken us to be well meaning and probably innocuous.

Returning in 1977, I found the walls ominously clean, and I did not feel at home. The era of good feeling had been a grim deception, and the slogans that were no longer scrawled on walls had been etched on faces.

My husband, Marty, and I had only a week to spend in Santiago and on the coast and a heavy agenda of people and places to see. After three years of courageous struggle and three bouts with the interrogators, my best friend, a journalist, had finally left the country. Other friends had been among the 300,000 or so who had escaped into exile during the first year of military rule. There were many more whose fate was unknown to me. It was most unlikely that my friends in the *poblaciones callampas* (literally "mushrooming" shantytowns), teetering then on the thin edge of survival, would have had the means to escape. They might be there still, if they had survived the holocaust. There were friends who had stayed behind to gnaw at the edges of inhumanity and some who had been unable to find a home in exile. And I had to face the painful possibility that some whom

I had considered friends might have stayed behind because they were thriving.

As Peace Corps Volunteers we had been able, in our working relationships as in our social ones, to hurdle the barricades of class in a manner that would not have been possible for us at home and that was not possible for Chileans in their own country. The Chileans had described themselves as a civilized people. They spoke scornfully of Argentina as the "long-play" country, in reference to its "33 revolutions per minute." Chile's president at that time, Jorge Alessandri, known affectionately or otherwise as "pelado" (baldy), walked alone every day from his modest apartment to his office in Moneda Palace. Chileans had never had a president assassinated, and they recoiled in horror at the level of social strife in the United States. As long as it was possible to believe that a "revolution in liberty," as Frei's campaign slogan promised, or a "peaceful road to socialism," as Allende had attempted, was possible, it had not seemed incongruous to have friends among the very rich as well as among the very poor. Surrounded now by the rubble of that shattered dream, it seemed a bit traitorous.

One of my first impulses in Santiago was to find out what had happened to TECHO, the urban community development organization that had employed a number of Peace Corps Volunteers. Most of all, I wanted to see Cecilia and her family in Población La Victoria, a shantytown on the outskirts of Santiago.

Cecilia had been in her late thirties when I lived in Chile. Her husband was an invalid, or so it was claimed, and Cecilia had had to raise the ten of her twelve children who survived infancy by herself. She was one of the driving forces behind our cooperative in La Victoria, where she worked as a seamstress. When we arrived in 1962, José Manuel, her baby of less than one year, was dying of dysentery; Bobbie, one of our Peace Corps nurses, saved his life.

Members of our production co-op generally lived much better than those of some of the other groups we worked with, such as the *papeleros* (paper-pickers) who collected, bundled, and sold the scraps of paper they could find on the streets. Cecilia's house had only two rooms and a dirt floor, but the walls were sturdy. Nevertheless, for her family survival was a daily challenge, and they met it with ingenuity, pride, and optimism. Physically, time had too soon taken its toll on Cecilia, as it was wont to do with the poorest of Chile's lovely women. But her children, without exception, were picture-book pretty. I had even had dark and never-spoken thoughts about trying to adopt one or two.

I had lost Cecilia's address soon after I left Chile and had had no word of the family since that time. La Victoria had not been among the very poorest of the *callampas*, but it had been among the better organized. Cecilia had been a Christian Democrat, but the Marxist parties had had a considerable following in the area. So when I heard about the occupation, shelling, or bombing— even napalming—of some of the *poblaciones callampas* in the course of the military takeover, I had a sickening fear for La Victoria and my Chilean family. Even if they had survived the open political strife, it was almost too much to hope that all of them had escaped the starvation that many observers claimed was now the more serious threat. At any rate, La Victoria was a huge shantytown. I didn't remember the layout, and I had little hope of being able to find Cecilia's family.

The TECHO office was listed in the telephone directory, though with a new address on the other side of the Mapocho River, so without any clues as to what we might find, we set out to pay it a visit. Except for the young man who answered the door and a middle-aged woman who was introduced as the executive secretary, the office was empty.

After I explained that I had once worked with TECHO, the executive secretary began to tell us in glowing terms about the prosperity of the organization and its wards. Stunned at such an upbeat report, I asked if TECHO still operated community centers and co-ops in La Victoria, José María Caro, Lo Barnechea, and other *callampas* I remembered. Her blank face suggested that she had never heard of these places. So I asked, where were their *callampa* operations? She replied that there are no *callampas* anymore—only clean, modern, prosperous communities. I was beginning to get the drift, and it became crystal clear when she went on to say that the women they worked with were learning that they wouldn't get anything by complaining—that they'd have to work for what they got. She worked herself into a frenzy talking about the horrors of the Allende government, particularly about how the poor people had refused to work anymore. She said that *rotos* (literally "broken ones") had put up shacks in her front yard in the *barrio alto*, that Allende supporters had pelted her with rocks when she participated in the March of the Empty Pots. And as the ultimate outrage, she, who had previously had servants of her own, had had to sell potatoes in the market in order to live.

I was aware that a great many of the popular institutions that had not been dissolved had been purged and taken over by the military regime, and I supposed, from the vehemence of her suppport for the junta, that she was a government agent. She said that the military had saved the country, that everything it had done had been absolutely necessary, and that she would do *anything* to prevent a resurgence of the "communists."

But an even more ominous thought occurred to me. In the surrealism of the situation, listening to this woman's near-hysterical monologue, I was reminded of a play presented by the University of Chile more than thirteen years earlier. "El Lugar Donde Mueren los Mamíferos" ("The Place Where Mammals Die") had dealt with the self-righteous, paternalistic upper-class ladies who fed their own egos by engaging in charity work with people for whom they had the utmost contempt. At the time I had thought it curious that the *callampa*-dwellers addressed Peace Corps Volunteers by first names and with the familiar pronoun "tu," while our middle-class Chilean counterparts were addressed as "Señora" and "Usted." Could it be that the "host country organization" Chileans we had worked with were of this caliber?

Frustrated and disoriented, I dragged Marty back across town and down to the Avenida Alameda toward Central Station in search of what had been the old TECHO office. I didn't remember the address, but Carrera Street looked familiar, so we walked down it until we came to a building I thought I recognized. A sign in the window bore the name of a cooperative that was new to me, so we gazed for a while, then turned to walk away. But I turned back again, wondering if I might be permitted just to glance at the interior and to see if the corn still grew tall in the patio. When the door opened, I thought for a moment that I was hallucinating. I was so caught up in my own attack of *déjà vu* I hardly noticed that the people who were gathering at the entrance hall were staring at me as if they were seeing a ghost. Then simultaneously we burst into screams and laughter and tears. It seems that when the TECHO office had moved, the workers, at least a great many of them, had stayed and formed their own co-op.

Their co-op had been relatively prosperous for a time—under the governments of Frei and Allende—but they were suffering very hard times now. All but one of the two dozen or so sewing machines were still. The previous year two customer firms had robbed them of the equivalent of about $5,000—one through a bad check and another through simply refusing to pay for merchandise delivered. When I asked if they had sought legal recourse, Alfonso, the manager, gave me a wry but benign smile that suggested that I was still a naive Peace Corps Volunteer. "There are no courts for poor people," he said.

It turned out that María, one of my old freinds at this co-op, had previously lived in La Victoria, and she and Alfonso offered to take us out in search of Cecilia's house. They had heard nothing of Cecilia's famly since the counterrevolution, so my heart was in my throat as we approached Población La Victoria. The neighborhood looked more livable in some ways than it had when I last saw it. Though most of the streets remained unpaved, there were sidewalks and even a few trees; but we saw no dogs or cats, not even the poor mangy and skeletal specimens that had been so abundant before.

The buildings that had housed TECHO's production co-op, clinic, nursery, and library were now being used by a center for Alcoholics Anonymous. The nearby chapel was understaffed; its regular priest had been imprisoned for refusing to inform on his parishioners. There was a relatively modern-looking government clinic in the community now, but its services, we were told, were available only to the fortunate few who had health insurance.

We finally found the little house where Cecilia had lived, and as we approached the gate it was opened by a pretty girl who appeared to be in her mid-twenties. With scarcely a moment's hesitation, she gasped "Juanita!" and threw her arms around me. Estela had been only twelve when I left, and they had heard nothing of me since, but even the newest member of the family, six-year-old Rosita, could recite all the stories about "Juanita"; and she insisted on occupying my lap or clinging to my legs the whole time I was there.

To my relief and amazement, Cecilia, her husband, and all nine of the children I had known were alive and well, and some now had children of their own. Cecilia's husband was there, no longer bedridden, but looking very old, along with Alejandro, the eldest son, about twenty, and José Manuel, now fourteen and looking remarkably healthy. But Cecilia and two of her daughters were away at the time, working as maids, and the other three children were scattered around the neighborhood.

Estela prepared *aguita* (boiling water over mint leaves) for us on a makeshift stove. She explained that they had had a real stove, but that times were bad and that only a few months after they bought it they had had to sell it again for only a fraction of what they had paid. She added that for the past two years her husband had been unable to find work, but that she had had piecework from time to time as a seamstress. We had to leave after a few minutes for an appointment downtown—ironically, at the new, luxurious Santiago Sheraton, which seemed to be light-years away—but we promised to return later when Cecilia would be at home.

We went back to La Victoria in a taxi, and I didn't realize that we had passed the house until Marty called my attention to a diminutive woman tearing down the street behind us. Cecilia had chased our cab for two blocks. This time all of the family had gathered in, and it was a highly emotional reunion.

They had not talked much earlier about their situation, perhaps because Alfonso and María had been with us, but now it all began to spill out; they had been living a nightmare. At the time of the overthrow of Allende, tanks had been stationed for a week on three sides of the intersection beside their house. Artillery shells had exploded in their front yard, breaking out the windows and imbedding shrapnel in the face and neck of Cecilia's husband.

Alejandro had been in the military at the time, but instead of shooting or arresting people who were caught out after curfew, he helped them to get home safely. For this he was accused of subversion and confined for three months in a box of about four feet by four feet; when he was finally released he had to be hospitalized for another three months. Several members of the family had been subjected to various indignities when they approached the Ministry of Defense to inquire about Alejandro. Cecilia herself had been imprisoned and tortured for fifteen days. She had scars on her back where she had been burned and on her head, which had been cracked open and stitched together again. She believes that she was finally able to convince her interrogators that she was not a communist when she produced pictures and letters from Peace Corps Volunteers. Cecilia's "crime" apparently had been her spunk. She wasn't about to let those animals in uniform push her around. And in this she was unreformed.

Cecilia's family had been more fortunate than some of their neighbors; they had survived. They told of seeing a three-year-old across the street machine-gunned to death. All of the men in the house next door had been dragged into the street in the middle of the night and beaten mercilessly. Another man on the block had been imprisoned and tortured for several months. He seemed to be mentally stable when he was released, but shortly thereafter he saw a mother strike a child, and he cracked up for keeps. There had been one man in La Victoria who was financially in much better shape than his neighbors. Convinced that he would prosper under the military regime, he celebrated the takeover by taking all his furniture out into the street and making a bonfire of it. Now he lives without furniture.

Just in case anyone had failed to get the message, the tanks reappeared, Cecilia said, each year on the anniversary of the counterrevolution, along with banners stretched across the streets, which said, "If the people rise up again, there will be another 11th of September." But the worst of the political terror had passed. The day-to-day source of terror was hunger. Some days, Cecilia said, they just don't eat. It had not been easy, when I was there in the early 1960s, for the men of communities like La Victoria to find jobs; now, they said, it was almost impossible.

Women had always been the backbone of such communities, partly because of the greater availability of jobs as maids. Most of the work to be found now was short term or piecemeal. And the workers were cheated in every imaginable way. Employers would advertise so many pieces or so many hours of work for so much pay, but when the work was done they might pay half of what had been promised, or whatever they chose to pay. Cecilia asked, rhetorically, what was the worker to do, where could he turn? There were no authentic unions, no courts, no government agencies open to poor people. There was only the Church, and it was overwhelmed with the most urgent cases and kept on a short leash.

As we started to leave, Estela retrieved copies of the Jesuit magazine *Mensaje* and of a sermon by the archbishop from their hiding places and urged us to take them back with us to the United States. There is among Chileans at all social levels a nagging fear that the rest of the world doesn't know what is happening to them, and an unfaltering faith that if the world knew it would make a difference.

The discussion that follows takes place for the most part on an abstract plane. The unpowerful are dealt with only in the aggregate. Nevertheless, the protagonists of this story are real people like Cecilia and her family.

Sentinels of
Empire

1

Confronting Nationalism and Social Change in Latin America

The nature of the relationship between the United States and the nations of Latin America has always been obscured both by official rhetoric and by the benign national self-image held by most Americans. Well-meaning Americans would like to believe that the policies adopted and actions undertaken by the United States toward Latin America are designed to promote the well-being of all the peoples of the hemisphere. In fact, however, "reasons of state" are rarely as they seem. Even more rarely do they reflect the preponderance of national will, or public opinion.

George Kennan warned in 1947 that the Soviet Union would continue to expand its sphere of influence wherever it met no counterforce, but the behavior of the Soviet Union in that regard is in no way unusual. The same principle has been applicable to the behavior of all great powers, including the United States. It has been reflected, in particular, in the behavior of the United States in the Western Hemisphere.

As one counterforce after another was defeated (Mexico in the war of 1846–1848, Spain in the war of 1898–1902) or edged out (Great Britain and to a lesser extent other European contenders, in the course of two world wars), the United States spread westward and southward. It more than doubled the size of its original territory and expanded its sphere of influence first into Central America and the Caribbean, then on to the Spanish Main, Brazil, and the Andean countries, and, finally, the Southern Cone. The period since World War II has witnessed the consolidation of U.S. hegemony, or dominance, over the furthermost reaches of the South American continent and the incorporation into the U.S. fold of Caribbean ministates, belatedly shifting from European (mainly British) to U.S. suzerainty.

The strategy for containing and controlling political change in the area was firmly established in the 1930s when U.S. marines, retreating from Central American and Caribbean countries they had occupied, left behind well-trained and well-funded local constabularies to protect the claims of U.S. corporations and the governments and political leaders favored by U.S. policymakers against challenges from less favored local contenders, particularly those who presumed to speak for the lower classes. These constabularies understood very well that their first-line base of support was the U.S. government rather than any element of the national population. The constabulary solution had not been the only means of keeping the Latin American states responsive to the wishes of U.S. governments, but until recently it had generally proved to be a very effective last resort.

Since World War II, no extra-hemispheric power has posed a credible challenge to the dominant role of the United States in any Latin American state except Cuba. The only remaining counterforce in the rest of Latin America is that of the Latin American people. Their only weapon is numbers and their only means of employing that weapon is through organization. Thus, just as it is not Western capitalism, but rather independent political and labor organization—the underpinnings of democracy—that threatens Soviet interests in Eastern Europe, it is not Soviet-style "communism," but rather democracy itself that threatens the dominance of the United States in Latin America.[1]

THE TRAPS FOR LATIN AMERICAN NATIONALISTS

There are many reasons for the failure of democracy to take root or to reach maturity in most Latin American countries. The interference of the United States is only one of them; but the obstacles posed by U.S. hegemony have become more apparent and more frustrating to Latin American nationalists as other obstacles have been overcome.

The highly stratified social and political systems of most Latin American countries can be traced to armed conquest. The system of exploitation based on the conquest of native Americans and the enslavement of transplanted Africans ultimately acquired a measure of legitimacy as it was moderated and condoned through the religious system imposed by the conquerors. The violent roots of inequality were gradually obscured as subsequent generations were taught that differential reward and punishment derived from divine purpose or merit. Those who dared to challenge that interpretation of the social reality were considered subversives.

In most Latin American countries, at least until the twentieth century, political participation was limited to a very small economic elite of European origin. Intra-elite competition—among landholding families and later between landholders and representatives of commerce and industry—was regulated through face-to-face encounters in social or business settings. When compromise failed, the outcome was sometimes determined by clashes between more or less private armies. The constitutional and legal systems that had been borrowed, after independence was achieved, from France and the United States served merely to legitimize political arrangements that had been reached in private—through intrigue or through force.

The dominance of the economic elite was underwritten, in general, by military and/or paramilitary forces, by the Roman Catholic Church, and by a colonial or hegemonic power. In providing force, material resources, or moral sanction to the ruling classes, these institutions and foreign powers acquired or maintained a measure of power in their own right in the emerging societies of Latin America. The conquering class was protected and "legitimized" by Spanish and Portuguese troops and clergymen for some 300 years. After independence, the hegemony that had been exercised by Spain and Portugal was assumed by other powers, predominantly Great Britain at first and later the United States.

Given the gradual demise of a rural subsistence economy, beginning in the nineteenth century, and increasing urbanization, education, and the spread of mass communication in the twentieth century, mounting pressure for fundamental changes in the social structure was to be expected. The question, then, was what the nature of that change would be. To the extent that the elite found it necessary to share power, accepting the participation of new groups in the political system, nonviolent change, mediated through more or less democratic systems, became possible. Where for reasons of extreme social distance, of prejudice and paranoia based on racial and ethnic difference, the aristocracy has concluded that it *dare* not expand political participation, and/or for reasons of reliable support from the United States government the elite has concluded that it *need* not expand political participation, the outcome has been either successful revolution or inconclusive cycles of insurgency and counterinsurgency. In fact, such intransigence on the part of elites has been most notable in Middle America and the Caribbean, the areas earliest and most overwhelmingly dominated by the United States.

In countries where the middle classes succeeded in their bids for participation, the rituals associated with electoral and parliamentary systems began to take on a serious function. Latin America's middle classes, however, have generally lacked independent sources of wealth; they have been salaried classes, derived from and dependent upon the expansion of commerce and government. Their bid for effective participation, beginning in the late nineteenth century in Argentina and continuing into the late twentieth century in Central America and the Andean highlands, could not rest upon their material resources or upon their own numbers alone. They found it necessary to incorporate the numbers and the potential disruptiveness of peasants and/or urban manual laborers into their power bases.

Middle-class bids for political power have generally been spear-headed by university students and intellectuals and carried to fruition by political parties, but they have rarely been success-ful unless they were believed to have the backing of organized labor. Thus the effectiveness of the ballot box has been pre-ceded by an effective demonstration of power on the streets, on the farms, and in the factories.

The effectiveness of democratic processes introduced with middle-class participation has been limited, however. Middle-class leaders have generally proved unable or unwilling to ex-tend full participation, through the electoral system, to urban workers and peasants. Even in those few countries where de-mocracy has appeared to be well entrenched, constitutional systems have been undermined by economic decline, which sharpened competition between middle and lower classes.

Uruguay enjoyed one of the world's most fully democratic systems and most highly developed welfare states during the first half of the twentieth century. That system began to un-ravel, however, when the country began to suffer economic re-verses in the 1950s. By 1973 it had succumbed to counterrevo-lution. Uruguay's early good fortune does not seem likely to be replicated in Latin America in the near future. Recent devel-opments in Latin America suggest that while a middle class may still rise to the full exercise of political rights through demo-cratic processes, it has become even more difficult, in the late twentieth century, for manual workers and peasants to do so.

At least in Latin America, and perhaps in most states under the dominance of major powers, limited democracy contains the seeds of its own destruction. The greater the proportion of the population participating in elections and other political pro-cesses and the longer the unbroken tenure of constitutional rule, the more policy will incline toward national self-determination and toward redistribution of wealth and opportunity. Such a course of events is seen as threatening not only by middle and upper classes of the country in question but by foreign inves-tors and the U.S. government as well.

The middle class, dependent upon salaries from the govern-ment or property-holding classes and insecure in its status, be-gins to align itself with the upper class. These classes, seeing their power ebbing away and their economic interests in jeopardy, lose confidence in the constitutional system. They enlist military and paramilitary forces and the government of the United States in the defense of their interests. The demise of the constitutional system and the abrupt constriction of political participation are then explained and justified as confronting the Soviet-Cuban menace and blocking the spread of communism.

Whereas in Latin American countries that have undergone successful revolution the link between the armed forces and the United States has generally been broken, military establishments in the countries that have followed a more or less democratic path of development have been increasingly trained and supported by, and consequently available to, the United States. Thus counterrevolution is most likely and most violent precisely in those systems that have achieved the highest levels of political development through democratic processes.

As the constitutional system is dismantled, the military establishment as a whole assumes the role of a ruling elite. Civilian instigators and supporters of counterrevolution soon find that military rulers are not content to become their pawns. Nor are such rulers content to become pawns of the United States. While economic policy initially conforms to the interests of U.S. investors, over time it increasingly reflects the institutional and personal interests of military officers themselves. Meanwhile, the systematic violation of human rights becomes an embarrassment to U.S. policymakers. The United States then becomes, in a sense, a hostage to the Frankensteins it has created but cannot control.

THE TRAPS FOR U.S. POLICYMAKERS

Why would the United States, which claims to seek peace and stability in the Western Hemisphere, commit itself to the support of intransigent elites in the least developed countries, thereby making nonviolent change impossible and violent change inevitable? Why would the United States, while purporting to seek democracy for Latin America, conspire with ambitious generals in the more highly developed countries to undermine and topple elected governments? How are we to explain a pattern in actual U.S. policy toward Latin America that runs counter to the founding principles of our own nation and that systematically defeats the goals of stated policy?

The Implications of the Security Issue

The general thrust of U.S. policy toward Latin America has varied little since the issuance of the Monroe Doctrine in 1823. That doctrine, utterly unrealistic and unenforceable at the time of its enunciation, expressed the ambition of drawing all of Latin America into the U.S. sphere of interest. Foreign intervention, political as well as military, was to be seen as threatening to the "peace and safety" of the United States.

While it is clear that security interests have always loomed large in the shaping of U.S. policy, it is less clear how such interests are defined and limited. The concept of security is eminently elastic. The boundaries of what is to be secured stretch to encompass whatever the policymaking body has, or thinks it has, or thinks it should have. Thus as the United States, over the course of the twentieth century, has expanded its stakes in Latin America—through private investment, through the emplacement of military installations, and through the cultivation of economic, political, and military elites—it has expanded concomitantly its security interests and the threats to those interests.

As U.S. power grew and the actual threat of European intervention in Latin America diminished, nationalism, expressed in resentment of U.S. influence, came to be seen by U.S. policymakers as essentially foreign-inspired and thus threatening to U.S. security. In combatting nationalism and incipient nationalist movements, the United States, in turn, has validated their arguments and contributed to their growth. United States hostility has also increased the likelihood that such movements would adopt "alien" creeds (e.g., Marxism) and, in some cases, seek alien support. In the manner of a self-fulfilling prophecy, this, in turn, reinforces the perception among U.S. policymakers of threat to the national security.

Given the elasticity of the concept of security, it is clear that it encompasses economic as well as military and other bureaucratic interests. Ultimately, of course, the limits of security interests and security threats must be sought in the minds of policymakers.

The Intertwining of Economic and Military Interests

A 1951 enumeration of U.S. military objectives in Latin America began as follows: "One is to secure the sources of strategic materials, such as the petroleum fields of Venezuela, the tin mines of Bolivia, and the copper mines of Chile; secondly to keep open the lines of access to those strategic materials . . . "[2] One means of securing such resources is to own them. Or was it, in some cases, that they had to be secured because U.S. companies already owned them?

United States policy toward Latin America has always stressed the maintenance of access to strategic materials, but open, friendly, and reliable trading relationships have rarely been seen as an adequate means of securing that objective. Instead, the objective has found expression typically in attempts to influence internal power relationships or to maintain access for private U.S.-based companies. The global exploits of U.S.-based companies have traditionally been viewed by U.S. policymakers as ensuring the availability of vital resources at "reasonable" prices, as impacting in a positive manner on the balance of payments, and as furthering U.S. foreign-policy goals. It is partly the case, however, that the foreign-policy goals which the activities of U.S. companies subserve are only policy goals because the power positions of these companies have made it possible for them, through the years, to assume a preponderant role in the very definition of the goals of foreign policy.

Thus U.S. foreign policy has traditionally stressed the promotion of open markets, free enterprise, and a welcome mat for foreign investments—goals which have been presented as in the general interest of mankind. The position of the national Petroleum Council, for example, that "the participation of U.S. nationals in the development of world oil reserves is in the interest of all nations and essential to our national security"[3] has typically been echoed by the Department of State. This symbiosis of public and private power has been continuously reinforced by the revolving door for personnel between the largest banks and corporations and the upper echelons of government.

The material interests to be pursued in Latin America have varied over the years in tandem with the evolution of the U.S. and international capitalist systems. From a concentration early in the century on the extraction of primary products, the purchase of government bonds, and the pursuit of markets for U.S.-manufactured goods, these interests were refocused in the 1950s and 1960s on direct investment in manufacturing for local consumption. In the 1970s and 1980s, U.S. interests have become more heavily involved in manufacturing for export and in the direct extraction of capital through stock market operations and interest on loans.

Competition for Latin American markets and for the fruits of Latin American land and labor increased markedly in the late 1960s and early 1970s as the economies of Western Europe and Japan recovered from World War II and leaped ahead in technology. Nevertheless, in absolute terms, the stakes of U.S.-based corporations in Latin American national economies have continued to grow steadily.

Official assessments of the U.S. strategic or security interests in the hemisphere have been based, to a considerable extent, on the material interests described above. However, as the role of protecting these and other interests has been assumed by various governmental departments and agencies, including in particular the Department of Defense and the various intelligence agencies, the bureaucracies involved have developed various interests of their own. These bureaucratic interests tend to go beyond the minimal requirements of maintaining a hospitable climate for foreign investment in systems otherwise free to choose their own forms of social organization to the idea of control for its own sake.

Moreover, as the roles of the Pentagon and the intelligence agencies in the making and implementation of policy have been strengthened vis-a-vis the roles of the Department of State and the various development agencies, the concept of control (generally referred to by the less intimidating term "influence") has been more tightly drawn and the categories of individuals, groups, policies, and ideas seen as threatening to U.S. security have been expanded.

The Perceptual Nature of Security

In the absence of an immediate military threat to the national territory of the United States, there is no such thing as an objective assessment of security threats. Security and insecurity lie in the minds of the strategists. Thus the Reagan Administration, in 1983, perceiving a threat to U.S. national security, launched an invasion of the tiny, distant island state of Grenada. The most nearly credible of the many rationales presented by administration spokesmen for that action was fear that if it did not invade the United States would be viewed as a "paper tiger."

The "paper tiger"or "pitiful helpless giant" insecurity complex has been cited at some point by virtually every U.S. administration since World War II to explain strategic goals and military actions that are otherwise inexplicable. It was cited repeatedly throughout the Vietnam War years and has been the fallback rationale for the mushrooming military involvement in Central America in the 1980s. If we cannot control the little countries in our own backyard, the argument goes, how can our allies and our enemies take us seriously? In fact, such evidence as is available suggests that what is in doubt among U.S. allies and enemies alike is not whether or not the United States will use its military power but whether or not it will use that power in a rational manner.

The first step for U.S. policymakers into this particular kind of credibility trap is the declaration that some distant or relatively insignificant and powerless state is "vital" to U.S. security. It follows that events in an area or a state that is vital must be controlled from the United States.

No rational person could discount the military power of the United States, but obviously there are limits to the efficacy of military "solutions" to political problems. Nor is there room for doubt that the American people have the political will to defend themselves. But there are clearly limits to the willingness of the American people to defend governments of dubious legitimacy in distant lands. If policymakers proceed, nevertheless, to make extensive commitments on the basis of such casual declarations of vital interest, their fears of loss of credibility may become self-fulfilling. It has commonly been the case that the individuals, groups, or nations whose wealth and power would appear to make them most secure are, in fact, most paranoid; by their frenetic attempts to ensure their security, they threaten to bring on their own destruction.

All U.S. administrations, whether Democratic or Republican, liberal or conservative, base their policies toward Latin America on considerations of security, including the security of U.S. business and banking interests. However, as we shall see, there are appreciable differences in the manner in which administrations from opposing extremes of the U.S. political spectrum assess security threats and respond to them.

VARIATIONS ON A THEME: THE RANGE OF U.S. POLICY

There are those who would say that the difference between liberal and conservative U.S. administrations in foreign policy, particularly toward Latin America, has been a difference merely of style. The objectives and long-term consequences, they would say, have been the same. That may well be true. But the short term is the term we live in, and in the short term that difference of style may mean the difference between life and death for thousands of Latin Americans. Thus it is worthwhile to try to understand the range of U.S. postures and the short-term differences in policies and consequences from one extreme of that range to the other.

The basic premises upon which U.S. policy is constructed are that: (1) what is good for U.S. business is good both for the United States and for its client states; and that (2) the United States must control the states within its sphere of influence in order that it not be viewed by allies and enemies alike as a "paper tiger." Thus the ends of policy—stability (good business climate) and influence (the option, at least, of control from the centers of power in the United States)—are not subject to reappraisal, but the means are. This latitude for debate over the means brackets the range within which U.S. policy fluctuates.[4] The former president of Venezuela, Rómulo Betancourt, speaking in Madrid on October 30, 1980, said, "There is a difference between Carter and Reagan which we Latin Americans readily appreciate. Whenever the Republican Party has governed the United States, the White House and the Department of State have favored dictatorial regimes."[5]

The distinction between the parties is not actually that clearcut. There have been Democratic presidents, Lyndon Baines Johnson, for example, who also, on balance, favored dictatorship. Furthermore, Republican administrations have occasionally elevated liberals to policymaking roles, and Democratic administrations have always included some policymakers of authoritarian bent. In general, however, Democratic administrations have been more inclined than Republican ones to tolerate democratic tendencies in Latin American and other client states.

The prototypical position at the extreme Right of the range of U.S. policy is one of militant "anticommunism," at the extreme Left a liberal stance of enlightened (and confused) national self-interest, and at the extreme Center, a position brazenly pragmatic, for interests both private and bureaucratic. The ideological Left—by definition, those who challenge the basic premises—is excluded from the debate.

The Ideological Right

The ideological Right exudes nostalgia for the straightforward imperialism of Theodore Roosevelt. A measure of the potential size of its domestic constituency, the populist Right, was to be found in the level of steadfast opposition to the Panama Canal treaties negotiated by the Carter Administration or the level of consistent support for Reagan's Central America policies. The ideological Right draws heavily upon national myths and symbols. Such myths, and the prescriptions that flow from them, reflect to some extent the interests of the domestic power elite but at an earlier stage in its evolution. Imbedded in folk culture, these myths have not changed with transformations in the spheres of international finance and transnational corporate enterprise.

The ideological Right yearns to show the flag, even when pragmatists would consider such display counterproductive. It favors military assistance but resists the proffering of economic aid, whereas pragmatists deal themselves into the aid programs. While pragmatists lust after a market of a billion consumers, the ideological Right would shun mainland China and deal only with Taiwan.

Adherents of the ideological Right, such as businesses that for one reason or another—size, immobility of assets, lack of vertical integration or global reach—lack flexibility,[6] can call upon a number of think tanks; among them is the Heritage Foundation, which provided much of the early policy planning of the Reagan Administration. But the most formidable standard-bearers of this position, in the making and implementation at least of policy toward the Third World, are to be found in the armed forces and in the clandestine operations branches of the intelligence agencies.

The first-line constituency of the U.S. ideological Right in Latin America is the military and paramilitary establishments (generally including the police) of the area. Like its constituents, the ideological Right tends to be impatient with the uncertainties and disorderliness of even the most limited and elitist democracies, preferring instead outright military dictatorship. The "excesses" of such dictatorships are readily excused as necessary to counter or prevent insurrection and the installation of communist regimes.

The Liberals

Prototypical liberals envision the evolution of the Latin American states, with the benevolent assistance of the U.S. public and private sectors, in the direction of an idealized conception of the U.S. political and socioeconomic systems.[7] Liberals, representing a relatively broad segment of the U.S. population (as suggested, for example, by public opinion polls in the mid-1970s favoring a human rights policy), respond, in turn,

to a relatively broad segment of Latin American populations.
Having links with academicians, journalists, clergymen, and
leaders of middle-class parties such as the Christian Democrats, U.S. liberals react strongly when the level of repression
in Latin American states rises to the point of threatening those
groups.

Liberals of John F. Kennedy's New Frontier argued that reform was an antidote to revolution and that democracy (ex-
cluding "Marxists," of course) would generate in the long run
more stable governments. Such governments would provide a
more predictable setting for U.S. business ventures than besieged dictatorships were able to offer. Furthermore, a posture
of support for democracy and social reform would reap a more
favorable attitude toward the United States on the part of the
Latin American people and, thus, more durable U.S. influence.
In the event that popular mobilization began to get out of hand,
U.S.-trained armed forces and police would maintain order.

When it appeared, however, that mobilization was indeed
getting out of hand, that reform might turn out to be a precur-
sor, rather than an antidote, to revolution, or that, at the very
least, effective democracy might not prove to be a boon to U.S.
investors after all, the New Frontier liberals were forced to admit defeat, to retreat or defect—in effect, to concede the upper
hand to the practitioners of *Realpolitik*.

The opportunity that had been available to the Kennedy Administration, of bulwarking democracy and promoting economic reform, was not available to the liberals of the Carter
Administration. It appeared that the most they might be able
to accomplish would be mitigation of the harshness of military
rule.

The position of the liberal contingent of the Carter Administration at its inception was most clearly articulated in the report
of the Commission on United States-Latin American Relations
(1974), chaired by Sol M. Linowitz. It condemned both unilateral U.S. military intervention, as directed against the Dominican Republic in 1965, and covert U.S. involvement in domestic
politics, as occurred in Chile in the early 1970s. It also argued
that genocide and other atrocities, apart from being morally rep-
rehensible, were counterproductive. "Such actions," the report noted, "generally lead to discord and instability."

As was true of the Kennedy-era liberals, it was the partial successes of the Carter Administration liberals, rather than their failures, that proved their undoing. Central American dictatorships, in particular, began to teeter when U.S. support was called into question; but the co-optable center the United States sought as a replacement was nonexistent. As the ultimate absurdity, 300 Salvadoran officers undergoing a special training program in counterinsurgency at the U.S. School of the Americas in the former Panama Canal Zone in the fall of 1980 were receiving instruction in human rights as well.[8]

To note that an administration that attempts to assume a liberal posture in foreign affairs is inevitably swallowed up sooner or later (and usually sooner) by its own contradictions is not to discredit the compassionate, courageous, and clearheaded among its ranks; it is merely to point out that the deck is stacked very heavily against them.

The prototypical positions outlined above mark the extremes of the range of acceptable debate. No administration can be expected to assume such a position in all, or even the majority, of its policies and actions. Positions on either extreme of the range are largely rhetorical—a matter of tone. Tone is not unimportant because it provides the cues from which Latin American constituencies proceed to extemporize.[9]

In fact, however, administrations launched from either extreme of this range are drawn more and more toward the center—that is, the pragmatic Right—as their terms in office progress. Whereas on the campaign trail the candidate must be mindful first of the party, then of the electorate as a whole, once in office a president and his coterie remain accessible to big business while distancing themselves from the unaffluent and unpowerful. Moreover, bureaucracies, in addition to being colonized by private interests, have interests of their own, and presidents tend to become captives rather than masters of their bureaucracies.

The Pragmatic Right

Unlike the tenants of the extremes of the range, the pragmatic Right has little popular following as such in the United States. It benefits, however, from the general inattention of the public to the business-as-usual of foreign affairs, from the carefully implanted notion that the affairs of state are too complex for the layman to understand, and from the obfuscatory bureaucratic code (not to mention outright lies) in which the debate is conducted. It benefits also from the general inertial resistance to innovative policy.

The pragmatic Right is the position of the modern-day robber barons—the giants of banking and transnational corporate enterprise—and the bureaucracies of business, government, and international financial institutions that serve them. Anchored neither to myths of an American past nor to visions of a Latin American future, architects of this position are free to protect assets and pursue profits in the manner befitting the moment.

The policymakers most nearly in tune with this position are those who bring to their roles little ideological baggage apart from a general predisposition to support big business. Like the liberals, pragmatists favor economic aid because they are, after all, the prime beneficiaries. They can be generous about turning the canal over to Panama; it was government property anyway. But the expropriation of private property is another matter. Like ideological Rightists, pragmatists would stop at nothing short of nuclear war to topple the government of Fidel Castro, but unlike ideological Rightists they seek to do business with his government in the interim.

Pragmatists do not oppose democracy in principle, only in practice. They can deal with elected civilian governments so long as they are narrowly based and sufficiently solicitous of foreign capital. Nor are they duty-bound to stand by tyrannical allies. They are willing to abandon a Trujillo or a Somoza whose atrocities are such as to give anticommunism a bad name, provided that a co-optable replacement can be found.

Pragmatists prefer subtle control to ostentatious muscle-flexing. They are concerned about their corporate images and about the image of the United States as a benevolent ally. They are not necessarily provoked by rhetorical anti-Americanism. Apart from expropriation, the prospects they fear most are default on foreign debts and effective labor organization.

A typical exposition of the position of the pragmatic Right, the report of the 1969 official mission of Nelson Rockefeller to

Latin America, featured recommendations for a liberalization of trade with the area and for increases in both economic and military aid. The fact that Rockefeller's visit to Brazil coincided with a period of dramatic increase in the systematic use of torture and in the activity of the death squads did not deter him from calling for a major expansion in U.S. assistance programs for Latin American military and police forces.

Likewise, a 1980 report of the Council of the Americas, which speaks for more than 200 corporations having interests in Latin America, recommended the extension of the Generalized System of Preferences to allow increased Latin American exports to the United States. It also recommended more generous funding for the Export-Import Bank and the Overseas Private Investment Corporation. It solicited greater U.S. government protection against expropriation and pointed out that politically motivated trade sanctions penalize U.S. companies. The report gave special attention to Central America and the Caribbean, calling for increases in both economic and military assistance in order to prevent "additional Cubas."

Beyond 1984: Big Brother Is a Pragmatist

True to the usual pattern of presidential accommodation, Reagan the ideologue has become a pragmatist on most of the matters of greatest concern to transnational corporate and banking interests. To the horror of his long-term loyalists on the ideological Right, he has embraced China; he has given generously of the taxpayers' money to the International Monetary Fund and to the hard loan programs of the World Bank and other international financial institutions; and he has greatly expanded some programs of economic as well as military aid, especially in the Middle East and in Central America and the Caribbean. He has also dealt sympathetically with many U.S. companies that have moved their manufacturing operations to areas of cheaper labor markets and now export their products back to the United States.

Reagan has continued to cater to his original base on the ideological Right, however, through his rhetoric, his massive arms buildup, and his direct military intervention in Central America

and the Caribbean. Flush from the popular victory of his invasion of Grenada, he entered the electoral arena in 1984 proudly
sporting his Teddy Roosevelt hat.

A Democratic victory in 1984 would almost certainly have
made a major short-term difference in foreign policy generally
and in policy toward Central America in particular. The covert
war against Nicaragua would probably have been de-escalated,
and eventually a modus vivendi with the Sandinista leadership
would have been sought. Efforts to undermine that leadership
by nonmilitary means, however, would have continued. A
Democratic administration probably also would have sought a
negotiated settlement to the conflict in El Salvador. The settlement and consequent civil peace would have been short-lived,
however, as the U.S. government attempted to co-opt the Center-Left political leaders and to detach them from their popular
bases.

The Democrats, however, never stood much of a chance to
gain the upper hand in the foreign policy debates of 1984. Those
Democrats who dared to try to reeducate the U.S. electorate were
automatically discounted as serious candidates for the party's
nomination. And the circumscribed and convoluted arguments
that characterize the prototypical liberal position lack the intel-
lectual clarity and moral force necessary to confront a combination of "Red scare" and the headiness of straightforward imperialism.

NOTES

1. Even Cold Warrior Zbigniew Brzezinski, President Carter's national security advisor, virtually conceded the point in a warning to
the incoming Reagan Administration. "There is a similarity of relationship," he said, "between the United States and Central America
and the Soviet Union in Eastern Europe . . . If the workers of Gdansk
have a right to demand decent wages and hours, the peasants of El
Salvador and Nicaragua have a right to demand land." *New York Times*,
January 13, 1981, p. 11.

2. Raymond Estep, "United States Military Aid to Latin America,"
Maxwell Air Force Base, Air University, Aerospace Studies Institute,
Documentary Research Division, September 1966, p. 58.

3. Michael Tanzer, *The Political Economy of International Oil and the
Underdeveloped Countries* (Boston: Beacon Press), p. 54.

4. Although this work focuses upon the relationship between the United States and Latin America, many of the generalizations set forth here regarding the means and ends of U.S. policies, the range of U.S. postures, and the consequences for client states are applicable also to U.S. relations with client states in other parts of the world. For a broader perspective on the issues raised here, see Noam Chomsky and Edward S. Herman, *The Washington Connection and Third World Fascism, The Political Economy of Human Rights*, vol. I (Boston: South End Press, 1979).

5. Latin America Report (London) November 7, 1980.

6. In general, capitalists of the national, as opposed to the transnational, arena.

7. A liberal, according to Prof. Brady Tyson of American University, is one whose interests are not at stake.

8. John Samuel Fitch discusses the contradictions inherent in any attempt to incorporate human rights instruction into a counterinsurgency training program in "A Latin American Perspective on Human Rights and the U.S. Military Training Program" (in manuscript, University of Colorado at Boulder, 1980).

9. Alan Riding reported that a few days after Reagan's electoral victory two bullet-riddled bodies were found in El Salvador with signs around their necks reading, "With Ronald Reagan, the miscreants and guerrillas of Central America and El Salvador will be finished." "Reagan Impact Felt in Central America," *New York Times*, November 16, 1980, p. 17.

2

Advancing the Southern Frontier

There have always been Latin American leaders willing to take the risk of rejecting U.S. arguments as to what constituted the major threats to national or hemispheric security and what steps should be taken to counter those threats. However, those who have fashioned U.S. policy have generally been able, especially since World War II, to find important sectors of the economic and military elites in each of the Latin American states who, for reasons of their own self-interest, have been receptive to U.S. concepts of security and the security threat.

LUST FOR EMPIRE

Long before the struggle for independence had achieved success in the southern part of the hemisphere, the United States felt that its newly won independence was threatened by the English, Spanish, French, and Russian presence on or near its borders. This apprehension was reinforced when the Napoleonic wars drew the embryonic nation into the War of 1812. Thus, once the territories of Louisiana and Florida had been acquired from France and Spain, respectively; an understanding had been reached with the British; and the Spanish had been routed from most of their former colonies, President Monroe issued, in essence, a warning to the countries of the Holy Alliance that the Western Hemisphere was no longer open to colonization.

The Monroe Doctrine, at the time of its enunciation in 1823, was not entirely new. The idea that the New World should be isolated from the tumult of the Old had been expressed by Thomas Jefferson, among others, and Henry Clay had gone so far as to propose the creation of a "system of which we shall be the center, and in which all South America will act with us . . . "[1] But the United States had neither the willingness to make binding commitments nor the wherewithal to protect (or, for that matter, to threaten) its southern neighbors. Only the British Navy had the capability of thwarting the designs of Spain and her associates in the Holy Alliance. The doctrine was important, however, as the germ of what was to become a more ambitious policy when the United States became a regional and, later, a global power. It was to be cited as if it were an expression of national rights and as if it carried the weight of international law.

The doctrine pledged the United States to refrain from interference in the affairs of Europe and of existing European holdings in the Americas, and declared that any attempt on the part of the European countries to extend their power systems to any portion of the Western Hemisphere would be considered dangerous to the peace and safety of the United States. The idea that political as well as military involvement of alien powers in the Americas posed a security threat was explicit in the doctrine.

Issued even before the decisive battle of Ayacucho had been fought, the Monroe Doctrine drew a mixed response from the Latin Americans. Some viewed it with alarm. The Chilean *caudillo*, Diego Portales, warned his countrymen to "be careful of escaping one domination at the price of falling under another."[2] Some pointed out that as a unilateral statement the doctrine was unrealistic, as such a quarantine could only be based on British sea power. Some greeted it enthusiastically, but the majority of the politically articulate simply viewed it with indifference.

The United States continued, despite the doctrine, to avoid entangling alliances with Latin America as strictly as with the European countries, and if some Latin Americans had been reassured by the Monroe Doctrine they soon had reason to become disillusioned. Europe did not stay out of Latin America. During the first half of the nineteenth century both the Spanish and the French made futile landings in Mexico. The British intervened to secure the independence of Uruguay and occupied the Falkland Islands, claimed by Argentina. The British and French jointly blockaded the Rio de la Plata. None of these incidents provoked so much as a firm protest from the United States. And when, as a result of the Mexican-American War, the United States annexed half of the territory of her southern neighbor, the Latin Americans began to read a more ominous interpretation into the Monroe Doctrine.

Despite its weakness during and after the Civil War, the United States did strongly protest some of the most blatant European interventions during the latter half of the century, including the establishment of the short-lived Empire of Maximilian in Mexico, but these protests were offset by such bizarre developments as the filibustering activities of William Walker in Central America and President Grant's scheme for annexing the Dominican Republic.

Meanwhile, some of the Latin American states had begun to think in terms of joint provisions for their own security. Many leaders of the revolution in South America considered the establishment of a single government for the former Spanish colonies the natural follow-up to driving out the *peninsulares*. Both José de San Martín and Francisco Miranda proposed the creation of a single vast monarchy ruled by an emperor descended from the Incas. It was Simón Bolívar, however, who made the most serious attempt to unite the Spanish American republics.

Although the league or confederation envisioned by Bolívar was to foster the blessings of liberty and justice, its primary purpose was to secure the independence of the former colonies from renewed attacks by Spain and her allies. In this endeavor he sought the protection of Great Britain and was reluctant to invite representatives of the United States, even as observers, to the congress of plenipotentiaries for fear that their collaboration would compromise the league's position with the British. Furthermore, he felt that the neutrality of the United States in the war between Spain and her former colonies would make its representation inappropriate, and that the existence of slavery in the United States would be an obstacle to the discussion of the abolition of the African slave trade. He acquiesced, nevertheless, when the governments of Colombia, Mexico, and Central America invited the United States to send observers.

Despite the sweeping implications of the recently enunciated Monroe Doctrine, President Adams, in deciding to send delegates to the Panama conference, was not disposed to obligate the United States to defend its southern neighbors. The delegates were instructed to refrain from participating in deliberations concerning regional security and to emphasize instead discussions of maritime neutrality and commercial intercourse. Nevertheless, there was much opposition in Congress to participation under any conditions, and by the time participation was approved it was too late for the delegation to reach the conference.

The Congress of Panama, which convened in June and July of 1826, was attended by four American states—Mexico, Central America, Colombia, and Peru—embracing an area now occupied by eleven states. The British and Dutch had unofficial representation. The "Treaty of Union, League, and Perpetual Confederation," drawn up at that congress, would have bound all its parties to mutual defense and to the peaceful settlement of disputes.

The treaty never became effective, as it was ratified only by Colombia, and the Liberator, having made several futile attempts to establish lesser federations, declared shortly before his death, "America is ungovernable; those who served the revolution have plowed the sea." Despite his disillusionment, however, he did not see U.S. protection as a viable substitute for collective security arrangements among the Spanish-speaking states. In fact, he is credited with having said, "The United

States seems destined by Providence to plague America with misery in the name of liberty."[3]

The launching of the Pan American movement in the last decade of the nineteenth century was by no means an indication that Americans north and south of the Rio Grande had come to recognize a mutuality of security interests. The movement, initiated by the United States, had little in common with its Spanish American predecessor. Although the original scheduling of the first Pan American conference was prompted by the War of the Pacific and reflected U.S. concern for establishing procedures for pacific settlement of disputes among the Latin American countries, the principal motive of the United States was the promotion of closer commercial relations.

From the beginning of this uncomfortable association of the United States of North America and the disunited states of Latin America, the principal motive of most of the Latin American leaders was that of limiting the interference of the United States in their affairs. They were soon disenchanted. The United States had become infected with an urge for empire.

This new mood was arrogantly expressed by Secretary of State Richard Olney in 1895: "Today the United States is practically sovereign on this continent, and its fiat is law upon the subjects to which it confines its interposition."[4] It was reinforced by the irrefutable victory over Spain in what John Hay described as the "splendid little war."

The Monroe Doctrine was dusted off and embellished with the Roosevelt Corollary, which assumed the right and duty of the United States to exercise an international police power over its unruly southern neighbors.

THE BIG STICK IN CENTRAL AMERICA AND THE CARIBBEAN

Unlike the Monroe Doctrine itself, the Roosevelt Corollary was no idle threat. The United States proceeded to assist in the "liberation" of Panama from Colombia and to establish control through treaties, customs receiverships, and/or military occupation over Panama, Cuba, Haiti, the Dominican Republic, and

Nicaragua. Gunboat and dollar diplomacy helped to keep other Central American states submissive, and the owners of United Fruit and other companies openly boasted of buying and selling presidents.

The inter-American conferences which took place between 1890 and 1933 were characterized by sharp conflict. The Latin American republics concentrated their energies on the adoption of resolutions designed to curb the aggressive policies of the "Colossus of the North," and the United States countered by attempting to confine conference agendas to nonpolitical matters, particularly avoiding the codification of international law aimed at outlawing intervention.

In 1917, when the United States became involved in World War I, eight of the Latin American countries declared war on Germany and five ruptured diplomatic relations. Seven remained neutral.[5] Seven of the eight countries that declared war were in the Caribbean and Central America, the area under the strongest imperialistic pressures from the United States. Among the Latin American belligerents only Brazil, which contributed to countering the submarine menace, took an active part in the war.

At the close of the war the Latin American countries did not choose to follow the United States into isolation. Fifteen of them became charter members of the League of Nations and all eventually joined. They saw in the league not only an opportunity for national recognition, but also a possible counterpoise to the United States. They soon became disillusioned with that organization, however, in part because it proved incapable of protecting their sovereign rights from abuse by the United States. In fact, Article 21 of the League Covenant in essence pledged the signatories to recognize the validity of "regional understandings like the Monroe Doctrine," despite the objections of Argentina and Mexico that the Monroe Doctrine was not a "regional understanding."

By the late 1920s, it had become apparent to U.S. policymakers that direct muscle-flexing in Latin America was not producing the desired results. United States occupation of the Dominican Republic, Haiti, and Nicaragua and intervention in Honduras, Cuba, and Panama had not produced reliable lead-

ers and stable political systems, nor had widespread intervention resulted in a receptive attitude toward U.S. trade and investments. As the subversive activities of Nazi and Fascist
sympathizers gained momentum in the 1930s, the United States
became concerned about the need for hemisphere "solidarity."

In his inaugural address in 1933, President Franklin D. Roosevelt enunciated the Good Neighbor policy. At the Seventh
Inter-American Conference in Montevideo the same year, the
United States expressed a qualified acceptance of the principle
of nonintervention; in 1936 the principle was approved without
reservation.

Nevertheless, as the U.S. marines retreated from their out-
posts in Central America and the Caribbean, they left behind
native constabularies trained and experienced in gathering intelligence, conducting unconventional warfare, and running
military government. Such unconventional warfare proceeded
from the assumption that the "enemy" was internal rather than
external. Enemies of the state, as identified by the marines, were
those who sought to upset the economic status quo, including,
of course, aspects of the status quo that benefited foreigners at
the expense of natives. It was understood that all natives were
to be viewed as "potential" enemies, that insurgents would be
indistinguishable from ordinary citizens, and that campaigns
against insurgents would endanger the lives and property of
friendly or neutral natives as well.[6]

WORLD WAR II: THE PRICE OF COOPERATION

Neither the Good Neighbor policy nor the economic influence wielded by the United States in Latin America was sufficient to persuade all of the Latin American countries to coor-
dinate their defense policies with those of the United States when
Europe became embroiled in the Second World War. Fear and
distrust of the United States had become deeply rooted, and
sympathy with the Axis was not unknown in Latin American
governmental circles. In fact, Argentina did not break relations
with the Axis until 1944 and only declared war in 1945 as the
price of admission to the United Nations.

Nevertheless, tentative collective measures in hemispheric

defense were taken between 1938 and 1940, and when the United States was plunged into the war in 1941 the Caribbean and Central American states followed close behind. In consequence of a meeting of foreign ministers in Rio de Janeiro in January 1942, all of the Latin American republics except Chile and Argentina severed relations with the Axis powers. Chile followed suit after a year of steady U.S. pressure.

Generally speaking, the new policy achieved the desired results. Disregarding the recalcitrance of Chile, the temporary problem with Bolivia, and the more serious standoff with Argentina, and winking at what some heads of state, such as Trujillo and Morínigo, actually did with their lend-lease acquisitions, it may be said that an acceptable multilateral framework was devised for the extensive bilateral defense arrangements.

Mexico and Brazil contributed military contingents to the fighting overseas, and several other countries indicated a willingness to do so. Communications between the Axis and the Hemisphere were largely severed, and air and naval bases were freely granted to the United States. The most significant collaboration, however, was in economic transactions. The United States attempted to meet Latin American demands for consumer goods, and Latin American countries accelerated production and shipment of strategic raw materials.

The consequences of the Good Neighbor policy and World War II cooperation for the inter-American system are usually discussed in terms of "hemispheric solidarity." Two additional consequences, however—increased economic dependence of Latin American countries on the United States and stronger bilateral military ties—did not bode well for the future of a system supposedly based on the principle of the sovereign equality of nation-states.[7] Moreover, the collapse of Europe had eliminated the possibility of playing off one hegemonic pretender against another.

The mounting evidence of Nazi and Fascist activity in Latin America had been partially responsible for the revived interest in that area heralded by the Good Neighbor policy, and those movements deemed to be influenced by the Axis became targets of the operations of such multilateral inter-American institutions as the Emergency Advisory Committee for Political Defense as well as of unilateral actions of the United States.

Like other innovative policies before and since, however, the Good Neighbor policy, according to David Green, was largely a response to a powerful and "dangerous" outburst of revolutionary nationalism.[8] It seems hardly coincidental that where alien political views had aroused the oppressed working classes and appeared to threaten U.S. economic interests, such as in Bolivia and Argentina, U.S. intervention in the domestic political affairs of Latin American states was most vigorous. Secretary of the Treasury John A. Snyder testified before the Senate Banking and Currency Committee in August 1949 concerning the importance of promoting investments:

As to the question of what is to be done to increase the volume of investments and to distribute them more broadly, we must address ourselves primarily to the problems of eliminating the obstacles which stand in the way of the investment of American capital abroad. It is essential that the task of removing such obstacles should be attacked both by foreign countries and by the United States. Foreign countries must, however, accept the major responsibility for clearing the existing obstruction to a broad and beneficial flow of private capital.[9]

Among the obstacles to which Snyder referred in his testimony were "the growth of ideologies favoring state ownership and control of industry" and "the existence of political instability and extreme nationalism." On the basis of a study of the actions and statements of U.S. agencies and officials in the 1930s and 1940s, Green concluded that the United States preferred allies in the Western Hemisphere who were dependable and weak.

The U.S. government, of course, embraced a great many agencies and individuals who were not necessarily pursuing the same goals or advocating or employing the same means. State Department records indicate, for example, that the U.S. armed forces faced stiff resistance from the State Department in the early postwar period before finally gaining its support for the initiation of an arms program for Latin America designed to consolidate U.S. military influence and exclude "foreign ideologies" from the hemisphere. In a letter to acting Secretary of State Dean Acheson, dated March 27, 1947, urging military aid, Secretary of War Robert P. Patterson wrote: "Thus will our ideals and ways of life be nurtured in Latin America to the eventual exclusion of totalitarian and other foreign ideologies." On April 17, he warned Acheson, "It would seem that we are playing into the hands of the Communists if by our own decision we disable ourselves from the tender of military assistance." Two weeks later, after General George C. Marshall had become secretary of state, Acheson announced that he had "overruled objections within his department" and would support authorizing legislation.[10]

The hemispheric ambitions of the U.S. armed forces suffered an additional temporary setback when the Inter-American Military Cooperation Act, providing for standardization of organization, training, and equipment, proposed by President Truman in 1946 and again in 1947, was twice defeated in Congress. Nevetheless, the cooperation of the war years and the assumptions it had nurtured had laid the groundwork for the extension to the whole of Latin America of a measure of the political and economic hegemony that had been practiced in the Caribbean and Central America. It was hardly the multilateralization of the Monroe Doctrine, as some have claimed, but rather the southward extension of the Roosevelt Corollary.

THE MESOAMERICANIZATION OF SOUTH AMERICA

The Allied victory in World War II marked an all-time high in inter-American relations. The leaders of most of the Latin American states were proud of the multilateral cooperation they had been able to achieve and were optimistic about their relations with the United States. Once the validity of regional arrangements had been recognized in the United Nations Charter, the American states proceeded to refine and give permanence to the patchwork of inter-American organs, procedures, and temporary expedients that had evolved over the previous sixty-year period.

The first order of business was to be the institutionalization of a collective security system for the hemisphere. The Inter-American Treaty of Reciprocal Assistance, asserting that "an armed attack by any state against an American state shall be considered as an attack against all the American states," was signed in 1947 in Rio de Janeiro and was eventually ratified by all twenty-one signatories. At the Ninth International Conference of American States in Bogotá in 1948, the principles and fundamental provisions of the Rio treaty were incorporated into a regional organization of general competence, the Organization of American States (OAS).

One of the fundamental principles upon which inter-American solidarity and cooperation were based was that of the sovereign equality of nation-states. Recognition, however, that political realities belied that principle is indicated in the stress placed on a broad interpretation of nonintervention in the charter of the OAS. Article 15 reads:

No state or group of States has the right to intervene, directly or indirectly, for any reason whatever, in the internal or external affairs of any other state. The foregoing principle prohibits not only armed force but also any other form of interference against the personality of the State or against its political, economic, or cultural elements.

In case any member state missed the point, Articles 12 and 16 were included. Article 12 reads: "The jurisdiction of States within the limits of their national territory is exercised equally over all the inhabitants, whether nationals or aliens." Article 16 reads: "No State may use or encourage the use of coercive measures of an economic or political character in order to force the sovereign will of another State and obtain from it advantages of any kind."

The community of interests and the generalized support for multilateral defense planning that were expressed in the Rio treaty and the charter of the OAS represented more nearly the culmination of an era than the initiation of a new one. The ink was hardly dry on the new charter before the cooperative spirit began to disintegrate.

It had been decided at the Mexico City Conference in 1945 that the Inter-American Defense Board, created in 1942 by recommendation of the Meeting of Foreign Ministers, should continue to function. This board, consisting of military officers from each of the American states, proceeded to draw up a list of recommendations for preserving and extending the military cooperation which had been achieved during the war. These included continued development and interconnection of civil and military telecommunication; the standardization of matériel; the full utilization of manpower through compulsory military service and other measures; the extension of U.S. standards of organization and training to the Latin American services through the use of military missions; and the creation of a permanent agency (on the order of the board) to promote coordination.

The United States military officials assumed, in light of these recommendations and of the Rio treaty, that negotiations for the retention of certain key bases, notably in Ecuador, Brazil, and Panama, would be in order. This proposition proved highly unpopular, setting off such public protest in the countries mentioned that agreement was impossible. By 1948 almost all bases and sites in Latin America that had been occupied by the United States during the war, including 134 in Panama alone, had been evacuated.[11]

However, the continuation of the Inter-American Defense Board was again authorized at the Bogotá conference in 1948, and the board was subsequently incorporated into the structure of the OAS to serve as a permanent organ of preparation and recommendation for collective security measures. The board, which has its seat in Washington, is composed of a Council of Delegates on which each country has one vote, the staff, the secretariat, and the Inter-American Defense College. The chairmanship of the council and the directorships of the staff, the secretariat, and the college are permanently held by the United States. The board has no armed forces under its control; its mission is defense planning only. It is virtually autonomous, as its recommendations go directly to the respective governments rather than via the OAS council as in the case of other agencies.

The most important function of the board has been that of providing the facade of multilateral sanction for the bilateral Military Assistance Agreements that have evolved since 1951.

These agreements have consisted of the provision, through grants and credits, of U.S. weapons and equipment, the stationing of U.S. army, navy, and air force missions in Latin American countries, and the training of Latin American officers in the United States and the Canal Zone.

In the 1950s, under U.S. prodding, the Inter-American Defense Board began to reconcile its hemispheric defense requirements with the exigencies of the Cold War and the concept of global strategy. As a direct attack in the southern part of the hemisphere was considered unlikely, Latin America's contributions to the defense of the "free world" were to be maintenance of internal order and prevention of subversive activities, defense of military and economic installations, provision of sea and air patrols, maintenance of communications, and production of raw materials.

Until the late 1950s the United States, obsessed with the military and political aspects of the Cold War, virtually ignored the pleas of the Latin Americans for economic assistance. President Eisenhower announced to Congress on January 7, 1954, "Military assistance must be continued. Technical assistance must be maintained. Economic assistance can be reduced."[12] Latin America was not excepted from this general posture.

The reaffirmation, solicited by the United States, by parties to the Military Assistance Agreements of their determination "to give their full cooperation to the efforts to provide the United Nations with armed forces as contemplated by the Charter,"[13] coming as it did at the outset of the Korean conflict, had caused some uneasiness in Latin America. The United States continuously reassured its southern partners that the bilateral arrangements were in accordance with multilateral agreements, that they would not promote a costly arms race, entrench dictatorial governments in power, or facilitate U.S. hegemony over the hemisphere. Nevertheless, Latin American leaders did not fail to note that in the spring and summer of 1954 Honduras and Nicaragua received substantial shipments of U.S. military supplies, as did the government of Castillo Armas in Guatemala after Arbenz had been overthrown. The staunchest allies of the United States in its anticommunist militance had been the hemisphere's dictatorships, but the massive demonstrations against

Vice President Richard Nixon and his party in Venezuela in 1958 gave some indication of the growing popular resentment against U.S. courtship of dictators.[14]

A wave of antimilitarism was sweeping the region, and by mid-1961 only one (Alfredo Stroessner of Paraguay) of the twelve military heads of state that had ruled in 1954 was still in office. Furthermore, and perhaps more importantly in terms of the challenges to U.S. policy, there was the Cuban Revolution. It was not overlooked by Latin Americans that President Kennedy's proposal of an Alliance for Progress preceded the abortive Bay of Pigs invasion by a single month.

The Alliance for Progress, as initiated by President John F. Kennedy and the New Frontiersmen of his administration projected goals that, within the context of Latin America, were contradictory: on the one hand, promotion of democracy and economic reform, and, on the other, promotion of more attractive incentives to American investors and the strengthening of internal security forces and other "anticommunist" elements.

In addition to the complex of schools established in the Panama Canal Zone in the 1940s and 1950s, more than 140 military installations in the continental United States offered military training, heavily salted with political indoctrination, to Latin American officers. Furthermore, by 1960 some 7,000 U.S. military officers had been assigned to Military Assistance Advisory Groups in Latin America.[15]

Aid to Latin American police forces, which had been initiated in 1954, was stepped up, and a new role for the armed forces—"civic action"—was added to the many activities grouped under the umbrella concept of "counterinsurgency." It was reasoned that U.S. law enforcement personnel would train their Latin American counterparts in more "humane" and yet more efficient methods of maintaining internal security.

It was also believed that the intensified linkage itself between the U.S. military and its counterparts, through more extensive training programs and through U.S. Military Assistance Advisory Groups working in the Latin American countries, would engender "democratic attitudes" on the part of Latin American military establishments. Furthermore, it was assumed that the military civic action projects would improve the image of the military while allowing it to keep tabs on potentially subversive groups in out-of-the-way places. It was also suggested that keeping the military establishments busy in that way might leave them less time and inclination to conspire against constitutional regimes. But the insurgents or potential insurgents they were being trained to deal with as the enemy were their own compatriots.

The Kennedy Administration introduced a recognition policy that was designed to discourage military seizures of power, but it was not consistently adhered to. After Kennedy's death it was abandoned altogether, and the contradictions inherent in the Alliance for Progress were resolved in favor of the big stick.

NOTES

1. Gordon Connell-Smith, *The Inter-American System* (London: Oxford University Press, 1966), p. 2.

2. Frederick Pike, *Chile and the United States, 1880–1962* (Notre Dame: University of Notre Dame Press, 1963), pp. 23–25.

3. Alonso Aguilar, *Pan Americanism from Monroe to the Present: A View from the Other Side* (New York: Monthly Review Press, 1968), p. 8.

4. John C. Dreier, *The Organization of American States and the Hemispheric Crisis* (New York: Harper and Row, 1962), p. 20. A New Orleans editor, James D. B. Debow, reflected the attitude of a large portion of public opinion in the United States between the end of the Mexican-American War and the beginning of the Civil War when he said, "We have a destiny to perform, a 'manifest destiny' over all Mexico, over South America, over the West Indies and Canada." United States attitudes toward manifest destiny in the hemisphere in that period are discussed at length in James Thomas Wall's "American Intervention in Nicaragua, 1848–1861" (Ph.D. diss., University of Tennessee, Knoxville, August 1974).

5. Brazil, Cuba, Costa Rica, Guatemala, Haiti, Honduras, Nicaragua, and Panama declared war. Bolivia, the Dominican Republic, Ecuador, Peru, and Uruguay ruptured relations. Argentina, Chile, Colombia, Mexico, Paraguay, El Salvador, and Venezuela remained neutral.

6. Ronald Shaeffer, "The 1940 Small Wars Manual and the 'Lessons of History,'" *Military Affairs*, vol. XXXVI, no. 2 (April 1972), pp. 46–51. See also Richard Millett, *Guardians of the Dynasty* (Maryknoll, N.Y.: Orbis Books, 1977), and Louis A. Perez, Jr., *Army Politics in Cuba, 1898–1958* (Pittsburgh: University of Pittsburgh Press, 1976).

7. For example, Brazil's exports to the U.S. in 1938 exceeded imports by 500 million cruzeiros. In 1952, imports exceeded exports by more than 2 billion cruzeiros. Brazil's short-term commercial indebtedness to the United States by early 1953 was $370 million. The increased dependence was particularly acute in such areas as spare parts and motor vehicles, machinery, and petroleum. See Ross K. Baker, *A Study of Military Status and Status Deprivation in Three Latin American Armies* (Washington: American University Center for Research in Social Systems, Government Printing Office, October 1967), p. 23.

8. David Green, *The Containment of Latin America: A History of the Myths and Realities of the Good Neighbor Policy* (Chicago: Triangle Books, 1971), p. 293–96.

9. Ibid.

10. U.S. Department of State, Historical Office, Bureau of Public Affairs, *Foreign Relations of the United States: Volume VIII: The American Republics* (Washington, D.C.: Government Printing Office, 1972), pp. 101–30.

11. A number of those bases in Panama were subsequently leased again to the United States.

12. Gordon Connell-Smith, *The Inter-American System*, p. 160.

13. Lloyd J. Mecham, *The United States and Inter-American Security: 1889–1960* (Austin: University of Texas Press, 1961), p. 336.

14. Venezuelan military dictator Marcos Perez Jiménez was deposed and the reformist Acción Democrática government of Rómulo Betancourt elected in 1958.

15. Paul Y. Hammond, David J. Louscher, and Michael D. Salomon, "Growing Dilemmas for the Management of Arms Sales," *Armed Forces and Society*, vol. 6, no. 1 (Fall 1979), pp. 1–21.

3

The Military Role Expansion of the 1960s

As the decade of the 1960s opened, it appeared that Latin Americans could look forward to a new era of democratic, constitutional rule. Victor Alba suggested that Latin American militarism was soon to wither away, as the military had no useful function and as there was an emergent generation of American-trained, technocratically oriented officers.[1] Between 1962 and 1969, however, eleven regimes that had held power constitutionally were toppled by the military, and several more fell in the 1970s, including those of Uruguay and Chile, which had firmly implanted traditions of civilian rule. Whereas in 1961 there were only three Latin American governments that were generally considered dictatorial, by 1976 there were only three or four that were generally considered democratic.

Martin C. Needler noted in 1966 that trends over the previous three decades of military intervention in domestic politics in Latin America had been toward: (1) veto coups, designed to preserve the status quo; (2) coups toppling constitutional regimes; (3) coups forestalling the election or inauguration of reformers; (4) coups resulting in an increase in popular resistance; and (5) coups occurring with greater frequency during periods of economic decline.[2] Those trends appeared to be holding, although with notable exceptions, until the late 1970s.

THE NEW PROFESSIONALISM AND U.S. PENETRATION

While the factors that contributed to the resurgence of political activism on the part of the military varied from country to country, some common denominators are to be found in changes in the institutional characteristics and self-interests of the military. Institutional self-interest varies in accordance with the threats posed or opportunities offered by the national and international environments at any given time. One of the threats posed by the international environment in the 1960s was that referred to by Alba—the loss of a legitimate function. For a number of reasons, not the least of which was the United States guardianship of the hemisphere, wars with neighboring countries were not feasible. But unless it is held in check by a strong civilian political apparatus or by its own internal cleavages, a well-organized, well-trained, and well-equipped military establishment will not just sit on its hands; it will make war or politics or both.

The threats and opportunities perceived in the national environment vary in accordance with the country's level of development, as we shall see in the following chapter. Changes in institutional characteristics can be explained in part by changes in the nature and extent of training. Prior to the Second World War, most of the military establishments in South America had been exposed to European training and strategic theory. European strategy was based on the premise that ally and adversary relationships were of a temporary nature. The focus was on the protection or extension of national borders.

With the onset of the Second World War, the United States acquired a near-monopoly on the training and equipping of the Latin American armed forces. In the postwar period, the United States began to teach a new global strategy, based on the need for a permanent alliance in the face of a presumably permanent war. The Cold War world-view held that the enemy was not merely a nation, or even a group of nations, but rather an ideology. In the wake of the Cuban Revolution, U.S. military training began to stress the idea that the enemy was not external but internal. So more traditional forms of training gave way to training for counterinsurgency and civic action. Counterinsurgency, by its very nature, involved the military in decisions as to what forms of political expression were permissible and left them with the conviction that those who did not share their views of the national goals were "the enemy." And civic action soon evolved into the far more ambitious concept of nation-building.

National Security was defined primarily in terms of the security of the military establishment, so that any criticism of the military, or any challenge to its perquisites, was regarded as subversive. Furthermore, as the enemy was assumed to be internal, the protection of the National Security called for maintaining control over all aspects of national life. Thus training was expanded to include economic planning, systems analysis, psychological operations, management, and other aspects of the art of governing.

One consequence of this exposure to advanced training in the social sciences was that officers became convinced that they were better prepared than the civilian political leaders to run the country. Another was the development of a stronger corporate consciousness; whereas traditional forms of foreign military training had involved only a small proportion of the Latin American military establishments, the focus on internal security involved a much larger proportion and contributed to the military's sense of alienation from civilians.

Thus the United States, through its programs of training and material assistance in the 1960s and early 1970s, contributed to the budgetary autonomy, the repressive capability, and the managerial self-confidence of Latin American military establishments. But the United States was not prepared to settle for indirect influence on the course of events; it engaged in direct reinforcement of the political ambitions of the military as well. The best documented cases of direct U.S. encouragement of military seizures of power in Latin America in the 1960s and 1970s are the cases of Brazil and Chile; but the general pattern of strengthening the Right, including military and paramilitary groups, dividing and weakening the Left, and frightening the middle class has been played out to varying degrees in most other Latin American countries as well.

The convergence of interests that results in a military seizure of power has many sources and many beginnings; we cannot isolate the variables in order to determine which were necessary and sufficient to produce successful coups. Even in the cases of Brazil (1964) and Chile (1973), motives of institutional interest have been apparent. In both cases military leaders resented political interference with the institution's seniority system; feared the subversion of military discipline as enlisted men dared to disobey the commands of superiors; feared loss of their monopoly of force, as popular militias were said to be forming; saw their economic security and social status being eroded by inflation; and perceived a general breakdown of law and order. Nevertheless, as we shall see, the United States both indirectly and directly nurtured the ambitions and anxieties of those leaders. Indeed, it is only through engaging the personal and institutional interests of military leaders that nonmilitary or nonnational conspirators can promote a coup.

Brazil's Security State

The Conspiracy Against Goulart. The complicity of the United States in the demise of Brazil's last constitutional government in 1964 and the establishment, in its place, of a military dictatorship is now a matter of record.[3] The long-term efforts of the United States in Brazil, as elsewhere in Latin America, to undermine movements springing from or appealing to the aspirations of the lower classes and to strengthen the military and other groups favorably disposed toward American capital had been infused with a new sense of urgency when reformist (but by no means revolutionary) João Goulart assumed the presidency of Brazil in 1961. The process of destabilizing his government involved a concerted effort on the part of virtually every agency of the U.S. government, in cooperation with the transnational corporate community and international financial institutions.

While U.S. banks and international lending agencies withheld credit, the CIA, the Agency for International Development (AID), and U.S. businesses channeled funds to political candidates, state governors, police and paramilitary groups, journalists, business, labor, and student leaders, and others who were conspiring against, or could be persuaded to conspire against, the federal government. Meanwhile U.S. military attachés and advisers encouraged and coordinated the plotting by factions of the Brazilian military of a coup d'etat. And against the contingency that the military conspirators might run into trouble, the United States had a naval carrier task force standing by.

The New Military Elite. The faction of generals, known as the Sorbonne group, that engineered the 1964 coup was distinguished from other active duty line generals in that significantly more of its members had fought, as the Brazilian Expeditionary Force, alongside the American Fourth Army in Italy; had established and staffed, with the assistance of a special United States Mission, the Superior War College; had graduated as number one in the class at one of the three major army schools; had attended foreign, mainly American, schools; and had been members of the technically most advanced branch of the army. Sons of military officers were also overrepresented among the generals plotting to overthrow the Goulart government.[4]

Nevertheless, in social terms, the military in Brazil had become a highly homogeneous institution. Recruitment had been increasingly from the middle class, at the expense of both upper and lower classes. There had been a high degree of recruitment from military families, and up to 90 percent of the 1960s generation of army officers entered the military academy system at about the age of twelve. Those who had reached the Superior War College (ESG) were being taught that the destiny of Western Civilization was severely threatened by communism and that the Cold War demanded governments with a centralized and hierarchic structure. They were also being told that the masses lacked a "critical sense of time and space" and that it was the duty of the "authentic elites of the global society" to direct the political community.[5]

Peru's Divergent Path

The Military Radicals. Peru had been second only to Brazil in the amount of American military assistance received between 1945 and 1960. Exposure to foreign standards of professionalism, including stress on hierarchy, discipline, and bureaucratization, enhanced the institutional self-confidence of the military as well as their impatience with what they viewed as the undisciplined behavior of civilian politicans. Furthermore, emphasis on internal security focused their attention on the country's socioeconomic and political structures.

Foreign assistance, in addition to a consistently generous portion of the national budget, enabled the military to establish its own extensive educational system and to enjoy considerable autonomy within the governmental structure. By the late 1960s many officers had come to the conclusion that the existing social and economic structures could not sustain a modern military organization. They felt that, in the face of the "incompetence" and "corruption" of civilian politicians, it behooved the paternalistic military vanguard to maintain internal security while promoting national development.

Unlike the Brazilian conspirators, however, several members of the core group involved in the Peruvian coup of 1968 had been trained in countries other than the United States, especially in Israel and at the school of the United Nations Economic Commission for Latin America in Chile. Their primary ideological commitment was to economic nationalism, and they opposed the civilian government not for its radicalism but for its moderation.[6]

A Costly Miscalculation. There is no reason to believe the United States encouraged, or even welcomed, the coup against Peruvian president Fernando Belaúnde Terry in 1968. In fact, the actions of the military regime that succeeded his constitutional government were inimical to powerful American interests, and the regime's foreign policy leaned toward nonalignment. Nevertheless, the United States contributed indirectly to that turn of events, not only by enhancing the strength, autonomy, ambitions, and self-image of the armed forces, but also by undermining the civilian government.

There had been various points of contention between Peru and the United States since the early 1960s, including Peru's claim to a 200-mile extension of territorial waters and its frequent seizure of American tuna boats within that zone. The most serious source of friction, however, was the status of the oil rights of the International Petroleum Company (IPC), a subsidiary of Standard Oil of New Jersey, which in the 1960s extracted more than 80 percent of Peru's petroleum. A 1922 arbitration award giving a British-owned company, which later sold out to IPC, subsoil rights to the La Brea y Pariñas oilfield in the northern coastal region had long been considered by Peruvian nationalists an infringement of sovereignty. The dispute was aggravated by the fact that for a long time IPC paid no taxes on the oil extracted.

Debate over nationalization and conditions of nationalization had been under way since the 1940s and was particularly virulent in the election campaigns of 1962 and 1963. In the 1963 campaign, candidate Belaúnde promised to solve the problem in ninety days if elected. Negotiations with the company began almost immediately after his inauguration on July 28, but by the end of October they had broken down. Therefore, on November 6 the Peruvian congress passed a law declaring the arbitral award of 1922 to be null and void.

Negotiations continued for five years. The major issue on the surface was the way in which profits would be split between the company and the government, but underlying it was the unresolved question of who actually owned the oilfields. The company offered to cede its ownership rights but insisted on retaining operating control and on a cancellation of its alleged debts. The government, however, having promised to recover a part of the national domain, insisted that the fields be ceded outright.

Meanwhile, economic aid under the Alliance for Progress that had been promised immediately after the 1963 elections was held up pending settlement with the IPC. In early 1966 the United States received assurance from Belaúnde that confiscation of the property was not contemplated, and aid was resumed. It was slashed again in 1967, however, when the Peruvian Air Force purchased supersonic Mirage jets from France (United States legislation called for a reduction in aid corresponding to the expenditure for sophisticated weaponry). Thus Belaúnde had been faced with a complete or partial suspension of aid for four of his five years in office. By 1967 a general economic decline and devaluation had combined with popular frustration over the delay in the IPC settlement to weaken the government.

The Act of Talara, signed by the government and the IPC on August 12, 1968, failed to assuage nationalistic antagonisms. The accord, through which the government was to drop its tax claims and grant a concession to IPC to continue operating in exchange for title to the property, split the governing coalition and even Belaúnde's own Popular Action Party and provoked intervention.

Bolivia: The Failure of Revolutionary Socialization

A Born-Again Military Establishment. In prerevolutionary Bolivia, the army had been an institution of the greatest importance in political life, its role in which had been largely directed toward the maintenance of the oligarchic status quo and the expansion of its own position in Bolivian society. In consequence, no other group except the oligarchy itself, known in Bolivia as the *rosca* (yoke), underwent such a rapid constriction of its power after the 1952 revolution.

During the twelve years immediately preceding the revolution, three of the republic's six chief executives had been military men, and the other three had effective army support, especially against the serious rebellion engineered by the National Revolutionary Movement (MNR) in 1949. On coming to power in 1952, the MNR, associating the army with the traditional order in Bolivia, consciously set out to nullify its power. Even the influence of the military group known as For the Sake of the Fatherland (*Razon de Patria*—RADEPA), with which the MNR was allied in the early 1940s, was negligible after 1952.

Apprehensive about any potential threat to its own government, the MNR moved rapidly against the army through forced retirement of about 80 percent of its commissioned and noncommissioned officers. With the counterbalancing force of the sudden growth of armed militias among the miners and the campesinos, the army was rendered virtually impotent in the first year of the revolution.[7] Military expenditures dropped from 23 percent of the national budget in 1953 to 6.7 percent in 1957.

On July 24, 1953, President Victor Paz Estenssoro issued a decree reestablishing the army and at the same time launched a program to remold the military in the revolutionary image. The army's military academy was directed to adopt admissions policies favoring lower- and middle-class candidates, and its faculty and curriculum were changed in an effort to ensure the inculcation of the party's revolutionary principles. At the same time, a supporting propaganda campaign was launched in the press. During 1953 and 1954 articles appeared frequently in *La Nacion*, the MNR daily newspaper, stressing that the army should reflect the new synthesis of social forces emerging under the revolution.

In 1954 there were other signs of government resuscitation of the military. Some career officers active in the prerevolutionary army were reinstalled in their former positions on the basis of thorough background investigation and in consideration of their taking an oath to support the MNR. The army's participation in construction and colonization projects in various parts of the country was favorably publicized.

In general, however, the military remained in a state of hibernation until 1958, when its fortunes changed abruptly. At that time the opposition of organized labor to the government's stabilization plan, largely imposed by the United States and the International Monetary Fund, led the MNR leadership to cultivate the military as a counterpoise to the armed militias. Military expenditures rose steadily after 1958.

In the early 1960s, Paz greatly increased defense expenditures and received a sharply increased amount of U.S. military assistance. By 1964 the defense budget had increased a dozenfold over its 1956 level, and twenty out of the twenty-three senior officers of the Bolivian army had been trained in the continental United States or at the United States School of the Americas in the Panama Canal Zone.

A number of officers had also been trained in other Latin American countries. And with the assistance of the United States and some Latin American neighbors, the Bolivian military had developed a system of educational institutions of its own far more complex than that of most countries of similar size and level of development. Training in the United States and in the country's own schools stressed various means of maintaining internal security, including counterinsurgency and civic action.[8]

Friendly Subversion of Bolivia's Revolution. The case of Bolivia suggests that U.S. "support" for a revolutionary government may be just as devastating to the goals of the revolutionary coalition as steadfast U.S. opposition. The United States had reacted to the Revolution of 1952 with predictable hostility, but shortly thereafter the Eisenhower Administration reversed its position and became the major benefactor of the MNR government. Whatever the strategy of the United States in this case, the consequences of heavy American influence were the undermining of the economic and political gains of labor, the splintering of the MNR, and the reconstruction of a politically powerful and predominantly reactionary military.

By 1954 the assistance program had grown to massive proportions, and by 1956 the United States was in a position to start turning the screw. From that time on further aid was made conditional upon acceptance of a stabilization plan that penalized labor and forced a retrenchment on social welfare legislation; on certain private investment incentives, including the opening up of the mines and oilfields to American investors; and on increasing defense expenditures. In 1957 and 1958 both the military and the police began to receive U.S. assistance. Meanwhile, the labor–middle-class alliance had been severed, and the middle-class MNR leadership began to use the peasants to assist the military in putting down strikes.

Hernán Siles Suazo, president from 1956 to 1960, later said that the United States had given him just enough rope to hang himself. Paz finally came to a similar conclusion. The U.S. Embassy had insisted that he run for reelection in 1964 in order to deny the presidency to the more radical Juan Lechín, leader of the powerful miners' union. Paz did and in the process accelerated the disintegration of the MNR, but he nevertheless suspected the U.S. military of conspiring with Air Force General René Barrientos to topple him later that year.[9]

The hopes expressed by Paz and other Movimientistas in the early 1950s that selection of officer candidates from lower-class backgrounds and nurture in the goals and principles of the revolutionary party would produce an officer corps respectful of civilian rule proved to have been mislaid; such factors made no obvious difference in either the political ambitions or the ideological orientations of the officers. Both Barrientos (president, 1964–1969) and Alfredo Ovando (president, 1969–1970), who conspired to overthrow Paz in 1964, had risen to their influential positions through the military reconstituted by the MNR. The proforeign investor, antilabor orientation of Barrientos, a *cholo* (mestizo), was very similar to that of Hugo Banzer (president, 1971–1978), an aristocrat; whereas both Ovando, an aristocrat, and Juan José Torres (president, 1970–1971), a *cholo*, assumed a populistic, nationalistic course in the presidency that would have been anathema to Barrientos and that was reversed by Banzer.

Ideological orientations within the officer corps between the mid-1960s and the mid-1970s tended to correspond to the increasing polarization of the larger political community. The populist, or nationalist, school, represented by Ovando and Torres, was the minority position among commissioned officers but apparently had strong support among the noncommissioned officers. These officers defined the internal enemy as that sector of the population allied with foreign commerce, and the external enemy as economic imperialism. They believed that the United States exaggerated the threat of international communism in order to manipulate and exploit its allies, and they viewed insurgency as a consequence of underdevelopment.

The ideological orientation of the majority of the commissioned officers favored economic growth without major structural change, and they advocated foreign participation in the economy to achieve that end. They viewed the insurgency threat as rising from an international communist conspiracy rather than from socioeconomic grievances, and they favored a foreign policy alignment with the United States in an ongoing cold war struggle. Most of the officers, including Barrientos and Banzer, who served as spokesmen of this position had been trained in the United States.

The most important conviction that appeared to be shared by officers at each ideological pole, at least until the late 1970s, was that the military was the only institution capable of governing the country. This elitism has been attributed in part to the many years of formal education that are an integral part of the officers' career patterns and to the strengths attributed by Bolivian officers and their counterparts throughout the hemisphere to the institution itself, such as discipline and administrative efficiency.

Chile: The Destabilization of a Constitutional Government

Until 1973, Chile had a tradition of constitutional democracy that was the envy of much of the hemisphere. Military intervention had been relatively rare, and most Chileans were convinced in the 1960s that the military was firmly under civilian control. Miners and urban working classes had begun to organize during the first decades of the twentieth century, and governments in the 1930s and 1940s had been based on a center-Left coalition of middle and working classes. However, political participation by lower income groups had not resulted in far-reaching redistribution of wealth.

In 1964, following the relatively conservative government of Jorge Alessandri, the country's traditional Right-of-center parties, lacking support, virtually collapsed. The presidential contest that year was between Eduardo Frei, representing the centrist Christian Democratic Party, and Socialist Salvador Allende, representing a Left-of-center coalition. Frei won the election but was not able to deliver on his promised "revolution in liberty." In 1970, a weakened Christian Democratic Party encountered a revived opposition on its Right, and the three-way split gave an edge to Allende, who had promised a "peaceful road to socialism."

The United States, then under the presidency of Richard M. Nixon, cut off most forms of economic aid to Chile, but military assistance was increased. In 1973, the Chilean armed forces murdered Allende and toppled his government in the bloodiest coup d'etat the hemisphere had yet seen.

In December 1975, the U.S. Senate Select Committee to Study Governmental Operations with Respect to Intelligence Activities, in a report entitled *Covert Action in Chile: 1963–1973*, revealed that the CIA had invested approximately $13.4 million between 1963 and 1973 in its attempt to shift the balance of power in Chile's political system to the Right.[10]

The report notes that the figure understates the value of these funds in Chile, where black market exchange rates amounted to up to five times the official rate. Furthermore, the figures represent only one category—covert action—of the activities of only one agency. They do not take into account, for example, intelligence or counterintelligence or other routine CIA operations. They do not include military aid and other forms of "assistance" geared to serve the same ends. Nor do they include the funds invested in the effort by ITT and other private U.S.-based companies. These figures, therefore, offer no more than a clue as to the magnitude of the effort.

The committee reported that the CIA had funded more than half of Frei's campaign in 1964. It also supported some candidates and conducted spoiling operations against others in the congressional elections of 1965 and 1969. Peasants, slum dwellers, organized labor, students, and the media had also been targets of covert action projects in Chile since the 1950s.

The senators stated that they had found no hard evidence that the United States was directly involved in the 1973 coup.[11] However, the committee found abundant hard evidence of indirect involvement, not to mention soft evidence of direct involvement. They found, for example, that the agency had covertly spent at least $8 million between 1970 and 1973 for a broad spectrum of activities, including manipulation of the media and support for opposition parties and private sector organizations. Money from these parties and organizations was in turn passed on to Right-wing terrorists and antigovernment strikers, including the truck owners whose strike was so damaging to the Allende government.

The select committee notes in *Covert Action* that in a "project renewal memorandum" after the coup the CIA boasted that *El Mercurio* and other media outlets supported by the agency had played an important role in setting the stage for the overthrow of Allende. The several committee reports cite various CIA projects that were designed to debilitate or discredit organizations of the Left and to strengthen and embolden those of the Right, as well as to influence elections. They also cite efforts to enlist international lending agencies and transnational corporations in a conspiracy, in the words of Nixon, to "make the economy scream."

As to the "military solution," the Senate report entitled *Alleged Assassination Plots Involving Foreign Leaders* explains in some detail that the so-called Track II, set in motion by Nixon himself after Allende's electoral victory in September 1970 to prevent him from actually taking office in November, was a direct attempt to promote a military coup.[12] Kissinger swore in congressional testimony that Track II had been terminated upon Allende's assumption of office, but, as noted in *Covert Action*, various CIA officials, including Deputy Director for Plans Thomas Karamessines, testified that as far as they were concerned Track II was not terminated until after the 1973 coup.

In *Covert Action*, the committee notes that after the failure of the United States to provoke a coup in 1970, the CIA and U.S. military attachés intensified their efforts to penetrate the Chilean military, and that by September 1971 a new network of agents was in place. United States officials were instructed to seek influence within the Chilean military and to be generally supportive of its activities without appearing to promise U.S. support "for military efforts which might be premature."

Stepped-up activities in late 1971 and early 1972 included subsidization of an antigovernment news pamphlet directed at the armed forces, a "deception operation" in which "real *or fabricated* evidence" of Cuban involvement in the army was passed to selected officers, and compilations of "arrest lists and other operational data" that would be necessary in the event of a coup. The CIA's Operating Directive for FY 1972 directed the Santiago station to: "sponsor a program which will enable the Chilean armed forces to retain their integrity and independent political power. Provide direct financial support to key military figures who can be expected to develop a meaningful following in their respective services to restrain and, perhaps, topple the Allende government."

By January 1972, the station was in contact with the leadership of a group it believed might mount a successful coup. The Senate committee report subsequently notes that "the CIA received intelligence reports on the coup planning of the group which carried out the successful September 11 coup throughout the months of July, August, and September 1973."

Nor does the story end with the coup itself. In the weeks that followed, while the junta unleashed a reign of terror unprecedented in the Western Hemisphere, the CIA, according to the committee report, renewed liaison with Chilean security and intelligence forces, allegedly for the purpose of assisting them in "controlling subversion from abroad"; assisted in the preparation of the *White Book*, justifying the overthrow of Allende, and in other means of projecting a more positive image for the junta, both at home and abroad; and helped the military government organize and implement new policies, including the overall economic plan.

The case of Chile represents an aberration only in the extent of violence accompanying the counterrevolution and in the extent of awareness and concern among private citizens in the United States. The Senate committee noted in *Covert Action*: "The pattern of United States covert action in Chile is striking but not unique. It arose in the context not only of American foreign policy, but also of covert U.S. involvement in other countries within and outside Latin America. The scale of CIA involvement in Chile was unusual but by no means unprecedented."

EXCEPTIONS TO THE RULE OF MILITARY INTERVENTION

Since military intervention and military rule have been the norm in Latin America in the past couple of decades, it might be worthwhile to look at the few Latin American countries that have escaped that fate and to ask why. Of the countries that were independent in 1960 (that is, disregarding a number of newly independent Caribbean states) only Mexico, Costa Rica, Colombia, Venezuela, Haiti, and Cuba have been spared military coups d'etat since that time.

Mexico: A Cold Shoulder to U.S. Military Assistance

Civilian supremacy in Mexico has been attributed in part to the mystique of the Revolution and its social goals, to the decisive defeat of counterrevolutionary military insurgencies in the 1920s, and to the strength and flexibility of Mexico's one-party system. Furthermore, as Mexico has a northern neighbor it can do little about and southern neighbors it need do little about, its military establishment has little ground for adventurism or arms races. Perhaps more importantly, Mexico, having lost half its territory to the United States in the nineteenth century and having endured endless U.S. intrigues during the course of its Revolution, has been the only Latin American country continually to shun participation in the U.S. mutual security pacts with their arms assistance and training provisions.

Mexico's military expenditures have been quite modest compared to those of other Latin American countries. Nevertheless, Mexico's military officers have been given political roles and attractive material perquisites as individuals. Furthermore, the military establishment has been given a relatively free hand in dealing with alleged subversives, particularly in areas of continuous rebellion, such as the state of Guerrero.

Venezuela: Postponing the Day of Reckoning

Likewise, the military establishments of Colombia and Venezuela have been praised and pampered and allotted a long leash. In Venezuela, oil prosperity has been a great asset for civilian governments. Petro-dollars have freed them to meet the most urgent demands of lower and middle classes without seriously taxing the rich. Thus would-be military conspirators have been denied the support of the local bourgeoisie.

The petroleum, however, has not been "sown" in agricultural development and industrial diversification fast enough to alleviate the effects of oil-induced inflation and to bridge the gap between rich and poor. Instead of investment in productive capacity, the oil bonanza has largely been absorbed by a bloated bureaucracy.

The experiences of other Latin American countries, particularly Uruguay and Chile, and of Brazil between Getulio Vargas and the generals, have shown that a large, unproductive middle class with acquired tastes, wholly dependent upon the government itself, can swiftly turn reactionary when the economic pie begins to shrink. Taxation of the foreign oil companies in Venezuela served in the past as a substitute for effective taxation of the local elite. The nationalization of the oil industry in 1976 suggests that the next confrontation will be an internal one.

Colombia: Creeping Militarization

The strength of the Colombian oligarchy and its traditional two-party system helps to explain the tenacity of civilian control in that country. The structures of the two parties, reflecting the pyramidal structure of the larger society, and the pervasiveness of party loyalty, has left little room for the emergence of modern parties organized along horizontal lines of common socioeconomic interests. Despite intense rivalry, the two parties have been able to present a common front at various times throughout their history when the dominant position of the oligarchy appeared to be challenged, whether by civilian or military insurgents. Furthermore, the Colombian oligarchy, like the Mexican revolutionary party, has made very effective use of cooptation to diffuse opposition.

Nevertheless, the grip of the traditional oligarchy has appeared more tenuous in recent years, and the military has become increasingly assertive, particularly since the inauguration of Julio César Turbay Ayala in 1978. The trade in illicit drugs, now the country's most important source of foreign exchange, has generated massive corruption and has brought the government into disrepute. Furthermore, the campaign against the drug trade, heavily supported by the U.S. Drug Enforcement Agency, has strengthened various security forces, including the military. In fact some military and paramilitary forces reportedly profit from the drug trade as well as from the campaign against it.

Periodically over the last two decades, the military has reported the capture or elimination of "subversive" groups, generally in isolated areas of the hinterland. In 1979 and 1980, however, the "antisubversive" campaign was accelerated and moved into the cities. Military intelligence agencies arbitrarily detained prominent professionals, as well as students and labor leaders, and torture of political prisoners became common. All of this occurred with the apparent acquiescence of the civilian president.

President Belisario Betancur, elected in 1981, has had considerable success in interrupting the cycle of escalating insurgency and repression. The two major guerrilla groups had accepted a government amnesty, repression against liberal dissidents had subsided, and a government crackdown on drug dealers had been relatively successful. Nevertheless, the armed forces continue to exert strong pressure for repressive powers, and they continue occasionally to defy dictates of civilian leaders and to take matters into their own hands.

Costa Rica: The Virtues of Nonprofessionalism

Although from the period of European settlement Costa Rica had many advantages over its Central American neighbors, including a more homogeneous and integrated population and a more equitable land tenure system, the country, like its neighbors, experienced military coups, dictatorships, and violent conflicts in the nineteenth century and the first half of the twentieth. Following a civil war in 1948, however, the victor in that stuggle, José ("Pepe") Figueres, disbanded the country's armed forces. From that time until the early 1980s, the country's only armed force had been a relatively unprofessional and modestly financed national guard or constabulary, which experienced a major turnover of personnel each time the presidency changed hands. Since the beginning of the Reagan Administration, however, civilian supremacy in Costa Rica has been threatened by a degree of acquiescence to U.S. pressure to transform the guard into a professional military establishment.

Haiti: Checks and Balances

Haiti's military emerged from the period of U.S. occupation as the dominant force in the country's political system. It was brought under control, however, after the election of François Duvalier ("Papa Doc") in 1957 and his establishment of a highly personal dictatorship. Papa Doc tamed the military by setting up an extensive network of armed bodies, each of which reported directly to him and served as a check on the others. Upon his death in 1971, this ghoulish governmental system was passed down to his son, Jean-Claude ("Baby Doc"). Baby Doc has carried out a limited degree of liberalization, but a portion of the paramilitary network has continued to hold the regular armed forces in check.

Cuba: A New Military Class?

The case of Cuba is particularly interesting for what it suggests about the relative influence of ideology and of institutional characteristics and self-interest on the evolution of the political role of the military, as well as about the domestic political consequences of Soviet—as opposed to U.S.—military suzerainty.

The guerrillas who had carried out the successful campaign against Fulgencio Batista found it necessary initially to be all things to all institutions. They became political organizers, economic planners, and administrators as well as military officers. The presence of these "civic soldiers," as Jorge I. Dominguez labeled them, on political councils did not imply that the military had assumed control of the political sphere any more than their presence in the military implied the civilianization of that body. It merely reflected the fact that the revolutionary generation was still in charge.[13]

The institutionalization of the Revolution in the mid-1970s, however, signaled a return to role specialization. The revolutionary generation was being eclipsed by a new generation of administrators and technicians distinguished less for their vision than for their training and experience. This development was reflected in increasing "professionalism" in the military as well.

The "new class" so evident in socialist states of Eastern Europe has not yet made a full-blown appearance in Cuba, but where evidence of such a class does appear it is often in connection with military officers or military institutions. The days of the "civic soldier," or of a distinctly "revolutionary" military establishment, are clearly numbered. Revolutionary rhetoric notwithstanding, Cuba's armed forces have been evolving since the late 1960s along the same lines as military establishments elsewhere in the hemisphere.

The revolutionary rank system has been abandoned in favor of the international one. Among the justifications for this change was the argument that Cuban officers must be able to interact on a basis of equality with their foreign peers. This newly graduated hierarchy was soon reflected in the establishment of military clubs segregated by rank and by other formal and informal trappings of a modern military elite.

There is now an extensive system of military schools. Most of the cadets graduating from military academies in the late 1970s had begun their training in military high schools. Military and civilian analysts alike are beginning to suggest that the military is the strongest institutional force in Cuba and the country's major pool of professional talent.

Furthermore, the military budget has been growing a great deal faster than the economy as a whole. Commitments in Africa have provided the rationale for a continuous expansion of the military establishment, and the cost of the military presence in Africa has predictably heightened the budgetary competition between the armed forces and some civilian ministries. Since the advent of the Reagan Administration, the threat of attack by the United States has served further to reinforce the military establishment.

Communist parties have managed to dominate national military establishments in most Eastern European countries in part because they have served as a direct link with the government of the Soviet Union and their positions have been backed by Soviet military might; but Cuba is not contiguous with the Soviet Union. Cuba, in fact, is still as much a part of Latin America as it is of the Soviet Bloc, and its prerevolutionary tradition, like that of most other Latin American countries, is one of frequent military intervention in politics. Furthermore, the case of Poland suggests that the Soviet Union, like the United States, has found that in the face of broadly based rebellion, a military establishment is a more reliable and effective guardian of the hegemonic order than a civilian political party.

The Soviet Union played no part in Cuba's liberation. Since the Revolution, the Cuban Communist Party has been dominated to a greater extent by Castro and his colleagues from the Sierra Maestra campaign than by the Soviet Union. The party thus has a firm base in Cuba's own revolutionary institutions. Therefore, it seems likely that the Soviet Union, like the United States, will choose to groom the military establishment as the guardian of its imperial interests.

It may be that as long as Fidel Castro and other members of the revolutionary generation are on the scene Cuba will be a special case, and the military will remain subordinated. But it is questionable whether the party in itself, lacking the charismatic leadership of Castro and the link which he and other revolutionaries provide between civilian and military institutions, will be strong enough to maintain civilian control in the long term.[14]

NOTES

1. Victor Alba, "The Stages of Militarism in Latin America," in John J. Johnson, ed., *The Role of the Military in Underdeveloped Countries* (Princeton: Princeton University Press, 1962), pp. 165–184.

2. Martin C. Needler, "Political Development and Military Intervention in Latin America," *The American Political Science Review*, vol. 60 (1966), pp. 616–626.

3. Comprehensive accounts of this relationship are found in Jan Knippers Black, *United States Penetration of Brazil* (Philadelphia: University of Pennsylvania Press, 1977), and in A. J. Langguth, *Hidden Terrors* (New York: Pantheon Books, 1978).

4. Alfred Stepan, *Authoritarian Brazil: Origins, Policies and Future* (New Haven, Conn.: Yale University Press, 1973).

5. Augusto Fragoso, "A Escola Superior de Guerra," *Problemas Brasileiras*, vol. 8, no. 88 (São Paulo, 1970), pp. 19–34.

6. Alfred Stepan and Luigi Einaudi, *Changing Military Perspectives in Peru and Brazil* (Santa Monica, Calif.: Rand Corporation, 1971).

7. Conversation with Victor Paz Estenssoro, Albuquerque, Spring 1978. Paz Estenssoro attributes the survival of the Bolivian revolution through its nascent years primarily to the militias.

8. For more information on the demise and resuscitation of the Bolivian military, see Cole Blasier, *The Hovering Giant: U.S. Response to Revolutionary Change in Latin America* (Pittsburgh: University of Pittsburgh Press, 1976), pp. 128–145; James M. Malloy and Richard S. Thorn,

eds., *Beyond the Revolution: Bolivia Since 1952* (Pittsburgh: University of Pittsburgh Press, 1971); and Charles D. Corbett, *The Latin American Military as a Socio-Political Force: Case Studies of Bolivia and Argentina* (Coral Gables, Fla.: University of Miami, Center for Advanced International Studies, 1972).

9. Conversation, Victor Paz Estenssoro, ibid. Several Americans who were in Bolivia at that time, including Bill Edwards, United States Peace Corps Representative, have expressed the same suspicions to this author.

10. U.S., Congress, Senate, Select Committee to Study Governmental Operations with Respect to Intelligence Activities, "Covert Action in Chile: 1963–1973," in vol. 7, *Covert Action*. Hearings, 94th Cong., 1st sess., December 4 and 5, 1975.

11. In accordance with Black's General Theory of Public Affairs—that no matter how bad the situation appears to be, it is actually worse—it is likely that direct U.S. participation in the coup of September 11 was much more extensive than the public record now reveals.

12. U.S., Congress, Senate, Select Committee to Study Governmental Operations with Respect to Intelligence Activities, *Alleged Assassination Plots Involving Foreign Leaders*. Rept. 94–465, 94th Cong., 1st sess., November 20, 1975.

13. Jorge I. Dominguez, *Cuba: Order and Revolution* (Cambridge: Harvard University Press, 1978).

14. The author's observations on trends in the political role of the military in Cuba are based in part on interviews with Cubans in various sectors and agencies, including members of the Central Committee of the Cuban Communist Party, and with foreign observers and officials resident in Cuba during a research trip in 1979. Some of these trends are also apparent in the Cuban military journal *Verde y Olivo*.

4

Military Rule and Public Policy

By the early 1970s, the idealism that had characterized U.S. policy toward Latin America in the early 1960s had given way to a more traditional stance, and the optimism that had infused scholarly analysis of trends in Latin America had been overtaken by events. The Johnson and Nixon administrations had built upon and reinforced the Kennedy Administration's apparatuses for the promotion and protection of U.S. investments and the maintenance of hemispheric security in the Cold War context. However, the Kennedy Administration's concomitant concern for socioeconomic and political reform had been abandoned. In fact, to both the Johnson and Nixon administrations, reformism, in itself, appeared threatening.

Meanwhile, the dominance of the military in Latin American politics, and particularly of the new category of "institutional" military regimes, led North American specialists in Latin American affairs to a new examination of the nature and consequences of military rule.

In general, the theories of development and modernization that had underpinned the scholarly work of the early 1960s had suggested that the choices for Latin America's future lay be-

tween peaceful, democratically adopted reform and violent revolution. As it became clear that the trend in the 1970s was toward
neither of those, but rather toward violent military-led counterrevolution, U.S. scholars began to look to the work of Latin
American academics for new approaches to the topic. The approach that soon gained supremacy was known as "dependency."

Dependency theory draws upon the Marxist theory of imperialism but assumes a Third World perspective. That is, while
the Marxist theory of imperialism seeks to explain why and how
the dominant classes of the dominant capitalist powers expand
their spheres of exploitation and political control, dependency
theory focuses on what this relationship of unequal bargaining
and multilayered exploitation means to the dominated classes
in the dominated countries. The theory assumes that the causes
of underdevelopment are not to be found in national systems
alone, but must be sought in the pattern of economic and political relations between dominant external powers (or "hegemonic" powers) and their client states. Perpetuation of the pattern within the client states is managed by a clientele class, which
might be seen as the modern functional equivalent of a formal
colonial apparatus. To the extent that economic growth takes
place under conditions imposed by an external capitalist power,
it is a distorted pattern of growth that exacerbates existing in-
equalities among both classes and regions within dependent,
or client, states.

A theoretical model known as "bureaucratic authoritarianism," which has come into use more recently, builds upon many
of the assumptions of dependency theory but serves to elaborate or refine our understanding of politics in dependent states.
Bureaucratic authoritarianism, according to its original expo-
nent, Argentine political scientist Guillermo O'Donnell, derives
from the process of social and economic modernization under
conditions of dependency. Such impersonal, institutional dictatorship is a defense against a perceived threat to the capitalist
system. Levels both of coercion and of economic orthodoxy imposed by the new dictatorial leadership depend upon the level
of perceived threat.[1]

Making use of these theoretical approaches, we will examine

some of the policy choices of military regimes in Latin America—income reconcentration or redistribution, nationalism and nonalignment or more avid courtship of the United States—and the circumstances that have determined which choices would be made. We will illustrate, in particular, the limitations on the range of choices.

COERCION, RECONCENTRATION, AND DENATIONALIZATION

A number of surveys of the comparative economic performance of military and civilian governments in the Third World, conducted in the 1970s and based on aggregate data, lent support to the view that regime differences were relatively unimportant for understanding policy differences. Apart from the problems of unavailability, unreliability, and incomparability of data that weaken the validity of these studies, such overviews usually derived from an unrealistic approach to development, which lumped indicators of economic growth and industrialization together with indicators of redistribution and social welfare.[2] When these indicators are disaggregated, some clear patterns of difference emerge, particularly in Latin America.

In the earliest of these surveys, Nordlinger found a weak correlation between military governments and per capita GNP growth in Latin America in the 1950–1963 period and a strong correlation with industrialization. However, he found that militarism correlated negatively with gross investment, agricultural productivity, educational enrollments, effectiveness of taxation, and commitment to economic development.[3]

Based on the most comprehensive survey to date, Philippe C. Schmitter concluded that military and other noncompetitive regimes were somewhat more successful in curbing inflation, increasing foreign exchange earnings, and promoting industrialization and economic growth. On the other hand, such regimes were less successful in extracting domestic resources for the pursuit of public policy, relied more heavily on indirect taxation, and spent less on social welfare. Schmitter noted, furthermore, that differences between the policies and consequences of military and civilian governments would be greater were it not for the fact that military seizures of power commonly occur to prevent major socioeconomic changes.[4]

A number of generalizations regarding the interplay between development and militarization have been advanced. For instance, Samuel Huntington has suggested that in the world of oligarchy, the soldier is a radical; in the middle-class world he is a participant and arbiter; as the mass society looms on the horizon, he becomes the conservative guardian of the traditional order.[5] This theory is partially validated by numerous surveys, both global and regional, which indicate that reform-oriented military regimes are more likely to be found in the least developed countries.

The experience of Latin America in the 1960s and 1970s suggests that the soldier is more likely to serve the traditional order, or to modernize without attempting to transform the social structure, regardless of the level of development. Nevertheless, when the Latin American soldier does emerge as a radical it is indeed from the world of the oligarchy. Of the military regimes that held power during this period long enough to develop and implement their own policies, only those of Peru and Panama had clearly redistributive phases.[6] The economic policies of most of Latin America's military regimes during the 1960s and 1970s were designed to promote accumulation or reconcentration rather than redistribution of wealth. While some were able to do little more than hold the line against threats to the status quo, others—those of Chile, Uruguay, and Argentina, for example—brought about a major transfer of income from wage-earning to capitalist classes, and one, Brazil, greatly modernized its economic system while generating economic growth and reconcentration.

The process of reconcentration has generally begun with a dampening of inflation through cutting back effective demand. Demand is cut through the pruning of social services, particularly those involving income transfer, and through wage freezes. Frozen wages, along with other indicators that the government has brought labor under control, can be expected to inspire the confidence of investors, both domestic and foreign. Other measures, however, such as credit, tax, and tariff policies, commonly favor foreign businesses over domestic ones. Domestic enterprises are absorbed by transnational ones, and a general denationalization and oligopolization occurs. The production system stresses exports, whether of raw materials or of manufactured goods. Domestic production favors consumer durables. Based on imported technology and product lines, its target market is the upper and middle classes. In fact, those of Uruguay, Argentina, and, particularly, Chile followed policies of deindustrialization that nullified several decades of economic development.

Having successfully completed the first stage of economic transformation, the regime may then turn its attention to the promotion of industrialization, rural modernization through high-technology agribusiness, and infrastructural projects such as highways, ports, and dams. In the case of Brazil, the military government, after the first half dozen years in power, began to play an important entrepreneurial role and to impose its own guidelines on foreign investors. Other reconcentrational military regimes in Latin America were not able to follow suit.

Like those military regimes that have been able to modernize the economy without undermining the traditional social structure, those that have carried out redistributional change have done so through expanding the state sector and increasing the power of the state itself vis-a-vis private economic sectors and interest groups. The expansion of the state sector signifies, in turn, the expansion of the middle class, albeit a highly insecure and dependent class. Most military governments, however, that have evidenced redistributional and nationalistic inclinations have been even shorter-lived than their civilian counterparts.

With the exception of Cuba, now heavily dependent on the Soviet Union and its socialist allies, neither civilian nor military governments of Latin America have escaped dependence on the international capitalist system in general and the United States in particular. Since military governments are less likely to have a sizable organized domestic constituency, they tend to be even more dependent than civilian regimes on external powers. The highest level of dependency is exhibited by military regimes in the early stages of counterrevolution.

Much of the consistency in the economic policies and consequences of military regimes might be explained not merely by the fact that they are military, but by the fact that a military regime was the only kind that could have effectively carried out political demobilization and a reconcentration and denationalization of wealth. It is not surprising then that repression has been most harsh in the countries that had enjoyed the highest levels of political participation: Chile, Uruguay, and Argentina. In these countries, as well as in Brazil, the military regimes that emerged in the 1960s and 1970s were of the "bureaucratic authoritarian" type, as they sought through force to neutralize a perceived threat to the capitalist system. The greater the proportion of the population that had come to participate in the political system and the more intensive that participation, the greater the violence required, at least initially, to dissolve organizations, eliminate leaders, and intimidate followers.

While bureaucratic authoritarian regimes are necessarily military or based on the exercise of military and paramilitary force, military regimes are not necessarily of the bureaucratic authoritarian type. The Peruvian military regime of 1968–1975, while bureaucratic and authoritarian in style of governance, proceeded, to some extent, from nationalistic and populistic motives. Its accomplishments were limited, however, by the country's inability to escape its economic dependence on the United States. Bolivia's military governments of the 1960s and 1970s followed a zigzag course on economic policy, but those leaders who favored foreign investors and kept labor under control were richly rewarded by the Johnson and Nixon administrations.

CHOICES AND CONSTRAINTS: FOUR CASES

Brazil

From "Colonial Fascism" to State Capitalism. In spite of American training and other assistance, economic nationalism and reformist inclinations had remained strong in the Brazilian military in the 1950s. However, by 1963 the economic crisis—a bad case of stagflation—had caused the upper and middle classes to square off against labor, assuming that its gains could only be at their expense. The military, in particular, felt that in terms of salary and status it was being reduced to the level of manual laborers. Moreover, groups representing lower-class interests had begun to break with the corporatist pattern. Members of the clergy were clashing with the Church hierarchy. Strikes and demonstrations had begun to go beyond the Labor Ministry's control, and rural unionization had become a free-for-all among the peasant leagues, radical Catholics, moderate Catholics, and Communists. Finally, noncommissioned officers had begun to be insubordinate to their superiors, reaching the point of actual mutiny in some instances.

The launching of Brazil's counterrevolution of 1964 has been called a bloodless coup. While that was not precisely the case (a dozen or more resisters were killed), the level of violence accompanying the military seizure of power in Brazil did not approach that which occurred in Chile almost a decade later. The development of political consciousness and independent organization, and the level of participation on the part of Brazil's lower classes, had proceeded only far enough to alarm the upper classes and their external allies; most of the poor remained passive, unorganized, and dependent.

Despite the near absence of organized resistance to the coup, more than 7,000 people were arrested within the week after it. During the months that followed several thousand more were removed from their elected and appointed positions. The labor and education ministries and the universities were purged. Labor and student organizations were dissolved or brought under government control. Nevertheless, the Brazilian military moved cautiously and methodically to consolidate its control of the political system. By allowing some civilians to participate while disqualifying others and allowing those who cooperated to profit from the demise of those who did not, the military rulers kept their opposition disorganized and disoriented.

It was not until almost five years after the initial coup that the military regime moved to silence its detractors and to crush the last vestiges of organized opposition. In 1969 it became clear that torture of political prisoners was systematic and that death squads operated with impunity. By the early 1970s the political surveillance that had become so pervasive in many civilian sectors had become common in the military as well, and officers were frequently removed from their posts for ideological deviation.

The political system that grew out of the military's so-called Revolution of 1964 was termed by Brazilian political scientist Helio Jaguaribe "colonial fascism." He maintained that the establishment of rigidly authoritarian rule and the preservation of oligarchical privilege could not have been carried out without external assistance, which was brought at the price of massive denationalization of resources.[7]

During the first three years after the military seizure of power, Brazil's economic performance continued to be dismal by anyone's standards. Inflation and unemployment were high, growth and direct new investment were low, and in response to the policy of "constructive bankruptcy" nationally owned businesses were wiped out or bought out at a dizzying pace. By 1968, however, the transnational corporate community had gained confidence in the Brazilian system, and, spurred by massive foreign investment, Brazil entered a phase that came to be known as the "economic miracle." The miracle was reflected for half a dozen years in annual growth rates of about 10 percent. Furthermore, a considerable proportion of the accumulated capital was invested in infrastructure projects that were to propel the country toward great power status. Considerable progress was made toward the physical integration of the country through the construction of the transamazon and peripheral highway systems. Human resources were not entirely uncultivated, as the provision of technical training was expanded. In addition, the fruits of economic growth that in the mid-1960s had accrued so heavily to foreigners eventually served to strengthen the Brazilian government as an economic actor.

Brazil's development model was erected, however, at great social cost. The increased prosperity of the few rested upon the further impoverishment of the many. The real minimum wage had dropped by 30 to 38 percent between 1960 and 1970, and in the latter year more than 60 percent of the population earned less than the minimum wage. According to Celso Furtado, the richest 900,000 Brazilians had the same total income in 1970 as the poorest 45 million.[8]

The "Special Relationship". Following Brazil's counterrevolution of 1964, both Brazilian and U.S. governments spoke unashamedly of their special relationship. While the military regime systematically dismantled democratic institutions and silenced its detractors, the U.S. government showered it with praise and public assistance. And American private investors responded enthusiastically to the highly favorable terms offered them. Following hearings before the Western Hemisphere Affairs Subcommittee of the U.S. Senate Foreign Relations Committee in 1971, Senator Frank Church suggested that the United States had pumped into Brazil more than $2 billion of the American taxpayers' money in order to provide a favorable climate for $1.6 billion in private investments.[9] Clearly, the network for political surveillance which the United States Public Safety Assistance Program helped to establish and the American Institute for Free Labor Development's training of "dependable" leaders of the labor movement contributed to a burst of economic expansion based on high profits and low wages.

As so often happens when the United States caters to a military regime, the role of the Department of State was eclipsed for a time by the Pentagon. United States Ambassador John Tuthill, who assumed the Brazilian post in 1966, took a dim view of the consolidating coup of 1968, in which the congress was closed for several months and remaining civil liberties were extinguished. Thus the Brazilian government and the American military mission virtually boycotted U.S. Embassy civilians and conducted the "delicate" affairs of state among themselves.

In December 1971, General Emilio Garrastazu Médici, Brazil's third military president after the 1964 coup, paid an official visit to the United States. Reports circulating in the international press of officially condoned death squads in Brazil and of the systematic use of torture on political prisoners did not deter President Nixon from saying of Médici that "in the brief time that he has been president of Brazil there has been more progress than in any comparable time in the whole history of that country." He added, "We know that as Brazil goes, so will go the rest of that Latin American continent."[10] (And so, in certain grisly respects, it did.) Other South American states that had come to fear Brazilian hegemony were hardly reassured when Sec. of State Henry Kissinger in 1976 publicly pledged to consult with Brazil on foreign policy initiatives contemplated by the United States—this at a time when he could scarcely be coaxed to consult with the U.S. Congress!

American bilateral development assistance, extended through AID, began to decrease in the early 1970s as Brazil's "economic miracle" unfolded. But overall foreign aid to Brazil was increasing as a consequence of increases in military assistance and in loans from the United States Export-Import Bank and international lending agencies. By the mid-1970s Brazil had become the best customer of the Export-Import Bank and the largest single recipient of loans from the World Bank. The Public Safety Assistance program was terminated by Congress in 1974, but many of its functions were assumed, in Brazil as elsewhere, by the Drug Enforcement Administration.

United States investment in Brazil continued to increase dramatically in the 1970s. But the proportion of Brazilian industry controlled by American investors dropped relative to both the shares controlled by transnational corporations based elsewhere and the portion controlled by the Brazilian government itself.

Chile

Until the counterrevolution of 1973, Chile had been one of the few Latin American countries to have enjoyed constitutional and more or less democratic government throughout most of its history as an independent nation. Political democracy had not been translated into economic democracy, however, although a rudimentary social welfare system and state participation in the economy had been developing over several decades. The election of socialist Salvador Allende to the presidency in 1970 had aroused hopes among the lower classes and fears among the upper and middle classes and their external allies that far-reaching redistribution of wealth was in the offing.

Violent Demobilization. Chile's counterrevolution began with the cold-blooded murder of members of the armed forces and police whom the conspirators suspected of loyalty to the constitutional government. Scores of officers and enlisted men were killed before the assault on the presidential palace.

There are no universally accepted casualty figures for the first days, weeks, or months following the military takeover. Casualty estimates for the first few days of organized resistance alone run as high as 25,000. The systematic use of torture began even before the tanks rolled into the streets. Public gathering places were transformed into prisons and morgues. A U.S. couple held in the Santiago sports stadium reported witnessing or hearing between 400 and 500 executions by automatic weapons of people brought out in groups of ten to twenty.[11] Within weeks of the military takeover concentration camps had been established throughout the remote areas of the country, and tens of thousands of workers and professionals whose commitment to anticommunism was less than fervent had been dismissed from their jobs.

Chile's universities had produced much of the original and influential theorizing about the constraints of "dependent" development, about the potential advantages of Latin American economic unity, and—yes—about U.S. imperialism; and they paid a heavy price for having been right. All the universities were thoroughly purged and placed under the direct control of military rectors. Thousands of professors and students were dismissed, and entire departments and research institutions were abolished. A foreign sociologist who visited Chile in 1977 was told by a smug Minister of Justice, "There are no sociologists here; they're all six feet under."

The Roman Catholic Church has been called upon to provide an umbrella for what remains of independent expression in the universities. Researchers have been somewhat less vulnerable to government reprisal if their work was sponsored by a Church-related institution or if a bishop could be persuaded to contribute an article to an anthology.

The Church is by no means invulnerable, but it is the only social institution that the generals have not dared to try to crush in a direct and all-out manner. They have preferred to attack it indirectly—for example, by imprisoning and torturing, or assigning their thugs to beat up, the lawyers and other laypersons who worked with the Vicaría de la Solidaridad, the Church's social arm. As a sort of countergovernment—the most reliable source of information, the only public defender and welfare agency at the service of the common people—the Vicaría has been overwhelmed, as well as harassed and closely watched.

Marginalizing the Masses. The process of reconcentration in Chile, following the 1973 coup, was similar to that of Brazil except that it was even more rapid and more extreme. Throughout the remainder of the decade, a large proportion of the population was engaged in a daily struggle against starvation.

In the weeks immediately following the coup, land and factories that had been transferred to, or seized by, their workers were returned to their original owners. Thousands lost their jobs, and wages were frozen while inflation climbed to rates among the highest ever experienced by any country in peacetime. Industrial production dropped dramatically, and corporate entities that had belonged to the state for more than a decade were sold to private interests.

By the late 1970s inflation was falling and production was rising, but nationally owned manufacturing industries and retail businesses were folding at the rate of several a day. Effective demand in the domestic market, never very "effective" for anything other than staple commodities, had all but vanished since the inception of military rule, leaving promise only in the export sector. The so-called Chicago boys (trained at the University of Chicago), who were managing the economy, had introduced a strategy akin to what the Chicago boys of Brazil's military dictatorship in the mid-1960s had called "constructive bankruptcy." They had virtually eliminated protective tariffs and had offered various incentives and advantages to foreign investors. This was resulting in the absorption of "inefficient" national concerns by "efficient" transnational ones. Furthermore, the generalized panic in the business community was enabling a group of speculators in the world of banking and finance, known as the *piranhas* (after the man-eating fish of the Amazon River), to rob the country blind.[12]

Despite the generous incentives offered them, new foreign investors were slow to indicate confidence in the Chilean regime. This was due in part to the generally disastrous economic performance of the regime's first several years. Furthermore, while the Nixon Administration embraced the regime, the U.S. Congress did not. Subsequently, the ambivalence of the Ford and Carter administrations toward the Pinochet dictatorship and its frequent condemnation by international forums cast doubt on its staying power. By 1980, however, the regime appeared to be comfortably entrenched, and the pace of foreign investment had increased substantially. Nevertheless, with its small size and limited resource base, not to mention the high level of repression that continued to be required, Chile was unable to move, as Brazil did, from this stage of "colonial fascism" to one in which the state itself had considerable power and leverage in international or transnational economic dealings. In fact, by 1983, as we shall see, Pinochet had accomplished, presumably unintentionally, what no socialist government could have: the utter destruction of the private domestic industrial and commercial sectors.

Peru

Military Radicals in the World of the Oligarchy. In the case of the Peruvian coup of 1968, the obstacle to military power was not the masses but the oligarchy. Despite considerable urbanization, industrialization, and other presumed indicators of social mobilization, Peru had yet to experience the "emergence of the middle classes." The country's income distribution in 1968 was among the most unequal in the world, but the bitter feud between the military and the major middle-class party, the American Popular Revolutionary Alliance (APRA), had enabled the oligarchy to use the military to protect its own interests.

The APRA, long considered the prototype of the national revolutionary party in the Western Hemisphere, had found that in order to share in power, even behind the scenes, it was necessary to postpone or abandon its more radical principles and programs. Meanwhile, the military establishment had itself undergone a far-reaching transformation. By the mid-1950s the officer corps was composed largely of mestizos from the outlying rural areas. Excluded by race and background from upper-class society and by occupation and political role from the middle and lower classes, they constituted a relatively isolated and alienated group. General Juan Velasco Alvarado, who spearheaded the coup of 1968 and assumed the presidency, was himself a mestizo from the province of Piurá. He had grown up, in fact, just outside the gates of the International Petroleum Company's Talara refinery, and he harbored deep resentment of the contempt and condescension with which the company's managers had dealt with his neighbors.[13]

Once in power, the military proceeded to confound civilian political leaders by carrying out reforms long promised by the APRA and other Center and Leftist groups. The expropriation of the International Petroleum Company was followed by measures curbing the power of the landowning oligarchy, channeling capital from land into industry, and extending governmental controls over industrial enterprises and financial institutions.

The Velasco government identified the petroleum and land reform issues as its most immediate concerns. On its second day in office it abrogated the Act of Talara. Five days later it seized the 416,000-acre oilfields and the refinery of the International Petroleum Company. It refused to compensate the company, maintaining that the company owed Peru more than half a billion dollars in back taxes, on the grounds that it had been operating illegally in the country since 1924. This action brought Peru into a protracted dispute with the U.S. government, but it provided the new government with a much-needed reserve of popular support.

Comparatively speaking, the repression practiced by General Velasco's reformist military government was mild. It dissolved congress, suspended political parties, and brought the communications media under control. It periodically arrested critics and political opponents, but repression was neither as extensive nor as harsh as was the case in countries undergoing counterrevolution.

The Velasco government sought, and apparently obtained, widespread support among peasants and workers. The populistic response it generated was strictly controlled, however, from the seats of authority. Autonomous grass-roots organization was not encouraged, and the mobilization of nonelite groups on their own behalf was not permitted.

The Limits of Nationalism. Velasco soon found that a certain level of accommodation with the United States could not be avoided. The United States, in turn, found it possible to deal with that government in a manner more moderate than that customarily accorded to reformist civilian regimes.

The president of the United States, under the Hickenlooper Amendment to the Foreign Assistance Act of 1962 and the 1961 amendment to the Sugar Act, was required to withhold foreign aid from, and suspend the sugar quota for, any country that failed to take appropriate steps to compensate American firms for expropriated property. In the face of widespread support in Latin America for the action of the Peruvian government, the United States government maintained that the legislation made allowance for protracted negotiations. When the deadline for application of the Hickenlooper Amendment arrived, it was announced that its application would be postponed indefinitely. In fact, however, U.S. aid, which had amounted to only $9.9 million in fiscal 1968, dropped to an annual level of about $3.5 million.

The continuing seizures of American fishing vessels by the Peruvian Navy led the United States in 1969, in accord with the Foreign Military Sales Act, to ban arms sales to Peru. Peru responded by evicting the United States military mission from the country.

Only after it became clear that the United States did not intend to invoke the Hickenlooper Amendment did the Velasco regime launch its most far-reaching reforms. In mid-1969, the government promulgated a series of land reform measures designed to distribute the land held in large estates, including the foreign-owned commercial plantations in the northern coastal area. Reimbursement was to be in government bonds unless the former owners agreed to invest 50 percent of an immediate cash payment in the industrial sector. The export-oriented coastal plantations, especially those in the northern departments of La Libertad, Lambayeque, and Ancash, were the first to be affected by the implementation of the land reform law. This was generally seen as a result of the government's determination to diminish the power of the sugar interests and to undercut Aprista strength, centered among workers in that area.

Novel approaches to industrialization were also adopted. The General Law of Industries, decreed in July 1970, established an order of investment priorities, beginning with heavy essential industries and dropping to essential services and consumer goods, nonessential goods, and, finally, luxuries. High-priority industrial sectors came under the state's jurisdiction, with private participation at the government's discretion. In addition, industries were required to distribute a certain percentage, varying by industry, of their net income before taxes to their employees and an equal amount to an "industrial community," whose board was charged with overseeing investment policy. Incentives were offered for the relocation of industry outside of the Lima-Callao area.

The banking system and the mining industry were also subject to reforms. Companies with mineral concessions were directed in September 1969 to file schedules for developing their prospects. A second decree in August 1970 required firms with large- or medium-sized holdings to present proof by the end of the year that they had secured the financing necessary to put their deposits into production. In the event of failure, the concessions were to revert to the state.

Other economic reforms included the marketing of major exports by the state and exchange controls prohibiting Peruvians from taking money abroad, holding funds in foreign banks, or possessing foreign currency. Economic growth, after lagging behind population increases in 1968 and 1969, approached 6 percent in 1970, in spite of the earthquake that struck Ancash Department and killed over 50,000 persons. Unemployment remained a problem, however, and by the early 1970s it was clear that there would not be enough investment capital, domestic or foreign, to finance all of the government's major projects.

Private U.S. interests had been adversely affected by reforms in agriculture, industry, and banking. The agrarian reform law, for example, decreed on June 24, 1969, resulted in the expropriation of sugar plantations owned by an American company. In this and in most cases, however, acceptable provisions were made for compensation. By the end of 1971 the Peruvian government had eased some of the restrictions originally imposed on foreign investments and had entered into contracts with a number of American companies for oil exploration, mining, and other enterprises.

Despite the redistributive domestic policies and independent foreign policies of the government of General Velasco, the United States never displayed the unrelieved hostility toward the Peruvian military regime that it did toward the contemporary civilian government of Salvador Allende in neighboring Chile. Velasco's charges of CIA involvement in the police strike and riots that immediately preceded the overthrow of his government, to this author's knowledge, have not been substantiated.

Nevertheless, the United States was clearly pleased by the 1975 coup that replaced General Velasco with the more conservative General Francisco Morales Bermúdez.[14] And the new regime was openly solicitous of improved relations with the United States. This rapprochement was facilitated by the new president's restoration of private enterprise in some previously nationalized sectors of the domestic economy and his proffering of new incentives to foreign investors. His policy was to manage the burgeoning foreign debt by increasing foreign capital inflows to develop mining and petroleum in joint ventures with the state enterprises. Under his government Peru, in Third World forums, ceased to champion an international moratorium on debts owed to the developed countries.

President Morales Bermúdez's government also backtracked on Peru's stance of nonalignment. Secretary of State Henry Kissinger visited Peru in February 1976 and reportedly expressed sympathy with Peru's financial straits but indicated that aid would hinge on an unambiguous stand in the Cold War.[15]

Bolivia

The First Throes of Counterrevolution. The case of postrevolutionary Bolivia, where military governments of reconcentrational and redistributional tendencies have alternated in power, is highly revealing of the grip of dependency. Under Barrientos, who seized power in 1964, the military occupied the mines, the labor movement was virtually dismantled, and American investors had a field day. In 1964 Gulf Oil produced three percent of the total Bolivian petroleum output and the state agency produced 95 percent. Three years later Gulf had 82 percent of that production and the state share had slipped under 20 percent. When Ché Guevara's guerrilla movement surfaced in 1967, the United States sent in a team of Green Berets to train a special counterinsurgency force that became known as the Rangers. The three Ranger battalions remained for a decade or more an efficient force for repression and a reactionary influence within the military.

Bolivian writer Sergio Almaraz Paz observed that "after the assumption of power by the North Americans . . . Bolivians began to feel uncomfortable with each other . . . Local functionaries did not know how to deal with their colleagues from another office because they didn't know the latter's relationship with the foreigner." [16] In 1968 his unease was shown to be well founded, as Minister of the Interior Antonio Arquedas, who had masterminded a large-scale crackdown on labor, students, and other leftist groups, admitted publicly that he had been a CIA agent and that the agency had penetrated all levels of the Bolivian government. [17]

Swings of the Pendulum. The two military presidents who followed Barrientos, Ovando (1969–1970) and Torres (1970–1971), attempted to gain popular support by appealing to economic nationalism. Ovando nationalized Gulf Oil and Torres nationalized two more American firms, including the Matilde Mine, owned by United States Steel, Phillips Brothers, and Engelhard Minerals. Neither ever gained the full confidence of the labor-Left, but Torres gave it enough freedom to scare the United States and its Latin American allies.

The conspiracy to overthrow Torres was apparently a multilateral affair involving Brazil, Argentina, and Paraguay, as well as the United States. The *Washington Post* (March 21, 1971) reported that a U.S. Air Force major had provided a radio receiver when the conspirators' communications system broke down. Gulf Oil was rumored to be involved, and a high official of Engelhard told this author that his company had had a man assigned to the conspiracy, but that he was caught before the coup and barely managed to get out of the country.

The coup itself turned out to be the bloodiest confrontation since the revolution and the Banzer regime one of the most repressive in Bolivian history. It also turned out to be one of the regimes most highly favored by U.S. assistance. About $14 million in "special emergency assistance" was extended immediately after the coup. Another $8 million was extended three months later. Banzer, in turn, decreed a new investment code that was particularly generous to foreign investors and moved to settle all the outstanding claims of American companies. In the case of the Matilde Mine, for example, he borrowed enough money from American banks to pay the former owners in cash even more than they had asked for.

In 1972, under pressure from the United States, the International Monetary Fund, and the World Bank, Banzer devalued the currency by 67 percent against the dollar. United States economic assistance for that year amounted to $60 million, more than at any time since 1964, and military assistance was $3.7 million, the highest ever. Economic assistance declined after 1972, but "security assistance" continued to rise. Direct grant military assistance for 1973 and 1974 was more than three times that extended to any other Latin American country. Bolivia received $47 million in loans between 1972 and 1976, twice the amount the country had received between 1962 and 1971, a period twice as long. Foreign investments increased from a total of $37 million during 1960–1969 to $46.5 million in 1971, $82.3 million in 1972, $28 million in 1973, and $41.9 million in 1974. Meanwhile real wages dropped 0.8 percent in 1972, 18.5 percent in 1973, and 35 percent in 1974.[18]

MILITARY SUPREMACY AND DEFENSE EXPENDITURE

A number of surveys based on aggregate data collected since the 1950s have confirmed what common sense suggests—that military regimes or political systems in which the military establishment wields power spend more on "defense" than do governments in which the military is clearly subordinated to civilian institutions. Drawing upon data collected by Nordlinger and Schmitter, Samuel E. Finer observed that between 1950 and 1967 defense expenditures in those Latin American states in which the armed forces were most nearly subordinated averaged only 9.3 percent of central government expenditures, whereas for those states that endured intermittent military intervention, defense expenditures averaged 14.1 percent. For those states ruled by the military around 1960, it averaged 18.5 percent. Between 1960 and 1965, the least militarized states increased defense expenditures by 2.8 percent annually, the group suffering intermittent intervention by 3.3 percent, and the group under military rule by 14 percent.[19]

Governments that do not respond to their constituencies, whether those constituencies are large or small, domestic or external, cannot expect to hold power for very long. The first-line constituency of an "institutional" military regime is, of course, the institution itself. Furthermore, the difference in military spending between military and civilian regimes would be far greater were it not for the fact that most civilian regimes in Latin America have been highly vulnerable to military intervention, and whatever the multilayered motives for a military seizure of power, those motives are translated, in the final analysis and in the final stages of coalition building, into defense of individual and corporate interest. In 1969 Victor Villanueva observed that every Peruvian government that had attempted to reduce the military budget had been overthrown.[20]

From 1968 through 1977, Latin American armed forces straightforwardly claimed an average of 12.6 percent of the budgets of their central governments.[21] During that period military expenditures for the region as a whole peaked in 1975 at U.S. $6.3 billion, up from $2.3 billion in 1968.[22]

U.S. Arms Transfers and Military Expansion

United States security assistance to Latin America increased dramatically after Pres. Richard M. Nixon waived the congressionally imposed ceiling on arms sales to the region in 1971. Between 1973 and 1975 the total value of military grants and credit sales more than tripled, from $72.5 million to $218.2 million. In 1975, the largest sum in grants was extended to Bolivia ($3.3 million), and the largest credit sales to Brazil ($60 million), Argentina ($30 million), Chile ($20 million), and Peru ($20 million)—most military dictatorships. During the same year Brazil's military expenditures amounted to 20.4 percent of the central government's budget, Argentina's 9.7, Chile's 17.2, and Peru's 21.5. By comparison, the civilian governments of Mexico and Venezuela devoted 5.7 percent and 5.8 percent, respectively, of their 1975 budgets to the military. In 1976, the year of Carter's election to the presidency, both the total military expenditure of the region and the average proportion of central government budgets allocated to the military began to drop.

The size of military establishments in Latin America in the 1970s varied greatly, from Brazil with 450,000 men under arms in 1977 to Costa Rica's 3,000-man national guard. Population size and resource base accounted for much of the variation, but regime type was clearly a factor as well. Mexico, with a population of 63.7 million in 1977, had an armed force of only 100,000 while Argentina, with 26.2 million people, had 155,000 men under arms.

Disregarding Cuba, which had more than one percent of its population under arms, the Latin American countries under military rule had about twice the proportion of their population (.5 percent) under arms in 1977 than the civilian-rule countries had. Those figures are not as revealing, however, as trends in the countries that had undergone military seizures of power between 1968 and 1977. Each of them had experienced an increase in the size of their armed forces. In some cases that increase was quite dramatic. The Chilean armed forces, for example, grew from 75,000 (.759 percent of the population) in 1973 to 111,000 (1.057 percent of the population) in 1977. Uruguay's militarization occurred more gradually; its armed forces grew from 15,000 (.54 percent of the population) in 1968 to 28,000 (.972 percent of the population) in 1977.[23]

Military Rule and Arms Control Prospects

The prevalence of military rule does not, in itself, increase the danger of interstate conflict in the short turn. Military governments who are occupying their own countries as if they were alien turf clearly need each other. In the 1970s, elaborate transnational intelligence networks were established. National secret police agencies tracked their prey across borders with the greatest of ease, and political refugees often met violent deaths in their newly adopted countries.

Virtually all of the Latin American countries have ongoing border disputes with at least one neighbor. Nevertheless, the specter of interstate conflict is most often raised when civil strife, particularly of an insurrectionary nature, occurs in areas where dictatorial regimes are contiguous with democratic ones. Most of the conflicts in the period since World War II that have been serious enough to warrant recourse to the Rio treaty of 1947 and the peacekeeping machinery of the Organization of American States have arisen in Central America and the Caribbean. In the mid-1980s, civil strife in El Salvador, Nicaragua, and Guatemala was threatening to embroil all of Central America in war.

The prevalence of military rule does not bode well, however, for the prospects for arms control and the maintenance of regional peace in the long run. We have seen that military regimes are prone to spend more than civilian ones on arms and armies. They are also less likely to initiate or to respond to arms control efforts. The issue of a regional approach to arms control has periodically been brought before the Organization of American States, in each instance save one by governments under civilian control.

The efforts of Costa Rica in 1958 and Chile in 1959 to promote, through the OAS, discussions of the possibilities of limiting expenditures on conventional arms came to naught. In preparation for the inter-American summit meeting of 1967, there was some discussion of working toward an agreement to shun certain categories of advanced weaponry. The heads of state, however, issued only a relatively meaningless declaration of intent to limit military expenditures as national security requirements permitted.

Finally, Colombia, in 1971, proposed that a committee be established to study means of implementing the 1967 declaration. The Colombian proposal had outlined several specific topics for study, but the resolution finally adopted by the OAS General Assembly merely authorized a study of the meaning and scope of the 1967 declaration. That limited study, undertaken by the Permanent Council, concluded that although the declaration remained in effect its application was left to individual governments, and the OAS assumed no oversight function.[24]

The issue was raised again in 1974, this time by the Peruvian government of General Juan Velasco Alvarado. Meeting in Lima on December 9, 1974, just eight months before Velasco was overthrown, the governments of Argentina, Bolivia, Chile, Colombia, Ecuador, Panama, Peru, and Venezuela signed the Ayacucho Declaration. This document, which pledged its signatories to "create the conditions which will make possible the effective limitation of armaments and an end to their acquisition for offensive purposes," was seen, in the first instance, as a step toward defusing the arms race between Peru and Chile.[25]

The most serious arms control effort undertaken by Latin America, or, for that matter, any area of the Third World, has been the Treaty of Tlatelolco. That treaty, signed by most of the Latin American states in 1967, declares Latin America to be a nuclear free zone. It came into being largely through the efforts of Mexico, with strong support from several other states at that time under civilian governments. Protocol I to the treaty requires those states with responsibilities for territories within the zone to apply treaty provisions to those territories. Protocol II requires nuclear-weapon states to respect the denuclearized status of the zone.

By 1980 the Netherlands and the United Kingdom had ratified Protocol I. France and the United States had signed but had not ratified. The United States, France, the United Kingdom, China, and the Soviet Union had ratified Protocol II. The treaty itself was in effect for twenty-two Latin American states. Brazil and Chile had ratified but were not bound by the treaty as they had not waived the entry-into-force requirements. Argentina had signed but had not ratified, and Cuba had not signed.[26] Brazil and Argentina were the only Latin American countries known to have advanced programs for the development of nuclear power, but Chile and Cuba had initiated such programs.[27]

Meanwhile, by the early 1980s the United States had lost its near-monopoly position as a supplier of arms to Latin American governments. Some individual decisions on the part of Latin American governments to look to Western European countries, to Israel, or even to the Soviet Union for arms can be traced to the advent of new governments in Latin America or of new policies in the United States and some to particularly attractive terms offered by extrahemispheric suppliers. On the whole, however, this shift in the arms trade has simply been a part of a larger trend, notable since the early 1970s, of expanding relations of trade and aid between Latin America and other parts of the world, particularly Western Europe. Of a total value of $5.5 billion attributed to arms transfers to Latin American countries in the period 1975–1979, the United States accounted for only $725 million. Other major suppliers included the Soviet Union, France, Great Britain, West Germany, Italy, and Canada.[28]

Also, in the course of the 1970s, Brazil and Argentina had entered the ranks of major arms exporters. Brazil, in fact, had become the world's sixth largest manufacturer and exporter of conventional weapons by 1984. The industry, which employs some 100,000 people in 400 firms, produces warplanes, missiles, tanks, hand grenades, pistols, and bullets; 95 percent of its armaments are exported. The products most in demand are its armored vehicles. The industry's sales, to some 33 Third World countries, were expected to bring in about $3 billion in 1984.

THE POLITICS OF ANTIPOLITICS

Of Latin America's many military regimes of the 1960s and 1970s, that of Brazil most nearly fits the stereotype of the new military governing elite. However, similarities in the formative experiences of this generation of military leaders, deriving in large part from their incorporation into the hemispheric strategy of the United States, tended to outweigh the differences deriving from national experiences and levels of development. Regardless of whether policy goals at any given moment favored nationalism or "internationalism," redistribution or reconcentration, there were common characteristics to be found that distinguished this generation from previous generations of military leaders. Cleavages within the military establishment and alignment of officers with competing groups of civilians were delegitimized; *caudillismo* was superseded by institutional rule.

The only norms that rulers dreaded to flout were those that preserved the discipline and hierarchical order of the military itself.

The prevailing ideologies varied, but the prevailing mentality was uniformly bureaucratic. Managerial skills were regarded as preferable replacements for the discredited political skills. Governance was viewed as an exercise in order and unity, the elimination rather than the resolution of conflict, and it was assumed that there were technical solutions to social and political problems. Modernization—expressed, for example, in industrialization, the development of infrastructure, and technological advancement—was a cherished goal.

Finally, this generation of military elites was characterized by sanctimoniousness. These standard-bearers of the postdemocratic era approached their mandate with the full assurance of the divine right of generals.

NOTES

1. Guillermo O'Donnell, *Modernization and Bureaucratic Authoritarianism: Studies in South American Politics*, Politics of Modernization Series No. 9 (Berkeley, Calif.: Institute of International Studies, University of California, 1973).

2. Karen L. Remmer summarizes and criticizes these findings in "Evaluating the Policy Impact of Military Regimes in Latin America," *Latin American Research Review*, vol. XIII, no. 2, 1978, pp. 39–54.

3. Eric A. Nordlinger, "Soldiers in Mufti: The Impact of Military Rule upon Economic and Social Change in the Non-Western States," *American Political Science Review*, vol. LXIX, no. 64, 1970, pp. 1131–1148.

4. Philippe C. Schmitter, ed., *Military Rule in Latin America: Function, Consequences and Perspectives* (Beverly Hills, Calif.: Sage Publications, 1973), pp. 117–187.

5. Samuel Huntington, *Political Order in Changing Societies* (New Haven, Conn.: Yale University Press, 1968), p. 221.

6. A junta of contradictory tendencies that held power in Ecuador for two and a half years between 1963 and 1966 developed a scheme for land reform but was not able to get past the initial stages of implementation. The briefer tenures of Ovando and Torres in Bolivia will be discussed in a different context.

7. Helio Jaguaribe, "Political Strategies of National Development in Brazil," in Irving L. Horowitz, Josué de Castro, and John Gerassi, eds.,

Latin American Radicalism: A Documentary Report on Left and Nationalist Movements (New York: Random House, 1969), pp. 390–439.

8. Cited in Eduardo Galeano, "The De-Nationalization of Brazilian Industry," *Monthly Review*, vol. 21, no. 7, 1969, pp. 11–30.

9. Dan Griffin, "Senator Church Assails U.S. Aid to Brazil Police," *Washington Post*, July 25, 1971, p. A-2.

10. "Visit of President Médici of the Federative Republic of Brazil," *Weekly Compilations of Presidential Documents*, vol. 7, no. 50, December 13, 1971, pp. 1625–1626.

11. Gary MacEoin, *No Peaceful Way: The Chilean Struggle for Dignity* (New York: Sheed and Ward, Inc., 1974), p. 179.

12. The author's information and impressions are drawn in part from conversations in Santiago in January 1977 with clergymen, academicians, jurists, journalists, businessmen, directors and members of cooperatives, slum dwellers, and others. For their own protection, their names will not be used.

13. Conversation with Victor Villanueva, Miraflores, Peru, January 1977. Villanueva has personal knowledge of Velasco's feelings on this matter.

14. The author met with U.S. Amb. Robert Dean and several members of the Country Team on a visit to Lima in January 1977.

15. Joanne Omang, "Peruvians Bury the Revolution," *Manchester Guardian*, September 12, 1976.

16. Cited by Cole Blasier in *Beyond the Revolution: Bolivia Since 1952*, James M. Malloy and Richard S. Thorn, eds. (Pittsburgh: University of Pittsburgh Press, 1971), p. 92.

17. Charles D. Corbett, *The Latin American Military as a Socio-Political Force: Case Studies of Bolivia and Argentina* (Coral Gables, Fla.: Center for Advanced International Studies, University of Miami, 1972), pp. 53–54.

18. June Nash, "Bolivia: The Consolidation (and Breakdown?) of a Militaristic Regime," *Latin American Studies Association Newsletter*, vol. X, no. 3, September, 1979, pp. 37–42.

19. Samuel E. Finer, *The Man on Horseback* (Hammondsworth, England: Penguin Books, 1975), pp. 234–238.

20. Victor Villanueva, *Nueva mentalidad militar in el Peru?* (Lima: Editorial Juan Mejia Baca, 1969), p. 194.

21. Under a military government, the portion of the budget over which military officers have direct discretionary power is always much greater than that appropriated for "defense."

22. U.S. Arms Control and Disarmament Agency, *World Military Expenditures and Arms Transfer, 1970–1979* (Washington, D.C.: Government Printing Office, 1982), pp. 97, 129.

23. Ibid.

24. Edmund S. Finegold, "Comments on Professor Kemp's Paper, 'Strategy and Arms Control in Latin America: A Framework for Analyzing the Military Dimension,' " prepared for the Conference on Arms Control, Military Aid, and Military Rule in Latin America, University of Chicago, May 26–27, 1972.

25. John R. Redick, "Prospects for Arms Control in Latin America," *Arms Control Today*, vol. 5, no. 9 (September 1975), pp. 1–3.

26. U.S. Arms Control and Disarmament Agency, *Arms Control 1979*, Publication 104 (Washington, D.C.: Government Printing Office, June 1980), pp. 26–28.

27. Alfonso Garcia Robles, "The Latin American Nuclear-Weapons-Free Zone," the Stanley Foundation, Muscatine, Iowa, Occasional Paper 19, May, 1979.

28. *World Military Expenditures and Arms Transfer*, pp. 97, 129.

5

The Trend to Military Withdrawal in the Late 1970s

The apogee in this cycle of military dominance was reached in 1976 and 1977. Thereafter the pendulum began to swing back in the direction of the ascendance of civilian regimes. In mid-1978 military intervention in the Dominican Republic to nullify the election of Antonio Guzmán, of the Center-Left Dominican Revolutionary Party (PRD), was thwarted, in part by the timely intercession of American diplomats and military officers expressing the displeasure of the Carter Administration with the initiative of the Dominican military. In July 1979, the Somoza dynasty, which with the support of the National Guard, its combined military and police force, had plundered Nicaragua for forty years, was felled in a revolution led by the Sandinistas. In August 1979, Ecuador, after seven years of military rule, inaugurated a popularly elected civilian president. A coup against El Salvador's repressive dictatorship in October brought to power a relatively moderate junta, which promised to enact reforms and to schedule elections (a promise which, as we shall see, it was unable to keep).

In Peru, where the military had held power since 1968, a popularly elected civilian president was inaugurated in July 1980.

The Bolivian government has changed hands eight times since June 1978, as civilians, with some help from the military, made a heroic effort to reinstate democratic rule; that effort, frustrated in particular by a coup in 1980, bore fruit in 1982. Finally, the trend known in Brazil as decompression, or the political opening, gained momentum in 1978. The fifth in that country's contemporary sequence of military presidents, inaugurated in March 1979, pledged to usher in a new democratic era.

It has been noted that the generation of military rulers of the 1960s and 1970s assumed the reins of government as if by divine right. What factors, then, could be expected to wean such an ambitious, self-confident, and closely knit elite from its grip on power? The answer appears to be factors not unlike those that weakened previous civilian regimes and cleared the way for military seizures of power. Among them are internal cleavage, economic stress, and external pressure.

The means of withdrawal is often identical to the means of assuming power in the first place—that is, a coup d'etat. In general, the military government that returns power to civilians is not the same one that displaced the civilian government, but rather represents a second or later phase of the military regime. Furthermore, just as the original conspiracy to seize power had civilian adherents, the coup that presages a return to civilian rule is instigated by an alliance of military and civilian elements.

FACTORS CONTRIBUTING TO WITHDRAWAL

Internal Cleavage

In contrast with the earlier phenomenon of *caudillismo*, Latin American military governments of the 1960s and 1970s attempted to maintain a convincing front of institutional, as opposed to factional or personal, rule. But the headiness of power and the spoils of office, not to mention the occasionally genuine conflicts of ideologies, are just as conducive to competition within the military caste as within a ruling civilian elite. Only the modern military establishment's general contempt for civilians has served to maintain the facade of unity.

Just as the preservation of the unity of the armed forces is often cited as a rationale for seizing power, it is also cited as a rationale for the withdrawal from power. This may mean that the actions of the prevailing faction are viewed by other factions as dragging the institution as a whole into disrepute. Or it may mean that a new generation of officers with new ideas and ripe ambitions is preparing to displace the existing hierarchy. But it is most likely to mean that power has become highly concentrated in the hands of an individual or a clique and that other factions or branches of the armed forces have ceased to profit adequately from military rule. For military governments, as for civilian ones, patronage has its limits, and for every individual or group rewarded or co-opted by high office there are many others left disappointed. Even in the Peruvian regime, extraordinarily autonomous between 1968 and 1978, only about fifty senior officers—less than 10 percent of the total of generals and colonels—held formal government positions at any given time.[1]

Cleavage may also result from competition among regions of the country or from differences among the three services and the various specialized branches. The navy, for example, tends to be the most racist and elitist of the services and to reflect the interests of the traditional oligarchy. The air force, highly dependent upon sophisticated technology and training, is especially sensitive to the mood of the external benefactor. The army, a more heterogeneous body, responds to a broader spectrum of the population.

Questions of succession in military regimes and issues such as whether to seize power or to withdraw from it are generally resolved by formal or informal polling among upper-echelon officers. Military elections, however, are not simulations of democracy but rather simulated battles, as votes are generally weighted in terms of command of firepower. The preference of a colonel commanding a regiment, for example, ordinarily carries more weight than that of a general in a staff position.

Once internal cleavage becomes pronounced, military dissidents may seek support from influential civilian groups in order to displace the ruling faction, or the ruling faction may seek civilian support to bulwark it against the plotting of military dissidents. In either case, the price of civilian support is likely to be a commitment eventually to return the government to civilian hands.

Economic Stress

The health of the economy and the nature of economic policy have a strong bearing on the survivability of military governments, as of civilian ones. Economic stress sharpens the competition and conflict among classes and economic sectors, creating a climate of instability. Such a climate obviates the claim of the military government to superiority over civilians in the maintenance of law and order. It also forces the regime to choose between adopting more repressive measures, which might generate an irrepressible reaction, or making concessions that appear to demonstrate weakness. In either case, the appearance of instability or weakness may shake the confidence of major domestic and foreign investors, whether or not their interests are immediately and directly threatened, causing them to withdraw their support from the regime.

Furthermore, a shrinking economic pie may exacerbate competition between military officers and institutions who have taken advantage of their governmental roles to establish profit-making enterprises or to extend their control over the economy and their erstwhile supporters in the business community. It may also sharpen discord among factions within the military over such issues as economic nationalism versus laissez-faire internationalism and reconcentration versus redistribution.

Finally, those military officers most concerned about the image of the institution will want to avoid presiding over a complete collapse of the economy. Whether recognizing the inadequacies of the institution or simply seeking to shift the blame, they will advocate an orderly transfer of power before it is too late.

The case for economic stress as a factor in the spasmodic retreats and advances of the military in Bolivia is less than clearcut because such stress has been the rule rather than the exception in Bolivia for several decades. In the cases of Brazil and Peru, however, the relationship is unmistakable.

External Pressure: The U.S. Role

In the 1970s, the abuse by governments supported by the United States of their own citizens (and in some cases of U.S. citizens as well) became so flagrant and extensive as to punish not only the inarticulate poor but also legislators, academicians, clergymen, and others with ties to politically articulate groups in the United States. This brought the U.S. Congress under intense pressure to terminate certain activities and programs, such as the arming and training of Latin American military establishments and police forces.

The legislative foundation for a human rights policy had been laid well in advance of President Carter's inauguration, but the Carter Administration was quick to grasp an idea whose time had come around again. Military assistance to several of the most flagrant violators of human rights was terminated, and other regimes preemptively renounced their interest in such assistance. The Military Assistance Program, under which 7,000 U.S. advisors had been stationed in Latin America in 1960, was trimmed in both function and personnel until by 1978 there were fewer than 1,000 U.S. officers assigned to Military Assistance Advisory Groups in Latin America.[2]

SOUNDING THE RETREAT: THREE CASES

Brazil's Decompression

Cracks in the Facade of Institutional Rule. As governing military factions begin to suspect other factions of disloyalty or conspiratorial behavior, they generally provide the press with resolutions affirming the unity of the armed forces. Such resolutions were being churned out at frequent intervals by the Brazilian Army's High Command in 1977 and 1978. Meanwhile the president, General Ernesto Geisel, made it kown that any active-duty officers caught discussing political trends with civilians would be arrested. General João Baptista de Oliveira Figueiredo, after assuming power in 1979,. carried the proscription a step farther to include retired and reserve officers.

Brazil's decompression, culminating in a 1979 amnesty for

several thousand exiles, persons who had been stripped of political rights, and most political prisoners, had many authors and many beginnings. Since virtually all civilians had been denied a role in decision-making, virtually all stood to gain through some degree of opening. The process owes much to courageous leaders in the Church, the unions, the media, the universities, the legal profession, and even the tightly leashed congress. However, President Geisel, inaugurated in 1974, must be considered also as one of the authors, as he chose to identify his administration with the movement.

Whether the new freedoms were granted or simply taken remains an open question. It may be that the government, confronting criticism or restiveness even from its limited constituency—the government of the United States, the transnational corporations, the national bourgeoisie, and a large portion of the salaried middle class—had little choice but to acquiesce. However, Brazilians who had ready access to military policymakers maintain that decompression policy was by no means the product of a confident and united military, but rather the policy of Geisel himself, who managed to centralize and personalize power to a greater extent than had any of his predecessors. Therefore, they trace the decompression to the presidential succession of 1969.

At that time General Albuquerque Lima, a self-designated insurgent contender for the presidency, had demanded a vote of the colonels commanding regiments, which he won. That should have settled the matter, but the more conservative generals of the Army High Command feared Albuquerque Lima's "socialist" leanings; so while he vacillated they closed ranks and purged his supporters.[3]

The deal that was struck within the highly factionalized high command gave the presidency to the "hardliners," who favored unvarnished dictatorial rule, with a guarantee that the more moderate Castelista faction (which took its name from the first in this series of military presidents, Humberto Castelo Branco) could have it next time around. The hardliners chose Emilio Garrastazu Médici as president, and the Castelistas installed Orlando Geisel as Minister of War to ensure that the bargain would be kept. The guarantee worked and Orlando's brother, Ernesto, who had been serving as director of Petrobras, the state-owned petroleum enterprise, succeeded Médici.

The hardliners expected to have another turn in power beginning in 1978, but by that time Geisel had very decidedly gained the upper hand. Following the torture death of journalist Vladimir Hertzog at the hands of São Paulo authorities in 1975, Geisel bypassed his hardline war minister, Sylvio Frota, and dismissed the commander of the São Paulo-based Second Army. The ultimate showdown with the hardline faction came in 1977 when General Frota's coup attempt aborted. Geisel was then able to select his own successor in 1978—General Figueiredo, the little known director of the National Intelligence Service (SNI)—though not without deepening the cleavages in the upper ranks.

The Brazilian military stood to lose a great deal in the relinquishment of power. Aside from the bloated budgets and other privileges that the institution had enjoyed, the highest-ranking officers had been able to anticipate lucrative positions upon retirement with private businesses, particularly the transnational corporations. They were also able to place their offspring in such positions, and lower-ranking officers could usually count on placing their offspring in responsible bureaucratic positions. Furthermore, there were military officials who had good reason to fear retribution at the hands of an unfettered civilian government.

Estimates of the proportion of "hardliners" within the officer corps in the late 1970s were generally low, although their power far exceeded their numbers. Hardliners of the Right were said to have stronger representation among colonels and generals than in the lower ranks, and to come disproportionately from the outlying areas as opposed to the metropolitan centers of Rio de Janeiro and São Paulo. Landowning families of the Northeast were overrepresented in this group, although there were also some officers of poor backgrounds who believed that they had raised themselves by their own bootstraps. Attitudes in this group were often based on racism. Its members were prone to claim or imply that because of the black admixture in the population, Brazilians were not capable of self-government.

Leftists were said to constitute a small minority of the officer corps, with greater concentration among the young in the lower ranks. Some favored a return to democracy, others continued military rule, but they were united in concern for the poor and in opposition to the privileged position of transnational corporations in the economy. Officers of this persuasion were found disproportionately in the Corps of Engineers and in other technical, administrative, and service groups that had been employed in the physical development of the interior. These officers, in general, had had more contact with civilians and more exposure to the problems of the lower classes than had those in some of the more traditional branches, such as cavalry and artillery. General Albuquerque Lima reportedly represented the authoritarian tendency within this socialist or populist orientation; retired General Euler Bentes Monteiro, an engineer who opposed Figueiredo in the rigged presidential election of 1978, represented the democratic one.

The locus of power within the military government, at least until the 1980s, had always appeared to be the eleven four-star generals of the Army High Command; in the event of severe disunity within that body, however, residual power lay precisely where it might be expected to in a government of force: in the command of troops. Thus, in a showdown power lay with the generals commanding the five military regions and with the approximately twenty colonels under them in control of *escolhas* or full-strength regiments of some 3,000 men.

Divisions within the high command, particularly between the Castelistas and Rightist hardliners, became even more pronounced after the Frota affair and Geisel's selection, without serious consultation with the high command, of his successor. But Geisel's strength reportedly lay in the support he enjoyed from regiment commanders. Whether or not Figueiredo inherited that support, as former director of the SNI he maintained a base of support in that powerful body. Nevertheless, many knowledgeable Brazilians believe that the SNI had become a sort of shadow government, scarcely responsible to the president, the high command, or any other authority. Each ministry had a special section controlled directly by the SNI. Furthermore, agents trained in the intelligence service's academy, ESNI, had been placed, unbeknownst to colleagues and superiors, in all branches of government ministries and in universities and other public and private agencies.

Members of the Castelista faction had always spoken of their theoretical adherence to democratic principles and of their intention ultimately to return the country to civilian rule. Their concept of democracy, however, was one of form without substance—of an orderly process involving a limited number of participants, all of whom are in accord with the "national objectives," as outlined by the Higher War College, and who accept the military's own interpretation of its "moderating role." Thus the common ground in the aims of the popular movement for decompression and the aims of the government itself was little more than a parade field.

The Carter Administration Weighs In. With the advent of the Carter Administration, U.S. relations with Brazil underwent a long-overdue reappraisal. Administration spokesmen made it known that Brazil no longer enjoyed a special status among U.S. Latin American allies. On an official visit to Brazil, President Carter made a point of meeting with São Paulo's Cardinal Evaristo Arns, a prominent critic of the violation of human rights in Brazil.

In discussions of the factors leading to the decompression— the new freedom of expression, even of organized dissent, that was given or taken in Brazil in the late 1970s—Brazilians rarely fail to mention President Carter's human rights policy. But whereas previous U.S. presidents, in attempting to destabilize democratic regimes or bulwark dictatorial ones, were able to mobilize the American business community and to concentrate the full force of government entities—military and civilian, overt and covert—to those ends, President Carter found it difficult to convert even the overt civilian element of his own foreign affairs apparatus. The author found a number of the officials of the U.S. Embassy and Consulates in Brazil in mid-1978 to be contemptuous of the human rights policy.

The Carter Administration's influence was further diluted by the fact that the Brazilian regime, by that time flaunting its own strong economic and military base, was attempting to declare its independence of the United States. This was demonstrated most notably in the purchase from a West German firm, over strong U.S. opposition, of nuclear reactors capable of producing plutonium. When the military government first came to power in 1964, criticism of the United States was treated as subversion. During the Carter Administration it was said that anti-Americanism was *de rigeur* within the military. Nevertheless, while the Carter Administration and important sectors of the Brazilian population could be led to believe that President Figueiredo and his relatively moderate "Castelista" faction intended to move the country, however slowly, in the direction of more humane rule and greater participation for civilians, the Castelistas stood to gain crucial support in their ongoing competition with both Right-wing hardliners and Leftist-nationalist groups within the military.

Creative Tension in the Economy. The Brazilian government claimed that having produced the economic miracle it was able in the late 1970s to begin to follow through on its original plan to step aside and return power to "responsible" civilians. But Brazilian civilians often cite economic problems among the reasons for the weakening of the regime and the increasing boldness of the opposition.

The working and would-be-working classes, who constitute the great majority of the population, always fared badly under military rule. However, by 1980 the middle sector, comprising 20 to 30 percent of the population, was feeling the squeeze of an annual inflation rate approaching 100 percent.

The so-called economic miracle collapsed in the wake of the energy crisis of 1973–1974. Since then even the most thriving businesses have been stalked by insecurity. The energy crisis only inflated what was already a staggering foreign debt. The servicing of that debt, exceeding \$50 billion as early as 1980, was absorbing more than half of annual export earnings; and people whose occupations and lifestyles would not suggest attention to such things seemed to feel genuinely threatened by it.

In the case of fuel costs, inflation was externally induced and could not have been easily avoided. In other cases, however, inflation had been a consciously generated byproduct of government policy. Many Brazilians trace the beginnings of a serious opposition movement to the government's decision to replace the bean crop for local consumption with soybeans for export; that decision led to scarcity and soaring prices for the most common dish of all Brazilians and the only source of protein for many. The cost of housing had also become a source of middle-class desperation. In some cities, apartments that had been designed for the poor were by the late 1970s scarcely within the reach of the affluent.

Uncertainty generated by the economic slippage also exacerbated competition and friction among the major economic sectors. Candido Mendes de Almeida, one of Brazil's most eminent social scientists, suggested in 1978 that the most "creative tension" in the country was that between the transnational corporations and the uniformed entrepreneurs of the state-owned enterprises.[4] The ability and willingness of the military government to sacrifice major sectors of national private industry had been essential to the program of the transnational corporations. By the late 1970s, however, some leaders of the transnational corporate community had begun to feel that their interests were threatened by the arbitrary power and the statist pretensions of the military government. Geisel proved more accommodating than they had anticipated, given his background as director of Petrobras, the state-owned petroleum company. But remembering the near victory of Albuquerque Lima, the managers of transnationals feared the economic nationalists who lurked in the lower ranks, and some had begun to think that they might be less vulnerable to surprises operating under a civilian government with limited powers.

Meanwhile, the national bourgeoisie had become increasingly vocal about its resentment of competition from both the transnationals and the state-owned enterprises. Most Brazilian industrialists, fearing the power of labor, supported the counterrevolution in 1964 with great enthusiasm. Like other capitalist sectors they profited from low wages and, until 1978, a docile work force. But on the whole they were played for suckers, and by the late 1970s some had begun to say so. The "creative bankruptcy" promoted in the early years of the regime was designed to weed out national firms and clear various markets for the transnational ones. The more recent mushrooming of the state sector has been, again, primarily at the expense of the national, rather than the transnational, private sector. Whether the rumblings of discontent from national businessmen reflected a large-scale withdrawal of support or merely an attempt to secure concessions from a seemingly weakened government, the uproar contributed to the momentum of the movement for re-democratization.

Peru: The Military in a Vise

Eclipse of the Reformers. The example of the Peruvian government of General Velasco contributed to the ideological or programmatic dimensions of factionalism within the military establishments of other Latin American countries. In some cases factions advocating a vanguard role for the military in the promotion of redistributive social change, an expanded social property sector, and a more nearly independent foreign policy even identified themselves as Peruvianist. But the Peruvian "experiment" was itself the result of a set of coincidences that allowed a minority faction to gain control of the military and thus of the government. The 1975 coup may be viewed, in part, as the eclipse of that faction.

The overthrow of the Belaúnde government in October 1968 was probably as much a consequence of the low threshold for military intervention in Peru as of the specifically reformist motivations of Velasco and his co-conspirators. Although Velasco, commander-in-chief of the army since January 1968, had begun to plot several months before, the IPC crisis so weakened the civilian government that Velasco was under pressure to move before other military factions preempted him.

Thus Velasco had by no means consolidated his position within the military before seizing power. His loyalists were obliged to place the army minister and the army chief-of-staff under house arrest before surrounding the presidential palace, and the coup prompted the resignation of several of the top-ranking officers of the navy and air force.

Nevertheless, through immediate nationalization of the IPC's Talara refinery, which generated widespread support within the military as among civilians, Velasco bought time to consolidate his position. This he did slowly, cautiously, and cunningly, through appointments, promotions, and resignations.

As most of his fellow conspirators had been colonels, majors, and even captains, Velasco found that the generals with whom it was necessary to fill the most visible and prestigious posts of his new government did not necessarily share his policy goals. Five of the seven generals appointed to his cabinet had been in direct command of troops before the coup. Through these appointments Velasco was able to conform to the protocol of "institutional" rule, while neutralizing those with the greatest potential for moving against him by removing them from command positions. He then moved the colonels who had been his major co-conspirators into the less prestigious but more crucial positions in command of troops, in the intelligence apparatus, and in the presidential advisory council, which was later to become the government's principal policymaking body.

In February 1979 Velasco began to reshuffle his cabinet, and in May he was able to issue a decree giving the president the discretion to retire senior officers before the completion of their normal terms of service. It was not until the balance had thus been shifted in favor of his reformist faction that Velasco undertook such major programs as the agrarian reform and worker profit-sharing.[5]

Velasco and his loyalists enjoyed considerable cooperation and passive support from civilian groups. Whether or not they were inclined to build a power base outside the military, however, their position within the military was never strong enough to allow them to do so.

Peru's currency, during most of the seven years of the Velasco government, remained relatively stable, and despite selective nationalizations and increased controls on foreign investment, the Velasco government actually attracted more foreign investment than had any of its predecessors. The national bourgeoisie, however, had shied away from substantial new investment. By 1975 a heavy trade deficit, caused in part by a steep decline in world copper prices and a thinning out of the schools of anchovy that provide fishmeal, and in part by extravagant spending on the military, had combined with inflation, strikes, food shortages, and shrinking international credit to drive the country into an economic crisis.

By 1975, Velasco, in failing health after the amputation of a leg, was under attack by disgruntled officers who charged him with having generated a personality cult. Although Velasco personally was not accused of corruption, there were charges of corruption in his regime. The impending eclipse of the reformists was signaled by a mini-coup in the navy that allowed its most conservative officers to regain control. This followed a revolt of the police, striking for higher pay, which the reluctant army had been expected to put down.

On August 29, 1975, General Velasco was replaced in a bloodless coup by his prime minister and army commander-in-chief, Gen. Francisco Morales Bermúdez. The coup was publicly endorsed by all five regional army commanders plus the navy, the air force, and the national police.

Morales Bermúdez, grandson of a former president and finance minister under Belaúnde as well as under Velasco, also enjoyed the confidence of the business community. Although Morales Bermúdez had been among those who originally conspired with Velasco, he purged from the government most of the members of the reformist faction and had some of them arrested or deported.[6]

Having purged the Left, Morales Bermúdez reportedly attempted to govern by consensus within the military, but as Peru's economic crisis deepened the regime found itself increasingly under attack from the Right. A coup attempted by a right-wing general who headed a military academy was put down in July 1976.

Contrary to the expectations of many conservative businessmen, the economic crisis did not abate after the overthrow of Velasco by Morales Bermúdez. Under pressure from the United States, private foreign banks, and the international bourgeoisie, Morales Bermúdez began to dismantle the social property sector of the economy, to reduce worker participation in management, and to impose severe austerity measures. United States Ambassador Robert Dean, speaking at the Center for Higher Military Studies (CAEM) in 1976, reminded the Peruvian officers that they were a part of the Western economic system and would have to put their house in order if they wished to attract loans and investments.

In order to spring loans of some $200 million from a consortium of American banks, Peru was required to prove its credit-worthiness by adequately compensating the American-owned Marcona Mining Company and reaching agreement with Southern Peru Copper Corporation. As vicious cycles go, these loans were needed primarily to meet interest payments that were due to the same banks. But military withdrawal was not seen by the United States at that time as a precondition for an orderly house.

The Morales Bermúdez government devalued the sol by 44 percent against the dollar in 1976 and cut spending on social programs. Prices of staple commodities were allowed to increase dramatically in the face of depressed wages and increasing unemployment. Still Peru's external economic position worsened. The foreign debt stood at $3.7 billion and the balance-of-trade deficit at $1.2 billion.[7]

By 1977 Peru was virtually mortgaged to two consortia of Western banks, but this was not enough; the banks were insisting that further assistance was conditional upon Peru's acceptance of the IMF's stabilization plan. Thus Peru became ever more desperate for direct U.S. assistance and for U.S. intercession with the banks and the IMF. However, with the advent of the Carter Administration, a new element—democratic process—had been added to the concept of an orderly house.

A New String Attached to Aid. There had been no mention of elections in Peru when Morales Bermúdez first seized power, and redemocratization was not among the strings attached to U.S. aid under the Nixon and Ford administrations. But Carter had occupied the White House less than a month when the Peruvian government announced plans to hold elections in 1980. General elections were to be preceded by the election in 1978 of a constituent assembly to draw up a new constitution. Restrictions previously imposed by the military on the media and on party activities were relaxed, although they were reimposed from time to time when the decibel level of protest rose.

Despite chagrin about Peru's large debt to the Soviet Union for weapons purchases, the United States ultimately came through with modest amounts of direct assistance. It also put quiet pressure on the IMF (with uncertain results) to modify its hard line, arguing that the strikes, rioting, and bloodshed certain to accompany additional austerity measures might provoke military hardliners to cancel the elections.

There was dissension within the Peruvian cabinet and among high-ranking officers over whether or not to accept the IMF stabilization plan in exchange for credits. While austerity had been imposed on the population at large, the military itself had continued its global shopping spree for the most modern and expensive weaponry; but the IMF plan called for a moratorium on arms purchases. Some officers opposed the plan because its implementation would heighten social unrest. There was also disagreement within the military over the extent of repression that was necessary and acceptable for dealing with this unrest.

Nevertheless, foreign reserves were exhausted, so in November 1977 the Peruvian government surrendered to the IMF. Hardliners argued that elections should be canceled, as only a military government could keep the consequent strikes and riots within bounds, but Morales Bermúdez and his military allies argued that the success of the strikes proved that the government was too weak to deal with the economic crisis without some cooperation from the unions and the parties that influenced them.

By 1978, when Peru finally reached refinancing agreements with most of its foreign creditors, foreign debt payments were absorbing half of the country's export earnings, inflation was approaching 80 percent, per capita income and real wages had dropped by some 50 percent in five years, and about 45 percent of the work force was unemployed or underemployed. The military government was so unpopular that many believed that only the prospect of elections prevented a popular uprising.

Strikes and riots in May 1978, resulting from a dramatic jump in prices, led to the imposition of "martial law," the arrest of hundreds of labor leaders, and military pressure on Morales Bermúdez to cancel the scheduled elections. The president's affirmation, in a nation-wide TV broadcast, that the armed forces were united in their approach to solving the country's problems confirmed suspicions of serious dissension.

President Carter, in April 1978, sent a letter to Morales Bermúdez applauding the scheduling of elections and pledging all "appropriate" support to that end. The United States increased bilateral aid to Peru to almost $140 million, a threefold increase over aid in the preceding two years.[8]

Elections for the constituent assembly took place on June 18 and resulted in a plurality for the APRA. The new constitution, which was signed by the 100 assembly members in mid-1979, stressed respect for human rights and civil liberties. The government accepted it with the qualification that some of its provision would become effective only after the inauguration of a civilian government in 1980.

By 1979 the basic cleavage within the upper echelon of the military appeared to be between the so-called hardliners who wanted to retain power and its perquisites and the "institutionalists" who argued that to avoid an open split in its ranks the military must relinquish power. Against the threat of insurgency by the hardliners in his own government, Morales Bermúdez became increasingly dependent upon the support of civilian party leaders who were counting on a return to democratic government.

Belaúnde was reelected to the presidency in 1980. Peru's external creditors were mollified as were the long-sidelined civilian political leaders, but the economic situation of the vast majority of the people remained desperate.

Bolivia: A Halting Retreat

The Constitutionalists in Ascendance. A few months before his government was toppled in 1971, President Juan José Torres commented that the biggest problem for a Bolivian president was survival. In fact, there is considerable evidence that the helicopter "accident" that killed General Barrientos in 1969 was staged by General Ovando. Torres himself was assassinated in 1977, presumably on the orders of Banzer, while in exile in Argentina.

Bolivia's military politicians have spoken as glibly of unity and of institutional rule as have those of Brazil, Peru, and other Latin American countries, but widespread accord on the vices of civilian leaders and the virtues of the military has scarcely resulted in unity. The frequency of military plots and counterplots in Bolivia must be attributed in part to personal squabbles and personal ambitions. As in Brazil, however, regional bases and generational ties have contributed to differing ideological orientations. Officers based, for example, in Santa Cruz, center of the new wealth of the 1960s and of American and Brazilian economic penetration, have tended to be more conservative than those based in La Paz, where the influence of the university and of labor unions is felt. Younger, less senior officers have tended to be more liberal than their entrenched superiors.

While the essential polarization of the 1960s and early 1970s appeared to be of Left and Right in socioeconomic terms with little dispute as to the appropriateness of military rule, observers in the late 1970s began to speak of a cleavage between hardliners, who would continue to occupy the palace, and constitutionalists, who would return to the barracks. Not surprisingly, constitutionalists, having a much larger civilian constituency, appeared to be more favorably disposed toward redistributive policies.

Bolivia has suffered more than 200 presidents in its 160 years of independence, most of whom assumed power and lost power through coups d'etat. Banzer held on to power longer than any other president to date in the twentieth century, but there were innumerable genuine plots against him, in addition to the many conspiracies that were apparently fabricated by his government to justify repressive measures, including internal purges of the military.

By the mid-1970s, Banzer had alienated a great many of his military colleagues by concentrating power in his own hands and defying institutional norms. Having found the role of commander-in-chief of the armed forces too threatening when held by another, he assumed it for himself. There were frequent conflicts over promotions, and many officers were offended by the corruption (or the monopolization of corruption) that flourished in the inner circle. Furthermore, the armed forces were particularly anxious to secure an outlet to the Pacific in compensation for territory lost to Chile a century earlier. Banzer's rapport with Chilean dictator Augusto Pinochet was offensive to anti-Chilean officers, and some felt that Banzer was not taking the steps necessary to secure U.S. support for Bolivia's claim.

Bolivian Civilians Look to Carter. When Banzer first seized control of the Bolivian government in 1971, he had persuaded members of two of the country's major political parties to serve on his cabinet in a feeble attempt to give his regime an aura of legitimacy. In 1974, however, the fig leaf of civilian participation in the military government was torn away. The system remained highly repressive, exploitative, and tightly controlled by Banzer and his military loyalists until the U.S. presidential election of 1976. On January 10, 1977, Bolivia's banned labor confederation published a letter it had sent to President Carter, congratulating him on his inauguration and supporting his policies in defense of human rights and in opposition to military dictatorships. The following day Banzer's press secretary felt obliged to comment that while Bolivia lacked formal democracy, its practical approach of informal consultation with civilians represented true democracy. Four days later, in a speech to railway workers, Banzer promised early restoration of political and trade union rights.

The actions of Banzer's government in succeeding months generated no credibility in his pledge. Meanwhile, the British government cancelled a £19-million loan to the Bolivian State Mining Corporation because of the ongoing repression of Bolivia's miners. In November Banzer announced that elections would be held in July 1978. On that occasion, he asserted: "This is an exclusively Bolivian decision in the service of Bolivian interests"—denying, in other words, that he was caving in to external pressures.[9]

The scheduling of elections in 1978 shook loose $75 million in U.S. food aid. Banzer, nevertheless, continued to hope that the Carter Administration was not serious. It was apparent that his original plan was to reinstall himself as an "elected" president. He allowed that some form of military tutelage would be maintained, and restrictions on political activity remained in force; but civilian opponents, encouraged by external support, took matters into their own hands. A hunger strike in December 1977 and January 1978, led by Hernán Siles Suazo and supported by the Catholic archdiocese, ultimately attracted some 1,300 participants. It also sparked a number of strikes and resulted in genuine concessions, including amnesty for political prisoners and exiles.

The process of civilian ascendance and military withdrawal continued haltingly through 1978 and 1979. In March 1978, as Bolivia was soliciting a large loan, Ambassador Paul Boecher made it known that future U.S. assistance was conditional upon the election process going ahead as scheduled.[10]

When it became clear that Banzer's antagonists in the armed forces were not going to allow him to have himself elected president, Banzer selected Air Force General Juan Pereda Asbun as the official candidate. In the elections of July 9, 1978, despite government rigging so blatant that the Electoral Court nullified the results, a Center-Left coalition led by Siles Suazo made a strong showing. Thereupon Pereda, declaring that "Communism will not triumph," attracted enough support among the armed forces to stage a coup on July 21. The United States officially expressed regret and hope that the interruption in the electoral process would be temporary. The only governments that recognized the Pereda regime within the month were those of Argentina, Brazil, Uruguay, Paraguay, and the Soviet Union.

Banzer's plan to perpetuate his grip on power through elections had eroded the last layers of his military power base. The imposition of an air force general was insult upon injury to the overwhelmingly dominant army. Most believed that Banzer had selected him on the assumption that he was weak and manipulable. Pereda himself must have come to that conclusion because by the time he seized power he had split with Banzer.

Pereda, an archconservative, had served as interior minister in Banzer's government, and had won U.S. favor through his prominent role in narcotics control. Like Banzer before him, his base was in Santa Cruz, and he was backed by the oil and cattle barons of the region. As an air force general and former Banzer protégé, however, his support within the military was weak and fleeting. He won on his gamble that the armed forces would let him assume the presidency rather than risk an open schism and "chaos," but his victory was not long to be savored. Military garrisons in Santa Cruz and other outlying areas had rallied to his uprising, but some of the commanders of military units in La Paz were conspicuously absent from his swearing-in ceremony.

Pereda ultimately promised to hold elections in May 1980, but that was not enough to mollify his antagonists. As spoiler of the electoral process, Pereda was opposed, in particular, by a faction known variously as the "generational group," the "constitutionalists," and the "democratic colonels." This group, under the leadership of Army Commander General David Padilla, was said to feel that the popular image of the military had been besmirched. On November 24, 1978, Pereda's short-lived government was toppled by General Padilla, who promised to restore civil rights and liberties and scheduled elections for July 1, 1979.

President Padilla delivered on his promises. Elections, this time relatively free of fraud, were held as scheduled in July. But neither of the major candidates, Siles Suazo and Paz Estenssoro, won the necessary majority, so the decision rested with the newly elected congress. There supporters of the two candidates were deadlocked, and the issue was finally resolved through the selection of Walter Guevara Arce, president of the senate, as interim president until elections could be held again in May 1980.

The interim civilian government of Guevara had been in power scarcely more than a month when military conspiracies began to surface again. On October 11, the army garrison at Trinidad, capital of Bení Province, demanded that his government be overthrown. More powerful army commanders in La Paz and elsewhere rejected the Trinidad proclamation but nevertheless warned congress to back away from its investigations of corruption practiced by military commanders. In the weeks that followed, Guevara was aware that a conspiracy against his government was gaining momentum, but the Army High Command refused to carry out his orders to retire or transfer officers he knew to be plotting.

Guevara's government, beset by economic problems and lacking a base of its own, lasted about three months. It was toppled on November 1, 1979, by Colonel Alberto Natusch Busch. The seizure of power by Natusch, commander of the military college, received strong support from army garrisons in Santa Cruz and Cochabamba and acquiescence, at least, from most other army garrisons, but it was opposed from the begin-

ning by some officers of both Left and Right, and opposition
from within the military grew as the death toll mounted. It was
also openly condemned by virtually all politically articulate civilian groups. Natusch claimed to be a Leftist-Nationalist, but
from civilian Leftists he gained no support, and he showed them
no mercy. Nor did his stand against "predatory terrorism" sat-
isfy Banzer and others who called for a reliably Right-wing regime. Most saw the coup as an expression of Natusch's personal ambition to follow the example of his uncle, German
Busch, who as a colonel had seized power in 1937, or as an attempt to forestall congressional investigations of his activities
as minister of agriculture under Banzer. Furthermore, a former
interior minister accused Natusch of plotting the murder of three
officers, including Padilla.

General Padilla, who sought to generate opposition to Natusch within the military, conceded that the officer corps had
not welcomed a return to democracy. Nevertheless, 250 officers
signed a proclamation urging Natusch to resign in order to avoid
civil war. Ultimately General Eden Castillo, commander-in-chief
of the armed forces, participated in negotiations with leaders of
congress and of the national labor confederation designed to
force Natusch's resignation.

The reaction from Washington to Natusch's seizure of power
was quick and sharp: all military and economic assistance except the Food for Peace program was suspended. The regime
failed to gain recognition by any foreign government. After sixteen days and more than 200 deaths, Natusch stepped down,
leaving the presidency in the hands of Lydia Gueiler, president
of the senate, who was to serve until the May elections. As we
shall see in chapter 7, that government, too, was to be short-
lived.

LINKAGES AMONG CONTRIBUTING FACTORS

We have seen that the new wave of military interventionism
that swept Latin America between the mid-1960s and the mid-
1970s was generated, in part, by external pressure and economic stress and facilitated by the internal cohesion of the mil-

itary institution. Of these, the factor of external pressure appears to have been most important. It contributed indirectly to internal cohesion, in that U.S. training gave rise to a new corporate consciousness and self-confidence, and counterinsurgency training subjected a much larger proportion of the armed forces to political indoctrination. Economic stress was in all cases related to dependency and was, in some cases, intentionally exacerbated by the United States.

Likewise, these three factors have been identified as contributors to the trend toward military withdrawal from power in Latin America in the late 1970s, and in withdrawal these factors—internal cleavage, economic stress, and external pressure—again are linked. External pressure may cause or exacerbate economic stress or internal cleavage. Economic stress may lead to internal cleavage and make a country or governing faction more dependent on external sources of support. Internal cleavage, in itself, makes the institution more susceptible to external pressure.

Of these three factors, external pressure appears to be the strongest predictor of the direction of change: to Left or Right and to palace or barracks. The external pressure that has weighed most heavily on the outcome of political competition in Latin America, at least since the Second World War, is clearly that of the United States. Although the United States is by no means the only source of external influence or pressure on Latin American countries, most private investors and Western financial institutions tend to follow the U.S. lead when its direction is clear.

Economic crisis often provokes a change of government. If the government in power happens to be a military one, there is a possibility that change will be in the direction of democratic process and civilian rule. But whether that possibility is realized or thwarted often depends on the predilections of the U.S. government. While the predilections of the Johnson and Nixon administrations strengthened authoritarian factions, the Carter Administration favored constitutionalist factions and at some crucial junctures made economic relief conditional upon military withdrawal. More importantly, perhaps, the Carter Administration's human rights policy gave encouragement to civilians who otherwise would have considered opposition to dictatorial rule to be both dangerous and futile.

NOTES

1. José Z. García, "Military Factions and Military Intervention in Latin America," in Sheldon W. Simon, ed., *The Military and Security in the Third World: Domestic and International Impact* (Boulder, Colo.: Westview Press, 1978), pp. 47–75.

2. Paul Y. Hammond, David J. Louscher, and Michael D. Salomon, "Growing Dilemmas for the Management of Arms Sales," *Armed Forces and Society*, vol. 6, no. 1 (Fall 1979), pp. 1–21.

3. My own source for the nullified "election" of General Lima cannot be cited. However, Brazilian scholar René Armand Dreifuss confirms this account on the basis of interviews with Lima and with Admiral Hannaman Grunewald Rademaker in 1976. According to Dreifuss, Lima, whose investments in the capitalist system were substantial, did not consider himself a socialist. Rather, he projected a socialist image in order to attract support from "young Turks" in the armed forces, elements of the press, students, and remnants of the organized Left.

4. Candido Mendes expressed this opinion in a conversation with the author in Rio de Janeiro in July 1978.

5. García, "Military Factions," pp. 58–72.

6. Meeting with United States Country Team, Lima, January 1977.

7. Manchester *Guardian Weekly*, September 12, 1976.

8. Judith Miller, "A Dilemma: Competing Aims Trouble U.S.," *New York Times*, May 24, 1978.

9. David Vidal, "Bolivia Is Promised Elections for '78" *New York Times*, November 11, 1977.

10. *Latin America Political Report*, March 17, 1978.

6

Back to the Backyard: Crisis in Central America

In the late 1970s, just as a number of South American countries that had been languishing under military rule began to see the ascension once again of civilian regimes, due in no small part to a U.S. policy of favoring such regimes, insurrectionary movements in Central America were gathering momentum. The crisis in that area was to threaten a turning back of the clock in U.S.-Latin American relations by more than half a century—to the era of gunboat diplomacy and straightforward military interventionism.

THE ROOTS OF INSURGENCY

The roots of insurgency in Central America are not hard to trace. In fact, the revolutionary ferment of the 1970s and 1980s was eminently predictable on several grounds. Revolutionary ferment has often been equated with popular mobilization—with increased political awareness and organization on the part of previously apathetic or acquiescent masses. But popular mobilization and the consequent pressures for change are not in themselves revolutionary. Revolution comes about only when the nonviolent pursuit of change has been blocked.

Perennial blockage of the nonviolent pursuit of change, and thus the maintenance of a very low level of political participation, may be attributed in part, in some countries of the area, to great social distance between Hispanic elites and Indian or mestizo masses. In such circumstances, elites are prone to feel that any concession, any break with tradition, threatens to topple their "house of cards." Thus rather than welcoming the development of an incipient middle class that might serve to diffuse class conflict and accepting marginal political changes, the elites systematically eliminate (often by assassination) spokesmen of middle-class interests and strive to maintain a vacuum in the political center. This pattern has been particularly clear in recent decades in Guatemala and El Salvador.

The role of the United states in Central America has reinforced this pattern. The backing of client-state oligarchies by the hegemonic power has served to offset pressures for incremental concessions to middle or lower classes. Furthermore, by maintaining a vacuum in the political center, those ruling classes are able to convince U.S. authorities that backing the existing order is the only alternative to revolution or chaos.

Finally, landlessness and the physical uprooting of subject populations (i.e., the proletarianization of the peasantry) have correlated with most incidents of successful revolution in the Western Hemisphere. Since the Iberian conquest of the New World, concentration of land ownership has been among Central America's most obstinate problems. Conquistadores and others favored by the Spanish monarchs carved out for themselves enormous estates complete with the previous native American claimants or imported African slaves to do the work. The land-grabs of the colonial period, however, pale by comparison to those inspired since the mid-nineteenth century by the growth of export markets for agricultural products—particularly coffee and bananas in the nineteenth century and cotton in the twentieth. By the beginning of the twentieth century, U.S. agribusiness interests had joined in the competition for peasant land and labor in Central America, and the U.S. government had aligned itself with landowners and others who resisted any change in a social structure built on conquest.

Many of the peasant uprisings of the late nineteenth and early twentieth centuries in Mesoamerica, including that led by Emiliano Zapata in Mexico, represented efforts to take back land that had been seized. In Mexico, alienation of the land was one of several factors that led to revolution in the first decades in the twentieth century.

In the case of the Mexican Revolution, as in the cases of all subsequent revolutionary movements and most reformist movements in Central America, representatives of U.S. business and of the U.S. government have charged that the impetus was external. Insurgents are often aided by foreign powers, of course, and since 1959 Castro's Cuba has been sympathetic with insurrectionary movements in various parts of the world; assistance to guerrillas in Central America from the maturing Cuban Revolution, however, had been modest. In toppling the Somoza dynasty, Nicaragua's Sandinistas ultimately received some material assistance not only from Cuba but from several other Latin American countries as well and moral support, at least, from several Western European countries. Nevertheless, revolution is not a commodity to be bartered in international trade. Only a truly committed capitalist could believe that revolution could be imported and exported.

Probably the most effective agent of change in Central America since the 1960s and the most powerful ally of the long-suffering masses, particularly in the rural areas, has been the Roman Catholic Church. The changing role of the Church in Central America has been reflective of a long-term global process of transformation, apparent particularly in the Third World and in countries—whether of East or West—governed by oppressive dictatorial regimes. The introduction of a new institutional role for the Church is often traced to the Second Vatican Council, convened by Pope John XXIII in 1962, which stressed the calling of the Church to minister to bodies as well as to souls.

The Conference of Latin American Bishops that took place in Medellín, Colombia, in 1968 placed the Church unequivocally on the side of the poor. The new alignment was reflected particularly in Church sponsorship of organization among peasants. This general trend in Church policy coincided in Central America with an intensification of popular opposition to oligarchic greed and military repression. Furthermore, as repression against peasant unions and other categories of dissidents increased in the 1970s, the Church came to be for many the only source of refuge. In providing refuge, the Church itself became vulnerable to attack and persecution and thus came to be identified with the resistance to incumbent regimes.

Meanwhile, in response to the contradictory impulses of the Alliance for Progress as well as to the relative prosperity and urbanization of the 1960s, both the forces of political pluralism and the forces of repression had been strengthened. Pressure for change intensified as urban workers became organized and political parties representing Christian Democratic, Social Democratic, and, in far smaller numbers, Marxist perspectives were established.

While the Kennedy Administration encouraged the organization of non-Marxist parties and the holding of elections (which, incidentally, were almost always either rigged or nullified by military or military-based authorities), it also armed and trained military and paramilitary forces in a modernized approach to counterinsurgency to ensure that opposition movements did not get out of hand—that is, that they did not become revolutionary or escape the control of the United States. Kennedy-era liberals had imagined that the military forces they were nurturing would block only extralegal, lower-class initiatives. In fact, however, those reinforced military establishments hastened to block any change that appeared to threaten their interests and the interests of their wealthy sponsors.

After Kennedy's death, the United States continued to strengthen military forces and to build military alliances, but it retreated from earlier policies of encouraging middle-class parties. In the 1970s, leaders of those parties, with decreasing hope of legitimized participation and under increasing threat of assassination, began to go underground or into exile, either joining, or leaving the field to, those who were prepared to seek redress by violent means.

The area also experienced a sharp economic decline during

the 1970s as a consequence of the soaring cost of imported petroleum, the dissolution of the Central American Common Market, climbing interest rates and debt service charges, worsening terms of trade for the area's exports, and, in some cases, ostentatious corruption. The prosperity of the 1960s had not been widely shared, and peasants and other deprived groups had suffered all the more as a consequence of the inflation induced by increased economic activity. With the decline of the 1970s, the groups that had shared in the prosperity of the 1960s found themselves competing for the remains of a shrinking economic pie. In some countries, economic elites were divided among themselves and were faced with increasing militance on the part of urban middle and working classes.

In Guatemala, these developments meant an acceleration in the slow-motion war that had been under way at least since 1954—some might say since the Spanish conquest. The level of violence—mostly official violence perpetuated against Indian peasants and those who dare to speak for them—has been climbing steadily since the mid-1960s, claiming tens of thousands of lives.

Guatemala: The Conquerors and the Conquered

Guatemala's history is a tale of two societies—unintegrated and unequal, conquerors and conquered. It is also a tale of intermittent conflict, of insurgency, and of crushing retaliation, as with each new generation and each new crop demanded by foreign markets, non-Indian landowners and entrepreneurs found new pseudolegal devices for further encroachment on Indian land and compulsion of Indian labor. It might be said that the period of conquest and wars against Indians that began almost five centuries ago has never really ended.

The land tenure patterns and farm labor arrangements in Guatemala have always been among the most unequal and oppressive in Latin America. The lot of the Indian peasant has improved little, if at all, since the pattern of Spanish settlement was crystallized in the seventeenth century. Relationships between landholders and tenants or itinerant wage laborers have been blatantly exploitative, and reform efforts have been bitterly fought by those who held effective political and economic power. It was not until the decade between 1944 and 1954 that the first—and last—concerted effort was made by the government to reconstruct economic relationships to the benefit of workers and peasants.

For several centuries a center of the Mayan empire, one of the most advanced pre-Columbian civilizations of the New World, the area that is now Guatemala became the seat of Spanish government for all of Central America. After independence, it was initially the seat of the short-lived Central American Federation.

As in other parts of the New World, the central feature of Spanish settlement was the establishment of large landed estates and a system of forced Indian labor for cultivating them. During the 300 years of the colonial period, these estates slowly spread along the fertile mountain valleys and across the more level stretches of the upland plateaus.

Then as now the extended Indian family cultivated corn, beans, squash, and other vegetables on small plots called *milpas*. These *milpas*, after a few years of planting, lose their fertility. Thus in pre-Columbian times each village controlled an area many times larger than the land under cultivation at any given time in order that plots might be allowed to lie fallow until they regained their fertility. As Spanish estates covered more and more of the highlands, however, this system became impossible. The lands not organized into Spanish or mestizo-owned estates were considered to be public domain and were cultivated as communal village property by the Indians, but the Indians neither sought nor were given legal titles to this land.

Under the *encomienda* system, which prevailed during the first part of the colonial period, Indians living contiguous to an estate were assigned by the local colonial authorities to the estate owner, to whom they had to pay tribute in kind from the output of their own fields and for whom they were forced to labor on the estate itself. The *encomienda* system began to decline in the seventeenth century and was generally replaced by the *mandamiento* system. Under this new system the local officials of the Crown were empowered to order every able-bodied Indian male to work for a period of approximately sixteen weeks a year on the lands of Spanish or mestizo owners. The estate owner was to pay the Indians a very low monthly wage or its equivalent in food and to pay rent to the local Crown official and to the Royal Colonial Treasury for each Indian assigned to his estate.

As the *mandamiento* proved inadequate for assuring the necessary supply of labor, another device was soon adopted to supplement it. The Indians were easily encouraged to contract money debts which they were unable to repay as they had little or no money income. Therefore, it was made obligatory for the Indians to repay these debts by labor. These two systems, the *mandamiento* and debt slavery, formed the basis of the Guatemalan economic system for more than 250 years.

Although legal slavery was abolished with independence from Spain, there was no change in the basic system of forced labor because few Indians had ever been held as outright slaves. After independence the cultivation of cochineal and indigo for export increased the demand for Indian labor, and the system of debtor servitude was expanded. Furthermore, the growth of commercial agriculture provided the impetus for the expansion of Ladino (non-Indian) landholdings, thus steadily decreasing the acreage of the "public domain."

From the mid-nineteenth century to the mid-twentieth, Guatemalan politics was dominated by a sequence of four *caudillos*. The first of these, Rafael Carrera, an illiterate peasant who was vigorously Catholic and conservative, rose to power in 1837—two years before the collapse of the United Provinces of Central America—and continued to be the dominant figure in Guatemalan politics until his death in 1865.

The second *caudillo*, Justo Rufino Barrios, a Liberal whose regime lasted from 1873 to 1885, was known to many as the "Great Reformer." He stripped the Catholic Church of many privileges, began an extensive public works program, introduced electricity in the capital, extended railroad lines, and established a national school system and a civil code. He also abolished the communal landholding system and introduced private property rights into the Indian villages.

The longest dictatorship was that of Manuel Estrada Cabrera, whose rule from 1898 to 1920 was notable for its corruption and its favoritism toward the privileged classes and toward foreign capital. Dictatorial rule was resumed in 1931 with the accession to power of Jorge Ubico. As corrupt as his predecessors, Ubico was also intelligent. He refilled the treasury coffers, balanced the budget, restored Guatemala's international credit, and built more roads and hospitals than all of his predecessors combined. He also pilfered more funds than his predecessors and executed more potential enemies.

Meanwhile, in the 1860s and 1870s the progress of European industry had put an end to the commercial importance of natural dyes, and Guatemala was forced to turn to other export commodities. This led to the introduction of new commercial crops, the most important of which were coffee and bananas. Coffee took the lead, and by the end of the nineteenth century the plateaus and mountain slopes on the Pacific side of the central mountain chain were dotted with coffee fincas.

The supply of Indian labor in the region of the coffee fincas was insufficient, so once again a new means of assuring a cheap labor supply had to be found. The means adopted for inducing Indians from the interior highlands to migrate temporarily across the mountains to the fincas for the seasons of heavy labor demand was the wage-contract system. This system, formalized by law in 1894, allowed agents of finca owners to travel through the highlands making money advances to individuals or groups of Indians, in return for which the latter contracted to work on the fincas for specified periods. Government officials were obliged to bring pressure to bear upon the Indians to accept the contracts and then to ensure compliance with them. With some modifications this system of securing agricultural labor predominated until the mid-1930s.

The Barrios regime, assuming power in the 1870s, had abolished the communal land tenure system. Village lands were permanently distributed among individual families; but due to fear of taxation as well as reluctance to deal with the Ladino population, few Indian families ever registered titles to their land. Thus Ladinos were free to stake out claims to Indian lands without fear of legal reprisal. In 1934, under the Ubico regime, the wage-contract system was abolished. In its place, however, a series of vagrancy laws were passed which compelled all Indians cultivating on their own account less than a specified amount of land to work as laborers for at least 150 days each year.

Ruling through repression in favor of the economic elite, Ubico, described as a policeman at heart, set the stage for what he dreaded most: rebellion and dramatic social change. An opposition movement begun by university students was ultimately joined by professionals, urban workers, and others, and the incessant clamor in the streets led to Ubico's resignation in 1944. An election later that year produced a resounding victory for a distinguished scholar and reformist, Juan José Arevalo.

Arevalo's term was characterized by the beginnings of economic planning, the extension of labor rights, and the establishment of a social welfare system. It was his successor, however, Colonel Jacobo Arbenz, elected in 1950, who succeeded in extending social reforms to the rural sector. His agrarian reform law of 1952 was hardly radical by modern international standards, but it was radical in the Guatemalan context, and it was offensive in particular to the U.S.-based United Fruit Company.

In 1954 an invasion of exiles, organized by the CIA and led by Col. Castillo Armas, toppled the Arbenz government. The subsequent counterrevolutionary regime rolled back most of the reforms of the previous decade. Land that had been distributed to Indian peasants was returned to Ladino estate owners, and labor and student groups and reformist political parties were systematically repressed.[1]

Castillo Armas was assassinated by a member of his palace guard on July 26, 1957. After a period of extreme confusion and political instability in which a provisional president was deposed and the election of another president was nullified, General Miguel Ydígoras Fuentes was elected to the presidency in January 1958. Ydígoras, an avowed conservative, proved unable to cope with worsening economic conditions and achieved widespread notoriety through flagrant graft and corruption. He was overthrown in March of 1963 in a military coup led by Colonel Enrique Peralta and supported by the Kennedy Administration.[2] It was feared that Ydígoras would allow Arevalo, who had just returned to the country, to enter the campaign for the presidential election that had been scheduled for the following December.

All but one of Guatemala's governments since the counter-revolution of 1954 have been headed by military men, and the one civilian allowed to serve a term, in the 1960s, was kept on a short leash. These governments have ruled on behalf of land-owning and industrialist classes, foreign interests, and the military itself. They have maintained a vacuum in the political center by eliminating, often by assassination, leaders of moderately reformist parties, along with labor leaders, intellectuals, Catholic clergy, and other reform-minded individuals. Repression directed against the Indians has been less selective. A counterinsurgency campaign in the mid-1960s, directed against a few hundred guerrillas, resulted in the deaths of several thousand Indian peasants as well.

Meanwhile, social relations in the countryside have remained frozen in time. Debt peonage and the century-old wage-contract system continue to serve as the guarantors of a labor supply. Army and police units continue to assist in the roundup of peasants allegedly indebted to the labor contractor. The contractor then sells the peasants, for the duration of the harvest season, to plantation owners. In some areas the assistance of army and police units is not needed, as plantation owners maintain their own armed bodies and detention centers.

The most notable change in the rural areas is the cumulative effect of the alienation—continual over five centuries—of the land from Indian and mestizo peasants and the ever greater concentration of landholdings. Many Indian villages continue to hold land communally and without legal title. Thus village property is vulnerable to expropriation by any pretender who can hire a lawyer and a military or paramilitary force. Of course, legal niceties are not always observed. It still is not uncommon for individual Indians or even whole villages to be murdered for their land. The consequent exodus from the countryside, in turn, serves to keep urban wages low.

In the mid-1970s the Guatemalan government began the construction of a road that was to run from the Atlantic coast to the border with the Mexican state of Chiapas. The road was to open up new tracts of land for farming and, near the Mexican border, for oil prospecting. Not surprisingly the best tracts of land were claimed by upper-echelon military officers. The Indian peasants who had been working the land were "relocated" to work camps or simply ejected.

One of the better publicized incidents of land-grabbing and massacre occurred in El Quiché in 1978. Villagers had announced that they would be coming into the town of Panzos on May 29 to protest that their land was being seized. When they reached the plaza, they were met by soldiers firing machine-guns. More than 100 men, women, and children were buried in the mass graves the soliders had dug two days earlier.[3]

Whereas the Indian population had proven difficult to mobilize in the early 1950s and had been virtually uninvolved in the insurgencies of the 1960s, the escalation of massacres and land-grabs in the 1970s served to drive a significant portion of the Indian population into active participation in guerrilla movements. Three peasant-based guerrilla organizations were operating boldly by the end of the decade.

Nicaragua: The Rise and Fall of the Dynasty

The fate of the native Americans of the territory that became Nicaragua was even more dreadful than that of the indigenous Guatemalans. A population of about a million was reduced within a few decades of the onslaught of the Spanish conquest to tens of thousands. Several hundred thousand Indians were shipped into bondage in other parts of the Spanish empire, particularly Peru. Others died in slavery on their own land, in battle, or in bouts with European disease. Since the middle of the sixteenth century, Nicaragua has been a predominantly mestizo nation.

Nevertheless, the pattern of absorption of peasant land and compulsion of peasant labor paralleled that of Guatemala and other areas of Mesoamerica. The Spanish interlopers and their descendants first used their ill-gotten land to produce dyes, beef, and hides, largely for export. But the domain of the landed oligarchy expanded dramatically in the late nineteenth century with the introduction of the coffee culture. Economic "reforms" of the era delegitimized the communal landholdings of the remaining Indian communities, and Indian lands, along with the lands of mestizo subsistence farmers, were absorbed by Nicaraguan *cafetaleros* and foreign investors.

Means of ensuring a reliable labor supply included debt peonage, vagrancy laws, work taxes, and a prohibition against the cultivation of basic subsistence crops. As elsewhere in Central America, such draconian measures were imposed by *caudillos* calling themselves Liberals or Conservatives. Ideological differences between the parties narrowed over time, but bloody competition between them continued unabated—this despite the fact that confrontations between landholders and peasants were increasing in frequency and intensity. A rebellion in 1881 by the Matagalpa Indians lasted for seven months before it was brutally crushed.

As if class conflict, intra-elite strife, and such curses of nature as earthquakes and volcanic eruptions were not punishment enough for the new nation, what might have been a blessing of nature—a river and lake system constituting a potential path between the seas—turned out to be a curse as well. The competing ambitions of Great Britain and the United States with regard to the construction of an interoceanic waterway began early in the nineteenth century to produce economic and military incursions. Railroad financiers, attempting to draw off profits from Cornelius Vanderbilt's transcontinental venture, underwrote the ill-starred filibustering activities of Tennessee's William Walker in the 1850s.

After construction was begun on the Panama Canal, the United States became even more concerned about controlling events in Nicaragua in order to prevent the construction of a competing canal. That, along with other concerns, led to military intervention and to occupation by U.S. Marines from 1912 to 1925 and from 1926 to 1933. The retreating marines left behind a well-trained and well-pampered National Guard, which knew very well that its source of sustenance—its political base— was not in any class or sector of Nicaraguan society, but rather in the United States. The command of that combined army and police force was soon assumed by a U.S.-trained businessman and opportunistic Liberal politician, Anastasio ("Tacho") Somoza Garcia, who founded Latin America's most durable dynasty.[4]

The Somoza dynasty plundered the country for almost half a century. Luis Somoza took over control of the National Guard and the country after his father's assassination in 1956. When Luis died in 1967, he was succeeded by his younger brother, Anastasio Somoza Debayle. A guerrilla war against that tyrannical rule had been launched in the early 1960s by students inspired in part by Marxism and in part by the liberation theology emerging from the Social Christian teachings of the Roman Catholic Church.

The National Liberation Front (FLN), predecessor of the Sandinista National Liberation Front (FSLN), was organized in 1959. A group of students, having despaired of terminating the tenure of the Somozas by legal means, placed their hopes in insurrection. In 1961, under the leadership of Carlos Fonseca Amador, the group added "Sandinista" to its name in honor of the insurrectionary leader of the 1920s and 1930s who had done battle with the U.S. Marines and who had been deceived and murdered by Tacho Somoza's henchmen in 1934.

The FSLN staged occasional guerrilla operations during the 1960s, but with little success. Several of its leaders were killed in June of 1969 in an exchange of gunfire with the National Guard. In the early 1970s, however, the group began to concentrate its efforts on political activities, particularly on organizing the peasantry, and its fortunes began to change.

In 1974, the FSLN called attention to its struggle by seizing twelve of Somoza's political associates at a Christmas party. They were held hostage until fourteen political prisoners were released. Somoza responded to the incident by declaring a state of siege, increasing repression in general, and redoubling his efforts to put down the still-limited insurrection.

Still lacking widespread support, the FSLN split over tactics in 1975 into the "prolonged popular war" tendency, which focused on political organizing in the rural areas, and the "proletarian" tendency, which sought links with the urban working class. Both of these tendencies found inspiration in Marxist thought. A third tendency, which came to be labeled *tercerista*, emerged in 1976. Inspired more by social democracy and lib-

eration theology than by Marxism, it forged links with middle-
class professionals and business groups.

Meanwhile, middle-class opposition to the tyranny was
mounting. The greed of Pres. Anastasio Somoza Debayle, demonstrated in particular by his haste to take personal advantage
of the devastating earthquake of 1972, and in so doing to take
over areas of the economy previously left to other businessmen, alienated even a large portion of the country's upper class.

The Nicaraguan clergy had been particularly incensed by the
lack of compassion shown by the government for the victims
of the earthquake and by government usurpation of relief assistance the Church had intended to distribute. Many priests
and nuns actively supported the guerrillas. By the time of the
FSLN's final offensive, the Church hierarchy had publicly condemned Somoza and had condoned the use of violence in
overthrowing his regime. The prominent role of Archbishop
Miguel Obando Y Bravo in orchestrating the movement against
Somoza reportedly prompted Somoza to vow that, if forced to
flee, his last act in Nicaragua would be to shoot "Comandante
Miguelito."[5]

In the 1970s the great majority of Nicaragua's radio and television stations and a sizable proportion of the print media as
well were controlled directly or indirectly by the Somoza family
or the National Guard. Most of the opposition press had been
effectively silenced. There was, however, one very important
exception: La Prensa.

The towering figure in the Nicaraguan press was Pedro Joa-
quín Chamorro. Descendant of a leading Conservative family,
Chamorro succeeded his father as publisheer of La Prensa, the
major Managua daily newspaper, in 1952. The battle that Chamorro waged with the Somoza dynasty was not confined to
newsprint. He had been arrested and exiled for political activities while still a law student in the 1940s and was imprisoned
at least four times thereafter in the 1950s and 1960s.

In the 1970s Chamorro became, in life and in death, both
symbol and synthesizer of the burgeoning opposition to the
Somoza regime. The prestige that Chamorro and La Prensa enjoyed at home and abroad left Somoza in a vise. His attempts

to censor the paper or to punish its editor cost him support abroad, particularly in the United States; but when he eased up on censorship, the paper lambasted him, revealing not only his crimes but also his weakness. After censorship was lifted in 1977, Chamorro was able not only to pass on to U.S. journalists the regime's misdeeds, but also, in turn, to inform the Nicaraguan reading public (limited in numbers, but influential) of the changing climate of opinion in the United States.

The assassination of Chamorro in early 1978, by assailants linked to the Somoza regime, is generally considered to have been a major impetus to the coalescence of anti-Somoza forces. Moreover, the newspaper continued to serve as a nucleus for the opposition movement. It coordinated the general strike that followed the assassination, and many of its reporters and editors doubled as Sandinista leaders.

Thus the insurrectionary movement gained considerable momentum in 1977 and 1978. A group of prominent businessmen, clergymen, and intellectuals, organized in 1977 as Los Doce (the Twelve) became highly successful in garnering foreign support for the campaign against Somoza. After the assassination of Chamorro, an opposition coalition of the political center, the Broad Opposition Front (FAO) was formed. But the intransigence of Somoza left no alternative to armed struggle, and in that the Sandinistas clearly had the initiative.

By early 1979, the FSLN claimed the loyalty of more than twenty student, labor, and neighborhood organizations, loosely affiliated in the United People's Movement (MPU). In March of that year the three Sandinista tendencies, having agreed upon the broad outlines of a political program, agreed also on a unified military strategy and command structure. As battles raged in city after city in the ensuing months, the approximately 2,000 Sandinista regulars were joined by thousands of young men and women, often no more than children, who formed loosely organized militias. By the time Somoza fled with the national treasury and the ragtag troops of the FSLN marched triumphantly through Managua in mid-July, it was hard to find a Nicaraguan who did not call himself a Sandinista.

When the smoke cleared on July 19, 1979, the people of Nicaragua basked in a sense of personal freedom and national dignity that most had never known before. The affluent and the indigent rejoiced together in the flight of a tyrant who had wanted all the wealth and all the power for himself. Haves and have-nots soon found, however, that it was far easier to agree on the kind of political and economic order they did not want than to agree on the kind they wanted. The leaders of the Western Hemisphere's first successful revolution in twenty years were well aware that the battle they had won in 1979 was only one of many formidable hurdles they were to face en route to the egalitarian society they envisioned.

The revolutionary triumph had been a costly one. During the final years of armed struggle, a desperate Somoza had resorted to genocidal tactics, including aerial bombardment of his own cities, in a futile effort to retain power. Thus the first tasks awaiting the survivors were hardly controversial; they had to treat the wounded, feed the orphans, clear the rubble, and find shelter for the homeless. Financial support for these tasks was available in the confiscated properties of Somoza and his collaborators as well as in the form of loans and grants from public and private entities around the globe—North and South, East and West.

The first source of tension, therefore, within the multiclass revolutionary coalition was the competition for power itself, rather than for the economic fruits of power. In that competition the wielders of economic power, represented by the Higher Council of Private Enterprise (COSEP) and by some of the traditional political parties, were overwhelmed by the hundreds of thousands of poor people who had been mobilized by the fighting, under the flag of the FSLN, and who in peacetime rallied to the Sandinista mass organizations of neighborhoods, workers, peasants, women, and youth.

The Governing Junta of National Reconstruction, installed on July 19, 1979, and the Council of State that convened the following May gave symbolic representation to the leaders of the private sector. The broad outlines of government policy, however, were set by the National Directorate of the FSLN, which retained direct control over the armed forces.[6]

El Salvador: The Generals and the "Fourteen" Families

The battle lines that have been drawn in El Salvador are not like those that produced the Nicaraguan revolution—multiclass opposition to a particularly obscene dictatorship. The dictatorship of General Carlos Humberto Romero, deposed on October 15, 1979, was indeed brutal, but his fall scarcely alleviated popular grievances. Nor was nationalistic opposition to U.S. imperialism a major impulse initially. The clash in El Salvador is straightforwardly a class struggle.

The symbolic enemies of the people are the "fourteen families" who have controlled the land and the government. In fact, the country's intransigent oligarchy now consists of some 300 to 400 families. Lands that had previously been worked communally, in keeping with Indian custom, were gobbled up by private landowners in the late nineteenth century. A modern military establishment and a rural-based National Guard were created at that time to ensure respect by the dispossessed Indians for the new landholding pattern. In many cases the guardsmen actually lived on the plantations and were paid by the landowners.

At the beginning of 1980, half of the land was controlled by less than 1 percent of the landowners. Most of the peasants had no land at all. They were paid only during the three months of harvest; the pittance they earned then had to last throughout the year. It could hardly be said that they were living at the level of subsistence, as so many failed to subsist. In the rural areas, three of every four children under five were malnourished and more than half of the children died before the age of two.[7]

Extreme concentration of landownership is by no means uncommon in Latin America, but it is uncommonly provocative in El Salvador since the economy is based on agriculture, particularly coffee, and more recently cotton production, and since the country, already the most densely populated in continental Latin America, experienced in the 1960s and 1970s an annual population increase of 4 percent, one of the highest in the world.

Furthermore, the same families who, at least until the reforms of March 1980, owned the land also controlled exportation and banking and a considerable portion of industry.

Repression often works, and Salvadorans had quietly endured varying degrees of it for several decades; but El Salvador also has a tradition of rural insurrection. Landless peasants staged bloody uprisings in 1872, 1875, 1885, and 1898. Another uprising in 1932 was suppressed so brutally, with the indiscriminate massacre of some 30,000 Indian peasants, that most of the remaining Indians, it is said, assumed the cultural traits of mestizos for the sake of survival. Urban workers showed their mettle as early as 1944 when they staged a general strike that toppled a government. It was also in the 1940s that the United States began to arm and train the Salvadoran military and paramilitary forces.

The military establishment has intermittently talked a reformist line, but, ruling uninterruptedly since 1932, its officers have in fact grown fat on institutionalized corruption and have generally yielded sooner rather than later to the co-optive tactics of the oligarchy. Meanwhile, the oligarchy has ensured itself against vacillation by the politicans in uniform by establishing its own vigilante networks.

Rural vigilantism reached new heights of audacity during the Romero regime in response to the beginnings of peasant organization inspired by the Catholic Church. Along with peasant leaders, members of the clergy and of religious orders became targets of the terror perpetrated by *ORDEN* ("order"), the most notorious and effective political arm of the landlords. Six priests were assassinated between December 1977 and August 1979.

The so-called security forces—the National Guard, the National Police, and the "Financiera" or Treasury Police—have backed up the vigilante groups in maintaining "order" in the countryside.[8] Although the leadership of these forces is supplied by the armed forces, they have separate identities and often take separate initiatives. By the fall of 1979 some of the younger, less senior officers of the regular army had come to feel that the arbitrary violence practiced by the security forces, along with the blatant corruption engulfing their senior officers, was blemishing the institutional image of the military.

This concern about institutional unpopularity was one of many motives that precipitated the move against Romero. A more pressing impulse, however, was the dissolution of Nicaragua's combined military and police force, the National Guard, following the Sandinista revolution. Instigators of the October coup had hoped that by initiating long-overdue structural reforms they might strip away the bases of the "popular organizations" of the extreme Left and forestall massive insurrection.

Furthermore, condemnation of El Salvador's record of human rights violations was on the agenda of the meeting of the Organization of American States scheduled for early November 1979 in La Paz. President Carter, reacting to the Nicaraguan Revolution and a brouhaha in Congress about Soviet troops in Cuba, had pledged increased military assistance to Central American regimes, but the *juventud militar*, or military youth movement, as the conspirators came to be called, feared that the human rights record of the Romero regime might make them ineligible for the increased assistance. Finally, it was clear to the younger officers that the top-heavy military hierarchy was blocking their access to the higher ranks. Enlisted men had little reason to be loyal to the hierarchy, as many of them had been kidnapped from their homes and villages and pressed into service.

The conspirators had polled and organized the junior officers—from the rank of captain down—of each barracks and had achieved a 90-percent consensus in favor of the coup. In its execution only one life was lost. The victors pledged sweeping reforms and a return to democratic process in the near future. But the government that emerged from the coup was one in which power was dispersed and lines of command were uncertain.

The governing junta included two military officers. One of these, Colonel Adolfo Majano, who headed the junta, was favored by the military youth movement. The second military member, the very conservative Colonel Jaime Abdul Gutiérrez, was the choice of the United States. Other junta members were Mario Antonio Andino, a representative of the private sector who was linked with Gutiérrez in a business relationship with a U.S. subsidiary firm; Ramon Mayorga Quiroz, rector of the

Catholic University; and Guillermo Manuel Ungo, leader of the Social Democratic Party (MNR), who also represented the Center-Left "popular forum," a loose amalgamation of political, student, and labor groups. The Cabinet was composed largely of young professionals representing the three major reformist parties—the Christian Democrats, the MNR, and the Communists—and other organizations of the Center-Left.

The military youth sought to institutionalize their participation in government through the establishment of the Permanent Council of the Armed Forces. An experiment in military democracy, this body was probably unique in the annals of Latin American militarism. Its twenty-six members included one representative each from the air force, the navy, the National Guard, the National Police, and the Customs Police, and one representative elected by the officers of each army barracks. All officers were eligible regardless of rank.

In addition to the several high-ranking officers who fled the country after the coup, some seventy officers, mostly colonels, were removed from active duty. Nevertheless, the rest of the military hierarchy remained intact, and many of the majors and lieutenant colonels who moved into positions of greater responsibility were drawn from the large and influential *tanda*, or military academy graduating class, of 1963. This class had been nurtured on U.S. military concepts of counterinsurgency and nation-building. These and other senior officers, not necessarily sympathetic with the goals of the lower-ranking military youth or of the new government, dominated the Army High Command and maintained control of the Ministry of Defense and thus of military policy and assignments.[9]

THE OPTIONS FOR U.S. POLICY

In late 1979, it was still possible to hope that major reforms might be carried out in El Salvador without resort to large-scale violence. However, such a solution would have required, at a minimum, that the United States cease to support and encourage those senior officers whose interests were linked to the oligarchy and the vigilantes, or "death squads," and who staunchly opposed structural reform. A relatively nonviolent solution would have been even more likely, at least in the short run, had the United States chosen openly to back those civilian and military leaders who were genuinely committed to reform and who enjoyed popular support.

In Nicaragua, despite the legacy of U.S. military occupation and U.S. backing of the Somoza dynasty, the new revolutionary government went out of its way to establish amicable relations with the United States. There was, in fact, no legitimate economic or strategic reason why a relationship satisfactory to the United States could not have been established.

That coexistence with a Latin American country that has undergone revolution is possible is amply demonstrated by U.S. relations with Mexico. The consequences of a posture of unrelieved hostility and of unsuccessful attempts to depose a revolutionary government are manifest in Cuba's adherence to the Soviet block. It should have been clear that the worst possible outcome for the United States, as for Central America, would be success in a military rollback strategy. The United States "succeeded" in Guatemala in 1954, and after more than 100,000 deaths that war is still being fought.

Had the Carter Administration's approach to foreign policy been a coherent one and had that administration been wholly convinced by its own rhetoric, much of the bloodletting of the late 1970s and the 1980s in Central America might have been avoided. The crisis in Central America offered to President Carter the greatest challenge of his administration—a chance to prove the efficacy of his human rights policy, to chart a new course for U.S. relations with Latin America, and to stake out for the United States a justifiable claim to moral leadership in a troubled world. The Carter Administration was tested and, as we shall see, found wanting.

NOTES

1. For a detailed account of the U.S. role in the Guatemalan counterrevolution of 1954, see Stephen Schlesinger and Stephen Kinzer, *Bitter Fruit: The Untold Story of the American Coup in Guatemala* (New York: Doubleday, 1982).

2. Susanne Jonas, "Guatemala: Land of Eternal Struggles," in Ronald

H. Chilcote and Joel C. Edelstein, eds., *Latin America: The Struggle with Dependency and Beyond* (New York: John Wiley and Sons, 1974), p. 195. See also Eduardo Galeano, *Guatemala: Occupied Country* (New York and London: Monthly Review Press, 1969), p. 55. Kennedy Administration support for the coup against Ydígoras has been confirmed by C. P., who was with a U.S. military intelligence unit in Guatemala at the time.

3. Thomas P. Anderson, *Politics in Central America* (New York: Praeger, 1982), p. 31.

4. The history of the U.S.-spawned National Guard and its role in bulwarking the Somoza fiefdom is traced by Richard Millett in *Guardians of the Dynasty* (Maryknoll, New York: Orbis Books, 1977).

5. Anderson, *Politics in Central America*, p. 162.

6. Good coverage of the Nicaraguan Revolution and the new Nicaraguan society is found in Thomas W. Walker, *Nicaragua: The Land of Sandino* (Boulder, Colo.: Westview Press, 1981); Walker, ed., *Nicaragua in Revolution* (New York: Praeger, 1981); and John A. Booth, *The End and the Beginning: The Nicaraguan Revolution* (Boulder, Colo.: Westview Press, 1981).

7. Conversation with a nun who worked in the countryside and who asked that her name not be used; and Gary MacEoin, "Reflections on the Salvadoran Struggle," in manuscript, 1980.

8. In fact, *ORDEN*, like the more recently organized vigilante groups or death squads, was comprised largely of retired members of the security forces, and active duty members, in or out of uniform, frequently took part in their terrorist activities.

9. Conversations with Jerry Walker, U.S. military attaché, San Salvador, January 1980. For more information on the roots of insurrection in El Salvador, see Thomas P. Anderson, *Matanza* (Lincoln: University of Nebraska, 1971); Cynthia Arnson, *El Salvador: A Revolution Confronts the United States* (Washington, D.C.: Institute for Policy Studies, 1982); and Tommie Sue Montgomery, *Revolution in El Salvador: Origins and Evolution* (Boulder, Colo.: Westview Press, 1984).

7

The Ambivalence of the Carter Administration

Any U.S. government of liberal or redistributive bent is bound to demonstrate ambivalence in both domestic and foreign affairs. This is a consequence of the country's power structure. But the Carter Administration was more ambivalent than most. The general policy thrust of the U.S. government was not settled at the ballot box in 1976. Nor was a middle ground sought between advisers and policies of Right and Left; rather, the competing tendencies continued to slug it out within the Administration.

THE U.S. HUMAN RIGHTS POLICY: A POSTMORTEM

A Timid Defense of Human Rights

From the beginning, the administration's implementation of its human rights policy was rather timid and inconsistent. Some types of military assistance were denied to some countries in some years. Where grants were denied, however, credit was extended, pipelines continued to flow, untimely renewals took place, and ostensibly humanitarian assistance was diverted to repressive ends.

When the U.S. Congress first banned military grant aid to the Chilean junta, for example, the Republican administration circumvented the intent of the legislation by stepping up other forms of aid. For a year or more, Chile received up to 80 percent of all Food for Peace assistance to Latin America, which enabled it to increase its arms purchases greatly. The Carter Administration put an end to that particularly cynical operation. However, the Chilean regime continued to receive a trickle of U.S. military assistance through the "pipeline" of appropriations for previous years.

Although AID's Public Safety Assistance Program, which strengthened the repressive capabilities of police forces, was terminated by Congress in 1975, many of its functions reverted to the CIA or were assumed by the Drug Enforcement Agency (DEA). Members of the U.S. Embassy staff in Santiago assured this author in 1977 that bilateral assistance to Chile in all its forms was being phased out. They neglected to mention, however, that at that moment only a few blocks away the DEA was launching a training program for the *carabineros*, Chile's now militarized national police force. The program was staffed largely by trainers drawn from the defunct Public Safety Assistance Program. Since Chile's traffic in narcotics was reportedly controlled by DINA, Pinochet's original secret police organization (officially dissolved in 1977 but still active), the *carabineros* could not have been expected to use their training against serious drug dealers. But the methods that were being taught for ferreting out drug offenders—infiltration, clandestine operations, and the like—would certainly be useful for trapping other categories of "subversives."[1]

The Liberals' Finest Hours

Despite its inconsistencies, however, the human rights policy proved to be remarkably successful—more so, no doubt, than some members of the administration had anticipated or intended. Apart from the countries in which the military actually withdrew from power, the systematic use of torture on political prisoners in countries still under dictatorial rule became less common, and a great many political prisoners were released as a consequence of U.S. pressures. Furthermore, in the Church, the media, the political parties, the academic and legal professions, and even in the severely repressed trade unions, advocates of constitutional rule were emboldened and dared to organize and to speak more freely because the great weight of U.S. influence appeared to have shifted to their side.

The quick, decisive, and well-coordinated response of the administration to the attempt by the Dominican military to annul the results of that country's presidential election in mid-1978 represented the finest hour of the administration's liberal contingent. After that time the administration, in the evolution and implementation of its human rights policy, increasingly lacked the courage of its avowed convictions.

It generally resisted congressional efforts to put more teeth in the policy. While bilateral assistance succumbed both to restrictions based on human rights and to the general unpopularity of supposed "give-away" programs, aid to Latin American countries from multilateral financial institutions was increasing dramatically. After many unsuccessful efforts, congressional liberals finally succeeded, in 1980, in passing legislation designed to introduce considerations of human rights and human needs into the U.S. vote in the IMF. Those efforts were consistently opposed by the Carter Administration.

The human rights policy had always been anathema to most politically active U.S. conservatives. Carter's vacillation with respect to human rights issues ultimately lost him the support of many liberals as well.

A Costly Diplomatic Victory

Another of the accomplishments of the Carter Administration, the signing and ratification of a set of new treaties governing the Panama Canal, also turned out to be very costly. The effort in the Senate was so great and the margin so narrow that Carter ultimately treated his victory almost as if it had been a defeat.

Attempts to renegotiate the treaties of 1903 had been under way for more than a decade. Riots and demonstrations in Panama stemming from resentment over U.S. policies had not been uncommon, but the rioting that occurred in January 1964 was uncommonly serious. A symbolic dispute over the flying of the Panamanian flag in the canal zone escalated into a free-for-all that persisted for three days; it resulted in the deaths of twenty Panamanians and four U.S. citizens, as well as in serious injuries to several hundred persons and property damage amounting to more than $2 million.

The controversy smoldered for almost a year after that riot, until President Johnson announced that the United States was prepared to negotiate a new treaty. Negotiations proceeded haltingly thereafter, breaking down on occasion, particularly over Panamanian objections to the continued presence of U.S. military bases and U.S. insistence on maintaining defense rights for an indefinite period.

Negotiations had lagged in the mid-1970s but were resumed in earnest after Carter's inauguration. In Washington, D.C., on September 7, 1977, with much fanfare and with most hemispheric heads of state in attendance, Carter and Panamanian leader General Omar Torrijos signed two new treaties. The Panama Canal Treaty, abrogating all previous treaties dealing with the canal and the zone, turned jurisdiction of the canal zone over to the Panamanians immediately. Panama was to assume full ownership and control of the canal in the year 2000. The treaty did not call for a reduction in the U.S. military presence, but did pledge that Panamanians would increasingly participate in defense activity. The accompanying neutrality treaty contained seemingly contradictory passages, guaranteeing "transit by the vessels of all nations on terms of entire equality" on the one hand and expeditious treatment of U.S. vessels on the other.

A plebiscite on the treaties in Panama on October 23, 1977, which drew a large turnout and returned a vote of two to one in favor, served as a fleeting reminder to North Americans that the Panama Canal issue was not strictly a domestic one. But the campaigns for and against ratification by the U.S. Senate raised such a furor that bilaterial issues and international implications were almost lost from view.

Administration spokesmen crisscrossed the country promoting the treaties; public opinion polls became more favorable and Senate head counts more encouraging in early 1978. The neutrality treaty was ratified in March and the canal treaty in April, both by votes of 68 to 32—one vote more than the two-thirds required. They passed, however, only after the adoption of a reservation, crippling from the perspective of many Panamanians, legitimizing U.S. military intervention in the event of interference with the operation of the canal.

Furthermore, with this initiative, it appeared that Carter had expended—or believed he had expended—too much of his presidential leverage. Thereafter he seemed less energetic in the pursuit of liberal goals and more hesitant to engage the conservative opposition in Congress.

Intelligence: Nothing Succeeds Like Failure

Beginning in the mid-1970s, the U.S. Congress undertook to place constraints on the activities of U.S. intelligence agencies. This move was by no means capricious. It came about in response to revelations of the involvement of the CIA and other intelligence agencies in the undermining of constitutional governments, in conspiracy to assassinate foreign leaders, in spying on U.S. citizens at home and abroad, in testing mind-bending drugs on unwitting human guinea pigs, and in infiltrating and subverting a myriad of organizations and professions, domestic as well as foreign.

The legislation actually passed was rather timid. The Hughes-Ryan Amendment to the Foreign Aid Authorization Act of 1974 provided only that no funds could be expended on a covert operation unless it was reported in "timely fashion" to eight congressional committees, four in each house.

With cooperation from the Carter Administration, the Senate's new permanent Select Committee on Intelligence began in 1978 to draft a charter to circumscribe the activities of the intelligence community. But a sequence of intelligence failures in 1978 and 1979 generated public frustrations, and the intelligence community was able to cash in on its own ineptitude. Blaming their poor performance on congressional reporting requirements, the CIA and other intelligence agencies persuaded the administration, and apparently most members of Congress, that what was called for was not less discretionary power and secrecy, but more.

Agonizing Success and Reappraisal

The years 1979 and 1980 witnessed the dismissal or defection of the most prominent liberals in the Carter Administration's foreign policy advisory team. United Nations Ambassador Andrew Young, widely considered the administration's conscience in foreign affairs, resigned under pressure in 1979. The departure of Secretary of State Cyrus Vance in the spring of 1980 left no doubt that the president's National Security Advisor, Zbigniew Brzezinski, and his security-minded allies had won the final round.

It was not the failures of the human rights policy, however, that undermined the influence of its authors and led to the reappraisals and backtracking of 1980; it was the policy's successes.

The most agonizing successes of the human rights policy were the Iranian and Nicaraguan revolutions of 1979. In both cases, the tone of disenchantment with dictators and concern for human rights set by the U.S. Congress in the mid-1970s and subsequently embraced by the Carter Administration threw the dynasties off balance and encouraged their opponents—but there the parallel ends.

There are, of course, innumerable factors—historical, cultural, and geopolitical—that have contributed to the differing moods and outcomes of the two revolutions. But the posture of the Carter Administration toward the two prerevolutionary regimes was also different. Iran was one of several states exempted from the punitive denial of military assistance for "security" reasons. Furthermore, whatever might have transpired behind the scenes, Carter's public expressions of support for the Shah were unequivocal until the bitter end. Thus Iran's fanatical revolutionary leadership backed the action of thugs, who seized the U.S. Embassy and took its occupants as hostages. The leadership of the Nicaraguan Revolution, by contrast, sought amicable relations with the United States.

The Carter Administration had by no means been supportive of the Sandinistas or comfortable with the prospect of revolution in Nicaragua. The Somoza regime, however, was one of those that had come to be identified in the United States as a systematic violator of human rights. Thus, by congressional mandate, direct military assistance was denied to it. (Until his capitulation, Somoza continued to receive military assistance from the Israeli government; it is scarcely conceivable that the Israelis would have continued such assistance in the face of U.S. disapproval.) More importantly, the appearance of a weakening in U.S. support for the dictatorship gave encouragement to Somoza's opponents. The political "space" opened up in part by U.S. ambivalence was generally considered to be one of the factors that had helped to make the revolution possible. Thus the Sandinistas were hopeful that relations with the United States might be if not cordial, at least correct.

Most spokesmen of the administration, responding to a generally favorable reaction by the U.S. media and public opinion, greeted the outcome of the struggle with serenity and good grace. But it was soon clear that that outcome—a revolutionary government led by avowed Marxists—was a trauma for the administration and a sort of Waterloo for its liberal elements. Rather than claiming a share of the credit for the demise of an indefensible regime, the Carter Administration accepted the judgment of its Right-wing critics that the Nicaraguan Revolution represented a devastating foreign policy failure.

Security Bests Human Rights

The Carter Administration's embarrassed reaction to the Sandinista victory was followed in short order by a great flap over Soviet troops in Cuba (troops that had apparently been there for more than a decade); by ominous warnings about unrest elsewhere in Central America and about the security threat from tiny Grenada, with its strategic production of nutmeg(!); by allegations that Cuba was once again fomenting revolution in the Western Hemisphere and the formulation of new strategies for dealing with that threat; and by the reinforcement of U.S. military bases at Guantanamo and in the Florida keys. At least in Central America and the Caribbean, concern about human rights had clearly taken a back seat to concern about security.

The administration's backtracking on human rights can also be seen in opportunities missed. In 1976, the Chilean government, according to testimony in U.S. courts, committed the ultimate outrage. Its secret police, DINA, arranged the assassination, in Washington, D.C., of a former Chilean official, Orlando Letelier. Letelier's U.S. assistant, Ronni Moffit, was also killed when his car exploded on embassy row. By 1978 the regime of General Augusto Pinochet appeared to be teetering as a consequence, in part, of the U.S. investigation of that crime.

The military regime undertook various cosmetic reforms after that assassination. In August 1977, when U.S. investigators began to zero in on the head of DINA, Chile's fearsome secret police, as the mastermind of the assassination conspiracy, the junta announced that DINA had been dissolved. But well-informed Chileans maintained that the organization, employing some 20,000 people, remained as strong and diabolical as ever, while a new secret police organization came into being.

In early 1979 an expatriate American and two anti-Castro Cubans were convicted of the actual killing of Letelier. A U.S. extradition request for three DINA officials, indicted as co-conspirators, remained stalled before the Chilean supreme court until early October, when the request was denied. The United States responded by recalling its ambassador from Santiago, but that recall also proved to be cosmetic. The United States had already begun to back away from previous pressures on the Chilean regime for respect for human rights.

The Letelier case was quietly dropped and the U.S. Embassy in Santiago, in early 1980, published a report lavishing praise on Chile's "free market" economic model. Foreign bankers and investors demonstrated increasing "confidence" in that government; the money poured in, but it did not trickle down. In September 1980, a confident General Pinochet staged a phony plebiscite on a new constitution that would leave him in power at least until 1989.

Meanwhile in Brazil, the democratic opening was suffering a temporary setback in 1980 as the government reverted to violent methods in cracking down on the metalworkers strike. Many strikers were fired, labor leaders were arrested, and the popular labor leader, Luis Ignacio da Silva (Lula), was banned from holding office in the labor movement. Right-wing terrorists burned down newsstands throughout the country where periodicals highly critical of military rule were being sold. The same terrorists were presumed to be responsible for an attack in August on a Jewish nursery, leaving obscenities and swastikas painted on the walls. The government denounced this wave of terrorist activities, but no arrests were made, and the government itself announced that it was working on legislation to impose "responsibility" on the press.

In 1980, the Carter Administration began also to mend fences with the repressive military governments of Uruguay and Argentina. Administration spokesmen asserted that, in light of Argentina's burgeoning trade with the Soviet Union, the United States could no longer afford to maintain strained relations with the Argentine government.

Bolivia, after holding presidential elections in 1980 in which Hernán Siles Suazo once again won a strong plurality, suffered yet another military coup. In mid-July, before the Bolivian congress could confirm the victory of Siles, a junta headed by General Luis García Meza, allegedly with strong backing from the Argentine government, ousted President Lydia Gueiler Tejada and seized control of the Bolivian government. García Meza's troops occupied poor neighborhoods, labor union offices, and the university in La Paz, and rounded up hundreds of political, labor, and student leaders. Siles managed to go into hiding, but Marcelo Quiroga Santa Cruz, Socialist candidate for the presidency, was murdered while the coup was in progress, and Juan Lechín, director of the central labor federation, was captured and held for several months.

Peasants throughout the country initially threw up roadblocks and tin miners went on strike. Within a couple of weeks of the coup, however, most of the miners, threatened with starvation and aerial bombardment, had returned to work. García Meza, likening himself to Chile's Pinochet, avowed that he would remain in power as long as necessary to "eliminate the Marxist cancer."[2]

The United States expressed extreme disapproval of the coup, recalled its ambassador, and froze all military and economic aid. There is no evidence, to this author's knowledge, that U.S. officials' opposition to the coup was less than genuine. United States officials openly accused García Meza of heading a major drug-smuggling operation. It seems unlikely, however, that the military conspirators had failed to note the general faltering of the democratizing trend in Latin America and in countries elsewhere that were under U.S. hegemony.[3]

The conflicting tendencies in the policies of the Carter Administration, which were an only somewhat exaggerated version of the tendencies to be expected in any liberal U.S. administration, were best highlighted in the U.S. approach to revolution and insurrection in Central America. Also highlighted was the plight of Latin American nationalists whiplashed by a reversal in U.S. policy.

BACKING THE PHANTOM CENTER

Nicaragua: Marching to Different Drummers

In the case of Nicaragua, the contradictory tendencies within the administration's foreign policymaking apparatus were set in relief long before Somoza's retreat. While some of Carter's advisers genuinely hoped for an end to the Somoza dynasty, others pressed only for the changes that they believed would allow things to go on as they were. When it became clear that Somoza had lost the support even of the business community that had helped to sustain him in the past, and that he could not hold on to power, some of Carter's advisers sought a new democratic order. Others, however, hoped that by sacrificing Somoza himself the old order enforced by the National Guard, *Somocismo* without Somoza, could be maintained. After it was already clear to most observers that the Nicaraguan political scene was terminally polarized between the Sandinista insurgents on the one hand and Somoza's shrinking entourage on the other, the Carter Administration was still frantically searching for a middle way—that is, for a government controlled by "moderates" beholden to the United States.[4]

As rebellion gathered momentum and spread throughout the country in 1978, the Carter Administration vacillated and sent out mixed signals. After the Sandinista offensive in September and the retribution exacted by Somoza's National Guard that left 2,000 dead and several cities in smoldering ruin, the United States instigated a process of mediation under OAS auspices. The process failed, however, either to intimidate Somoza or to isolate the Sandinistas; ultimately it served only to discredit the "moderate" elitest elements of the anti-Somoza coalition who had been willing to go along with the U.S. initiative. By early 1979 it was clear that the issue would be settled by armed conflict and that if Somoza was to be routed it would be by the Sandinistas.

Nicaragua's new Sandinista government, facing geopolitical realities and desperate economic needs, as well as responding to the general Nicaraguan climate of goodwill toward North Americans, attempted to convey to Washington its willingness to bury the past and its eagerness to establish amicable relations. The foreign debt was a particularly prickly issue, since the leaders of the new Nicaraguan government were hard-pressed just to meet the most urgent needs of their war-weary people and since they were convinced that the creditor banks and lending agencies had been well aware that Somoza would use their loans simply for his personal enrichment.[5] However, they could ill-afford an international credit freeze. Therefore, they entered into negotiations with a thirteen-bank steering committee representing about a hundred banks.

Nicaragua was in no position to pledge payment of the debt at the interest and on the schedule that had been agreed to by the deposed government. The banks, however, were uneasy about the specter of a Nicaraguan default and the precedent that would have been set. Thus, the negotiators were able to come to terms. The agreement reached in September 1980 called for repayment at reduced interest rates over a twelve-year period, with a five-year grace period.

The Carter Administration, despite its embarrassment over the outcome of the Nicaraguan conflict, decided that a U.S. posture of hostility would only tend to drive the Nicaraguan government farther to the Left, perhaps even to the Soviet bloc. A policy of qualified generosity was seen as providing the United States with greater possibilities for influencing the course of the Revolution. Thus, in the immediate aftermath of the fighting, the United States joined many other countries in providing disaster relief supplies. In subsequent months, the "pipeline," containing millions in loans that had originally been appropriated for the Somoza government, was unstopped and allowed to flow again.

Finally, the Carter Administration proposed, and Congress authorized, an aid package—albeit a package tightly wound with strings to bulwark private enterprise and to ensure payment of Somoza's foreign debts—of $75 million for the new Nicaraguan government. However, attributing the delay to a tight budgetary ceiling, Congress held up appropriation of the aid until October 1980. The beginning of the actual disbursement of funds was further delayed until President Carter was willing to certify that the Sandinista government was not supporting terrorists or violence outside Nicaragua, a reference to the insurrectionary struggle under way in neighboring El Salvador.

Meanwhile, not surprisingly, the issue that proved most divisive for the revolutionary coalition was that of the extent to which the nation's wealth was to be redistributed and the speed with which that redistribution was to take place. The veteran Sandinistas, along with most of their closest allies during the fighting and their newer adherents in the mass organizations, were committed to moving in the direction of a socialist regime. They were also committed, however, to maintaining unity within the revolutionary coalition as long as possible.

They concluded that maintaining production levels on the land and in the factories taken from Somocistas would be challenge enough for a new group of leaders untrained in government or in business management. Furthermore, they were anxious not to alienate the managers, professionals, and technicians whose services would be greatly needed. Thus, the FSLN leadership assured the owners and managers of the approximately 60 percent of the economy that remained in private hands that they were to be an integral part of the New Nicaragua. But they also warned that the revolutionary government was to be at the service of all the people, and that private interests would not be allowed to override the public interest.

Some members of the business community accepted that proposition as reasonable, if not inevitable. Many others, however, were greatly disturbed by it and by such developments as the nationalization of the banks and of foreign trade operations. Without denouncing the Revolution or "Sandinismo" as such, they expressed alarm about the concentration of power in the hands of the Sandinistas and about the rapid growth of the mass organizations. The fact that about half of the economic assistance extended by the United States was earmarked for the private sector strengthened the resolve of the business community to resist the initiatives of the revolutionary government. The election of Reagan in 1980, of course, signaled to that sector that they need not conform to the new order.

El Salvador: No Way Out

The Carter Administration's efforts to find a middle way between Somoza and the Sandinistas had clearly been too little too late. However, the administration hoped that there might still be time to locate a political center to back in El Salvador, and thus to thwart the mounting insurrection in that country.

The full extent of U.S. involvement in the coup of October 1979 remains undisclosed, but it is clear that U.S. officials were briefed in advance on the conspirators' plans and that the United States was quick to recognize the new government and to offer its assistance. United States officials, however, considered the military youth unreliable and the initial postcoup junta and cabinet too close for comfort to the "popular organizations." Therefore, at least until the resignation of that government and the advent of the Christian Democratic one, the United States lent its strongest support to the senior military officers, particularly Colonel José García, who, with U.S. backing, had become Minister of Defense. In the face of continuing unrest in the countryside, U.S. officials urged the Defense Ministry to get the upper hand and to maintain "law and order."

During the first week of 1980 most of the civilians in the cabinet and the junta, declaring that the Defense Ministry was frustrating their attempts to initiate reforms, presented an ultimatum to the Permanent Council on the Armed Forces. Unless that body was willing and able to restrain the Defense Ministry, they would resign. The council was not, and the cabinet and junta civilians resigned en masse. At that point, most of the Salvadorans this author encountered could only shake their heads sadly and say, "No hay salida" (There is no way out).

According to Dr. Guillermo Manuel Ungo, the MNR leader who resigned from the junta, military commanders in the rural areas were reinforcing a revived vigilante network in terrorizing the peasants. He maintained that the well-meaning military youth, confused and naive, were not able to stand their ground against the senior officers who had been bribed and co-opted by the oligarchy. Furthermore, even the military youth, while seeing the oligarchy as the enemy in theoretical terms, continued to see the Left as the enemy in immediate, concrete terms. Thus, although in the case of civil war some of the military youth would undoubtedly defect to the rebels, the military establishment as a whole was sure to continue to play a counterrevolutionary role.[6]

On the day following the cabinet resignations, the Christian Democrats, with encouragement from the U.S. Embassy, called a press conference and set forth their conditions—agrarian and labor reform and nationalization of the export and banking sectors—for joining the military in putting together a new government. The military accepted.

With some justification, the Christian Democrats felt that they were the rightful heirs of political leadership. In the presidential election of 1972, their standard-bearer, José Napoleón Duarte, was denied victory through the customary electoral fraud and driven into exile. (His coalition's vice-presidential candidate on that occasion, representing the MNR, was Ungo.) Christian Democrats controlled most of the country's municipal governments, but they had lost much of their popular base to organizations of the extreme Left.

Adolfo Rey Prendes, Christian Democratic mayor of San Salvador, explained to the author in 1980 that the party had grown out of the electoral process, which began to be taken seriously in 1964. After 1972, however, it became clear that the oligarchy and its military collaborators were not going to allow reformers to come to power through elections. The party, not prepared to adopt the methods of clandestine and violent opposition, was eclipsed by groups that were. Now that the country is undertaking the restoration of the democratic process, he said, the formerly clandestine groups will have to learn the methods of electoral politics or drop the ball.[7]

The "popular organizations," however, were by no means prepared to drop the ball and allow the Christian Democrats to profit from the gains they had made through years of risk and sacrifice. Even the Center-Left and the Church appeared to view the Christian Democratic initiative as futile at best, treasonous at worst.

The cabinet crisis of early January served as a catalyst to bring about unity among the three major popular organizations: the United Popular Action Front (FAPU), the Popular Revolutionary Bloc (BPR), and the Popular Leagues of February 28 (LP-28). Each of these organizations had a mass base made up of groups organized along sectoral lines, whose members did not necessarily engage in illegal acts; but each also had clandestine affiliates which engaged in acts of insurrection. The FAPU was strongly rooted in urban organized labor. The BPR had a sizable component of peasant organizations, many of which were initially mobilized by the Church. The LP-28 was newer and younger, composed largely of students. A few months after the popular organizations united they were joined by the social democrats (MNR), the communists (UDN), a sizable faction of the Christian Democratic Party, and several other groups, including one representing proprietors of small businesses, in the Revolutionary Democratic Front (FDR). The affiliated guerrilla groups were also united in the Frente Farabundo Martí de Liberación Nacional (FMLN).

The upheaval in El Salvador has been viewed in some quarters as a clash between the government and the Catholic Church. The most prominent victim of the unceasing violence has been Archbishop Oscar Romero, 1979 nominee for the Nobel Peace Prize, who was gunned down by unidentified assailants while saying mass in March 1980.[8] Archbishop Romero had denied that the clash was one of church and state. The conflict, he said, is between the government and the people, and the Church is with the people.

Monsignor Urioste, the late archbishop's deputy, told the author that he had met earlier on the day of her visit in early 1980 with the U.S. ambassador and had urged him—in vain, he realized—not to bring in more weapons for the military. He had also been visited that day by leaders of an organization representing about 20,000 peasants. They wanted his advice on whether or not to join a group committed to violent revolution. He had urged them to have patience, to continue for a while longer to seek a peaceful solution, but he had conceded that ultimately each individual had to make that decision for himself.

In early March, the junta decreed the nationalization of the country's banks and a land reform program that, if fully implemented, would ultimately redistribute 35 percent of total farmland and about 60 percent of the best land. All farms larger than 1,240 acres were to be nationalized immediately. Landowning families adversely affected were to be generously reimbursed in cash and long-term government bonds.

Officials of El Salvador's Land Reform Institute (ISTA) protested, however, that both their institute and the Ministry of Argriculture had been bypassed, as the American Institute for Free Labor Development (AIFLD)[9] and the Salvadoran security forces assumed complete control of the program. The Legal Office of the Archbishopric and spokesmen of several university and professional organizations charged that military occupation of rural communities, in the name of agrarian reform, was actually undertaken to reward members of ORDEN and to identify and eliminate actual or potential peasant leaders. Even the Unión Comunal Salvadoreña (UCS), a peasant union created by AIFLD to divide the rural labor force, denounced official repression in eight of the country's thirteen departments. Eight UCS leaders were massacred by members of the security forces on May 30. By August, the land reform programs, as such, had virtually ground to a halt.

Those members of the Christian Democratic-military junta who actually sought to implement reforms were unable to dominate the junta, much less to control the military field commanders or the security forces. The junta, as constituted, increasingly came under assault from both Right and Left. As Right-wing coup plots continued to surface periodically, it appeared that the junta's only solid base of support was the United States.

A coup attempted in March by Major Roberto D'Aubuisson, on behalf of the oligarchy, was blocked by the United States. But the junta's attempt to incarcerate D'Aubuisson was blocked, in turn, by the Salvadoran military hierarchy. The military, in fact, responded by demoting Colonel Adolfo Majano and elevating Gutiérrez to the leading role on the junta. As the junta was little more than a facade, the Carter Administration had become a hostage, in effect, of the real wielders of power—a corrupt and repressive military establishment.

As was often true in the case of the Nicaraguan insurrection against Somoza, Carter's policy in the face of the Salvadoran conflict appeared unintegrated or ambivalent. United States Ambassador Robert R. White straightforwardly accused Salvadoran landowners and businessmen of underwriting Right-wing terrorism. Furthermore, the United States made available to the Salvadoran government an economic assistance package amounting to at least $50 million for the explicit purpose of supporting the reforms of March.

The overriding objective of U.S. policy, however, was not reform for its own sake, but rather the stemming of the revolutionary tide, and to that end the United States also sought to enhance the counterinsurgency capabilities of the Salvadoran military. To the publicly voiced dismay of both the late Archbishop Romero and Christian Democratic junta member José Antonio Morales Erlich, the Carter Administration announced its intention to provide to the Salvadoran military more than $5 million worth of equipment as well as counterinsurgency training in-country and at the U.S. School of the Americas in Panama. The United States also urged European and Latin American allies to share the burden and the blame for this new counterinsurgency offensive. Some Christian Democratic parties and regimes—particularly the Venezuelan government—rallied to the cause, but European and Latin American social democrats and several European governments, including those of West Germany, Holland, Sweden, and Norway, openly supported the opposition Revolutionary Democratic Front.

By June 1980 it was clear that a new offensive had indeed taken shape. The army had set up roadblocks and checkpoints throughout the country and had launched a large-scale anti-guerrilla campaign in the area north of San Salvador. It had also strengthened its ties with counterinsurgency forces in Guatemala and Honduras. In response, the FMLN escalated its own offensive, combining strikes in the cities with attacks on military installations in the rural areas. Both the FMLN and the army distributed leaflets in San Salvador advising residents of how best to protect themselves in the event that full-scale fighting should break out.

Casualties, which mounted at an average rate of twenty or more a day during the first half of 1980, rose even faster during the last half of the year. Some 9,000 people—mostly peasants, workers, and students—were killed between the cabinet crisis of early January and the U.S. presidential election in November. Vigilante groups continued to take their toll, but the Legal Aid Office of the archdiocese of San Salvador estimated that some 80 percent of the victims had been killed by the regular army or the security forces. In fact, as the reorganized vigilante groups, now proudly calling themselves death squads, grew stronger and bolder, it became clear that many of their hit men were members of the security forces in civilan clothes.

Reagan's election had begun to change the political balance, particularly in Central America, even before his inauguration. Acting Archbishop of San Salvador Arturo Rivera y Damas warned that "right-wing fanatics, inside and outside the government, may now feel openly encouraged to increase repression."[10] And a U.S. diplomat commented that the Right felt after the election that it had a "green light" to purge the Christian Democrats and the reformist Colonel Adolfo Majano from El

Salvador's supposed-to-be-governing junta. Those assumptions turned out to be accurate.

In November, six leaders of the FDR, the Salvadoran political opposition, were seized by soldiers at a public meeting; their mutilated bodies were found shortly thereafter. (Dr. Ungo then accepted the presidency of the FDR.) After surviving an assassination attempt in November, Colonel Majano was purged by the Military hierarchy in December. He subsequently went into exile.

The complexion and structure of the junta underwent another transformation in December. Morales Erlich, the more liberal of the two Christian Democrats on the junta, was demoted, as Duarte assumed the presidency and Gutiérrez the vice-presidency. Morales Erlich was, at any rate, under "control," as one of his sons was being held by the military as a guerrilla.

Among the victims of the escalating violence in December were four American women, three nuns and a social worker, tortured, raped, and murdered, allegedly by members of the security forces. Two more U.S. citizens, working for the American Institute for Free Labor Development, were murdered on January 4, 1981, together with the head of the Salvadoran agrarian reform institute. Their assailants were later found to have been acting under the orders of Army Captain Eduardo Avila, who, incidentally, had close personal ties to the U.S. military attaché.[11]

President Carter suspended military aid to El Salvador in December 1980 as a gesture of protest over the murder of the four churchwomen, but the aid pipeline, containing some $64 million, was unstopped in mid-January. During his final days in office, in response to a major offensive by the Salvadoran guerrillas, President Carter approved the disbursal of another $10 million in emergency military assistance. He also dispatched to San Salvador twenty U.S. military "advisers."

A CASE OF INFANTICIDE

Trend reversals in U.S. foreign policy tend to foreshadow rather than merely to reflect changes in administration, and the change ushered in by the presidential election of November 4,

1980, was no exception. Carter's human rights policy was already succumbing to infanticide months before the presidential campaign got under way. In his attempts to disown the successes of his human rights policy and to flee from its ultimate implications, Carter contributed greatly to generating the opposition to his own administration.

The Carter Administration had not pursued its human rights policy with equal force in all Latin American countries at all times. In fact, it had on several occasions and issues opposed legislative attempts to eliminate ambiguities in that policy and to make it more effective. Furthermore, a policy explicitly aimed at mitigating the harshness of dictatorial rule is a weak fallback position compared to the goal of promoting democracy, espoused (though ambivalently and inconsistently pursued) by the Kennedy Administration of the early 1960s. But the experience of the late 1970s suggests that democratic government is, after all, the logical conclusion of the process of institutionalizing respect for human rights and that for Latin America, at least, a little bit of U.S. human rights policy can go a long way.

NOTES

1. This information was provided to the author by a Chilean who was participating in the DEA training program, Santiago, January 1977.

2. Warren Hoge, "Brazilian Rightists Begin Terror Drive," *New York Times*, August 24, 1980, p. A3.

3. Democratizing trends in Taiwan and South Korea, for example, had been abruptly reversed in late 1979 and early 1980.

4. The author's impressions are based on conversations with several officials of the Carter Administration in 1978 and 1979.

5. Conversation with Reynaldo Tefel Vélez, director of social security, Managua, January 1980.

6. Conversations with Guillermo Manuel Ungo in San José and Managua, January 1980.

7. Interview with Aldolfo Rey Prendes, San Salvador, January 4, 1980.

8. The Salvadoran judge who heard the case (and has since taken refuge in Costa Rica) reported that the crime was committed by members of the Cuban exile group, Omega 7, in the pay of Salvadoran Maj. Roberto D'Aubuisson. D'Aubuisson, a graduate of U.S. military train-

ing programs in the former Panama Canal Zone and the International Police Academy in Washington, D.C., has been identified frequently as a Right-wing death squad commander.

9. The AIFLD has been funded primarily by the U.S. government, with token support from the AFL-CIO and from major U.S. corporations. Government funding has been channeled through AID and, at least during much of AIFLD's history, through the CIA. Roy Prosterman, author of the agrarian reform program for El Salvador, had designed a similar program for South Vietnam.

10. Alan Riding, "Reagan Impact Felt in Central America," *New York Times*, November 16, 1980, p. 17.

11. The author made the acquaintance of Captain Avila at the home of U.S. Military Attaché Jerry Walker in San Salvador in January 1980.

8

The Return of the Rough Riders

In stark contrast to the Carter Administration, the Reagan Administration has been remarkably consistent in its foreign policy agenda and its attempts to follow through on campaign pledges. It has sponsored the country's largest ever military buildup. It has generated the highest level of tension in U.S.-Soviet relations since the 1962 missile crisis, resulting, for several years, in a hiatus in communication at virtually all levels on virtually all issues. It has reinforced the various intelligence agencies, expanding both surveillance and paramilitary capabilities, reinstating the practice of CIA surveillance of U.S. citizens at home and abroad, treating any agency of government and any private organization or profession as legitimate "cover," and introducing new measures to protect secrecy and punish whistleblowers.

The Reagan Administration has redefined development in such a manner as to stress private enterprise and private profit over governmental responsibility and public interest. It has offered moral and material support to authoritarian regimes and has brought indecorous pressures to bear on democratic ones.

Finally, the Reagan Administration has escalated U.S. military involvement in Central American conflicts continuously, mindless of overwhelming popular opposition to its policies at home and in allied countries of Europe and Latin America; mindless of multiple opportunities for negotiation and compromise; and mindless, finally, of the certainty of ignominious failure.

OLD INTERVENTIONISM AND THE NEW COLD WAR

Reagan's prepresidential stance was unashamedly in the Theodore Roosevelt mold. In 1975, he had recommended that U.S. tuna boats fishing within the 200 miles of territorial waters claimed by Ecuador be accompanied by U.S. Navy destroyers.

On the Panama Canal, Reagan reportedly said, "We bought it, we paid for it, and they can't have it." Advocating retention of direct colonial rule in the canal zone, he, along with several retired generals, led the opposition to the Carter Administration's Panama Canal treaties. On the campaign trail, in 1980, he urged military blockade of Cuba as a means of responding to the Soviet invasion of Afghanistan.

Reagan's Cold War rhetoric has been of a type rarely heard in public discourse since the 1950s. "Let us not delude ourselves," he said in a preelection interview, "the Soviet Union underlies all the unrest that is going on. If they weren't engaged in this game of dominoes, there wouldn't be any hot spots in the world." He labeled Latin America, in particular, a battleground in the Cold War, and he insisted that Castro was trying to turn the Caribbean into a "red sea."[1]

Throughout the presidential campaign, Reagan and his surrogates criticized Carter's use of the human rights issue in the hemisphere, berating his administration in particular for "bullying" Brazil and Argentina. Appearing on CBS Evening News on November 15, 1980, Jeane Kirkpatrick, later appointed the Reagan Administration's ambassador to the United Nations, said that extending aid to "moderately repressive, autocratic governments" was preferable to allowing those regimes to succumb to insurrection supported by Cuba. The Reagan coterie's intention to roll back the revolutionary tide was heralded in the

Republican Party's 1980 platform as reported in the *Latin America Political Report*, WR-80-28, July 18, 1980:

We deplore the Marxist Sandinista takeover of Nicaragua and the Marxist attempts to destabilize El Salvador, Guatemala, and Honduras. We do not support United States assistance to any Marxist government in this hemisphere, and we oppose the Carter Administration aid program for the government of Nicaragua. However, we will support the efforts of the Nicaraguan people to establish a free and independent government.

ESCALATION IN CENTRAL AMERICA

During its first days in office, the Reagan Administration rejected overtures for negotiation from both the Salvadoran revolutionaries and Nicaragua's Sandinista government. All assistance to Nicaragua was suspended and military assistance to El Salvador and Honduras was dramatically increased. Assistance to El Salvador included a contingent of some twenty-five additional military "advisers," consisting largely of Green Berets. Circumventing a congressional ban on military grants and loans to Guatemala, the administration sent helicopters, trucks, and jeeps, redesignated as "civilian" equipment.

It appeared, early in 1981, that the administration approached the conflict in El Salvador with exhilaration, that it viewed that conflict as one in which American military power might be revindicated and the so-called Vietnam syndrome forever laid to rest. The administration soon found, however, that the U.S. public was less than enthusiastic about its crusade. In fact, polls showed Reagan's support slipping, especially with women, as a direct result of it. Thus the strategists decided to "low-key" the issue. After Sec. of State Alexander Haig complained to the media that coverage had been excessive, El Salvador virtually disappeared from the news for several months.

The crusade has not been popular on Capitol Hill either. Salvadoran Pres. José Napoleón Duarte was unable, during his visit to the United States in September 1981, to make a convincing case to the U.S. Congress that his government was viable or that his armed forces were using their U.S. military assistance

in an acceptable manner. Congress resolved that further extension of such aid should be conditional upon assurance by the
President of the United States that the Salvadoran government
was demonstrating greater respect for human rights. Reagan
himself, apparently impressed by the arguments of Mexican Pres.
José López Portillo, hinted at that time of a willingness to consider a negotiated settlement of the hostilities.

Scarcely two months later Haig, having concluded that the
fighting had led to a stalemate that might eventually mean the
defeat of the government forces, brought El Salvador back into
the news. He was said to be urging a reluctant Defense Department to prepare for direct military intervention in El Salvador and for some forms of military action against Cuba and
Nicaragua as well. The argument for including Cuba and Nicaragua in the hostilities was the familiar one; they were accused of aiding the Salvadoran rebels.

Haig refused, on November 12, to give a disturbed House
Foreign Affairs Committee assurances that the United States
would not attempt to overthrow or destabilize the Nicaraguan
government or institute a military blockade against it. At the
same time the administration was trying to convince Latin
American governments that Cuba and Nicaragua were assisting the Salvadoran rebels and that collective military action was
called for. In conjunction with the armed forces of several Latin
American countries, the U.S. began conducting maneuvers off
the Honduran-Nicaraguan coast.

For some time exiled members of Somoza's Guard had been
training in Argentina and in Floridian swamps and making frequent armed incursions into Nicaraguan territory from Honduran bases. It became known in March of 1982 that their activities, along with others, such as insurrection among the
Miskito, Sumo, and Rama Indians on Nicaragua's Atlantic Coast,
were being orchestrated and funded by the CIA. One sup-
posed-to-be covert CIA project, leaked to the media and widely
publicized, funded at $19 million, involved the sponsorship of
commando forces comprised of Latin Americans. These forces,
who came to be known as counterrevolutionaries, or *contras*,
operating from base camps in Honduras, were to undertake acts
of economic sabotage against Nicaraguan targets such as bridges

and power plants.² Such hostile acts were in addition to the provision of financial support for Nicaraguan businessmen and others who were conspiring against, or might be persuaded to conspire against, the Nicaraguan government.

Both the fighting in El Salvador and the U.S. involvement in that conflict continued to escalate in early 1982. Despite well-documented reports of a massacre of some 1,000 peasants in Morazán Province in December by U.S.-trained Salvadoran troops, President Reagan declared in late January that the government's human rights performance was improving. On the strength of that declaration, he released $26 million in military assistance that had been appropriated conditionally and extended $55 million more in presidential emergency assistance. Furthermore, the administration made it known that more U.S. "advisers" and several hundred million dollars more in military assistance would be needed in the months ahead.

Battle Lines on the Domestic Front

From the beginning, the Reagan Administration presented the conflict in Central America as a proxy war between the Soviet Union and the United States. Secretary of State Haig testified before a congressional committee that the revolution in Nicaragua represented only the first stage in a Soviet plot that included the conquest of El Salvador, Guatemala, and Honduras, and that ultimately threatened Mexico and perhaps the United States as well.

In El Salvador, U.S. and Salvadoran forces searched in vain for a body—dead or alive—to prove their charges of Soviet and Cuban involvement. They finally caught a Nicaraguan and paraded him before a press conference in the United States—only to be rebuffed when he denied all charges of involvement in guerrilla activities before the cameras and added that he had confessed only under torture. In fact, most of the foreigners who had been killed in El Salvador were U.S. citizens, murdered by forces of the government the U.S. supports rather than by the guerrilla forces that oppose that government.

By 1981, both the U.S. National Conference of Bishops (Catholic) and the National Council of Churches (Protestant) had roundly condemned U.S. military involvement in Central American conflict, as had a great many professional organizations, including particularly scholarly ones in the social sciences and the humanities. Hundreds of organizations sprang up across the country, based particularly in the churches and the universities, to mobilize opposition to U.S. policy and to assist victims of the U.S.-backed governments.

An organization headed by movie and television actor Edward Asner was one of several that began to send medical supplies to peasant villages behind guerrilla lines in El Salvador. United States Catholic and Protestant churches, adopting a practice that had already become common in Central America, began to offer refuge to Central Americans fleeing the savagery of their own governments—this is defiance of U.S. law as interpreted by the Immigration and Naturalization Service. (By early 1985 more than 200 U.S. congregations and several U.S. cities had declared themselves "sanctuaries.") Committees of lawyers were also organized in a usually vain attempt to prevent the U.S. government from sending apprehended refugees back to their countries of origin. By 1982, churches and other organizations were sponsoring "peace vigils" on the border between Nicaragua and Honduras in an effort to dampen any prospect of a U.S.-Honduran invasion and to prevent escalation of the attacks by U.S.-backed mercenaries based in Honduras and Nicaragua.

The spreading conflict had also sharpened divisions within both parties, between the Republican-controlled Senate and the Democrat-controlled House, between the Congress and the administration, and within the executive branch. On the whole, members of Congress remained skeptical but timid, essentially giving the president what he wanted, but covering themselves by voting for conditions without teeth.

Haig's replacement by George Shultz as secretary of state in mid-1982 was accompanied by some change in rhetoric and strategy, but not in the overarching goal of military victory. Shultz's Assistant Secretary of State for Inter-American Affairs, Thomas O. Enders, a veteran of the diplomatic battles of the Vietnam War, felt a need for winning "hearts and minds" in El Salvador and, more importantly, in the U.S. Congress. Enders's strategy called for promoting reform, denouncing the death squads, and isolating the far Right. But he had underestimated the strength of the far Right both in El Salvador and in Washington. In early 1983, after U.S. Amb. to El Salvador Dean Hinton called the death squads a "mafia," both Enders and Hinton were fired, and control over policymaking toward Central America was moved from the State Department to Reagan's "hard-line" confidantes in the CIA and the National Security Council.[3]

When National Security Adviser William Clark was shifted to become Secretary of Interior later in the year, some observers expected the administration's stand to become more conciliatory, but instead it simply became more ambivalent—or perhaps more hypocritical. Since 1981, Congress had made the extension of military assistance to El Salvador conditional upon presidential declarations that the human rights situation there was improving. And every six months, with shameful disregard for what was actually happening in El Salvador, Reagan had declared that the situation was indeed improving. In late 1983, however, he vetoed the legislation containing conditionality and extended military aid under one of the many devices he claimed as executive authority. At the same time, he sent Vice-President George Bush to San Salvador to lecture the generals about the need to clamp down on the death squads.

In 1983, two international groupings entered the arena. Under U.S. prodding, the Central American Defense Council (CONDECA), formed in 1963 but dissolved in 1969, was reestablished. The new incarnation was announced on October 1, 1983, by the defense ministers of El Salvador, Honduras, and Guatemala. At that formative meeting, attended also by General Paul Gorman, head of the U.S. Southern Command, options for military intervention in Nicaragua were discussed.[4]

Weighing in on the other side, the foreign ministers of Mexico, Venezuela, Colombia, and Panama began to meet to draw up proposals for the peaceful settlement of the area's various conflicts. As their first meeting took place on the Panamanian island of Contadora, they became known as the Contadora group. Their proposals centered on nonintervention, the withdrawal of all foreign military advisers, and termination of arms transfers on the one hand and open-ended negotiation on the other.

The Reagan Administration claimed to welcome and support the efforts of the Contadora group but, in fact, sabotaged and undermined those efforts. Its conditions for peaceful settlement with the Salvadoran rebels—that they lay down their arms and participate in elections sponsored by the existing government—amounted to surrender, if not suicide. As to the Nicaraguans, the administration turned a deaf ear and a blind eye to their overtures and concessions and continued its counterrevolutionary push on the pretext of stopping the flow of arms from Nicaragua to El Salvador.

On the home front, as a means of squelching debate and of marginalizing critics in Congress, Reagan appointed a bipartisan commission, headed by former Sec. of State Henry Kissinger, to report on Central America. The Kissinger Commission report, a rehash of old myths and contradictory proposals, was released at the beginning of 1984. Despite the report's advocacy of conditioning military aid to El Salvador on human rights improvement, to which Kissinger himself took exception, and the dissenting opinions of two Democratic commissioners, who opposed further aid to the *contras*, the report appeared to have served its purpose.

El Salvador: Stalemate on All Fronts

Total direct U.S. assistance to El Salvador jumped from $172 million in 1981 to $235 million in 1982. The explicitly military portions of that assistance were $35 million in 1981 and $81 million in 1982. Most of the military assistance for those years was extended through presidential emergency powers and was not submitted to Congress at all.[5] So-called economic aid, furthermore, has been primarily aid to the war effort, since by 1981 most other aspects of government in El Salvador had broken down.

Meanwhile, it had become increasingly apparent that the Salvadoran junta was a powerless pseudogovernment serving only as the diplomatically presentable link between the U.S. government and the real foci of power in the country: a tiny oligarchy living in posh exile in Miami and the armed forces. That pseudogovernment had been denounced by the United Nations and by Social Democratic governments around the world, including such important U.S. allies as West Germany, France, and Mexico. More importantly, public opinion polls in the United States continued to oppose military support for that government, and the U.S. House of Representatives, with its Democratic majority, was becoming increasingly obstructive.

Thus, with much fanfare, elections for a constituent assembly were scheduled for March 28, 1982. The choice for the electorate was between the moderate Right, represented by the Christian Democrats, and the criminal Right, represented by a new party known as ARENA. It was hardly surprising that others chose not to participate. The experience of recent years had made it unmistakably clear that any candidate who presumed to speak for the wretchedly poor majority would have been murdered, along with all of his identifiable supporters and a lot of uninvolved bystanders.

It is scarcely credible that the Reagan Administration expected such elections to legitimate the system in the eyes of Salvadorans. After all, electoral fraud in El Salvador was a folk art, and it was precisely because every past election had been fraudulent and every means to peaceful change had been blocked by those in power that insurrection was underway. Nor were America's European allies swayed; most of them refused even to send observers. It is most likely that the elections were intended to legitimate the Salvadoran regime in the eyes of U.S. citizens and, more importantly, the U.S. Congress. In that, the elections were successful—to a degree and for a while. Observers representing the media interpreted a large voter turnout as indicative of faith in the election, or even opposition to the guerrillas (who had hoped to sabotage the elections) rather than simple prudence. (One who failed to show evidence of having voted might have been suspected by the authorities of being sympathetic to the guerrillas.) Thus, the administration's critics in Congress suffered a setback—this despite the fact that the outcome of the election proved highly embarrassing to the United States.

The winning coalition was headed by ARENA, a party

formed—with considerable advice and material assistance from Right-wing groups in the United States—through a coalescence of several Salvadoran death squads. Its leader, Major Roberto D'Aubuisson, had been openly charged by former U.S. Ambassador Robert White and others with having masterminded the assassination of Archbishop Romero.

Allowing D'Aubuisson to serve formally as interim president would have virtually ensured that the U.S. House of Representatives would balk on the extension of further military aid. Thus the United States partially nullified the results of its own celebrated election. It conspired with the Salvadoran military to push D'Aubuisson aside and to appoint to the presidency a little known banker, Alvaro Magaña, who had handled the banking needs, in particular, of military officers. D'Aubuisson retained the presidency of the General Assembly, where he and his cohorts were able to roll back most of what remained of the land reform of 1980.

While the U.S. government assured the U.S. public that the Salvadoran government it bulwarked with arms and advisers enjoyed popular support, the Salvadoran government itself was less sanguine. It assumed that virtually all civilians were potential "subversives," and it acted accordingly. For more than two years, it had conducted a campaign of abduction, torture, and murder against members of religious orders, peasant and labor organizations, professional associations, and political parties. In short, members of all organizations that did not actively support the government had become prospective victims.

The number of combat casualties had been small compared to the thousands who had been seized, unarmed, from their homes or places of work. Under the guise of carrying out agrarian reform, Salvadoran security forces had slaughtered peasant families in their fields, or as they fled, or even in the supposed safety of Catholic refugee centers. Dozens of teachers had been machine-gunned in the classroom in front of their students. Priests had been murdered in their churches and doctors and nurses in their clinics.

By the middle of 1982, some 35,000 casualties had been recorded. The Salvadoran government was attributing half of the atrocities to Leftist guerrillas and the other half to Right-wing death squads over which it claimed to exercise no control. The

U.S. government echoed that claim, but the legal office of San Salvador's Roman Catholic Archdiocese reported that the government's own security forces had been responsible for some 80 percent of the murders. Likewise, Amnesty International had documented hundreds of individual cases in which official military and paramilitary units had been responsible for summary executions of unarmed citizens.

It was also reported that the Salvadoran armed forces, like Somoza's National Guard in the last months of the Nicaraguan Revolution, had swept through villages and shantytowns killing all the males they could find in a certain age group. They had done this on the supposition that young men were likely to be, or likely to become, guerrillas. As self-fulfilling prophecies go, the ranks of the guerrillas had been swelled by young men who preferred the risk of dying in battle to the prospect of dying unarmed.

Many young men who were unable to flee and who escaped execution as suspected guerrillas were forcibly pressed into the government's armed forces. Not surprisingly, such troops often proved unreliable in battle. The unreliability of front-line troops and massive corruption in the officer corps were among many factors that worked to the advantage of the FMLN.

By 1983, the guerrillas had become a very effective fighting force and were making steady advances, despite the infusion of more than $100 million in U.S. military assistance. This turn of events prompted the removal of General José García as defense minister and his replacement by Gen. Eugenio Vides Casanova, former head of the National Guard whose close ties to the United States antedated the 1979 coup. But Vides Casanova proved no more capable than his predecessor of halting the advance.

In the fall of 1983, the guerrillas, now numbering 8,000 or more, swept down from their strongholds in the north and northeast to attack some 130 towns, holding more than fifty of them and extending their control to six of the country's fourteen provinces. In November, an entire company of 135 soldiers surrendered to the guerrillas without a fight. In December, the guerrillas destroyed a major U.S.-designed base at El Paraíso and the Cuscatlán Bridge on the Pan-American Highway, crucial to east-west traffic.

By the end of 1983, the death squads, after a several-month lull, had been reactivated, targeting in particular both urban and rural labor leaders. Verification of the full scope of political murder had become increasingly difficult, as human rights workers were also among the preferred victims of the death squads, but it was believed that the toll had climbed to some 45,000.

In March of 1984 a former high-ranking Salvadoran military officer who, fearing reprisals, asked to remain anonymous, briefed several members of the U.S. Congress on the inner workings of the death squads. With a hood over his head, he was also interviewed on CBS network news by retired anchorman Walter Cronkite. He said that the network of death squads was shaped by the highest ranking Salvadoran military officers, including former Minister of Defense José Guillermo García and Chief of the Treasury Police and former Deputy Defense Minister Col. Nicolás Carranza. Actual organization of the death squads in late 1979 was assigned to then Major D'Aubuisson, who, according to the informant, was continuing to direct the squads. The informant also said that current Defense Minister Vides Casanova, formerly commander of the National Guard, had directed the coverup of the murders of the four U.S. churchwomen in December 1980. Those murders had been ordered, he said, by Vides Casanova's cousin, who is a colonel.[6]

Another of the allegations of the Salvadoran informant, that Carranza had been drawing payments of $90,000 annually from the CIA, was confirmed by U.S. officials, although the CIA's official spokesman refused to confirm or deny that Carranza was on their payroll.[7] Although Carranza was removed from his post two months later and dispatched to Madrid as military attaché, there was no indication that either the Congress or the media was following up on this connection between the CIA and the death squads.

Attention was soon redirected toward El Salvador's presidential elections in March, which were followed by a run-off election in May. The choice once again was between José Napoleón Duarte and Roberto D'Aubuisson. Duarte was declared the winner by a comfortable margin. D'Aubuisson's charge that Duarte's campaign had been supported by CIA money was echoed by Sen. Jesse Helms (R-NC), who was in turn censured by the Senate Foreign Relations Committee for leaking classified information. Nevertheless, the election and Duarte's subsequent visit to Washington, followed immediately by another of Reagan's televised addresses to the nation, had the effect of disarming congressional critics and prying from the House of Representatives in late May $62 million in emergency military aid to El Salvador that the Democratic leadership had held up for several months. At the same time, the trial and conviction of five National Guardsmen in the 1980 murders of the U.S. churchwomen, the country's first trial for political murder in more than four years, resulted in the release of another $20 million in military assistance that had been appropriated conditionally. The issues of orders from and coverups by higher-ranking officials were not raised at the trial.

In the fall of 1984, President Duarte made a bold move; he invited the FDR-FMLN to meet with him for unconditional peace talks. The guerrillas immediately accepted his offer. The timing of the initiative, the fact that it was first announced before a meeting of the UN General Assembly, and the initial reaction of the Reagan Administration, suggested that it had not been cleared with the United States. The earliest official U.S. reactions were hesitant, confused, and ambivalent, but President Reagan, in the midst of his campaign for reelection and, in particular, gearing up for a televised debate on foreign policy, could not afford openly to oppose such a peace initiative.

The meeting took place in mid-October in the little town of La Palma, in rebel-held territory. Guillermo Ungo and Rubén Zamora spoke for the FDR, Ferman Cienfuegos and Comandante Justo for the FMLN. Duarte was accompanied by Defense Minister Vides Casanova and two political advisers. Archbishop of San Salvador Arturo Rivera y Damas and three other Church officials acted as witnesses. The meeting produced little of substance. The rebels held to their demands for some power-sharing arrangement and a restructuring of the armed forces. Whether or not Duarte and the Christian Democrats would have considered such a proposition, it was clear that the Salvadoran military and its U.S. patrons would not. Nor was the Salvadoran military prepared to consider a ceasefire; a ceasefire would have acknowledged and perhaps legitimized rebel control of about one-third of the national territory. Never-theless, the meeting itself set a useful precedent. A joint com-mission was appointed to maintain the dialogue and arrange further formal talks.

Following the election on March 31, 1985, for the sixty-mem-ber national legislative assembly and for the country's 262 may-ors, Duarte attributed the strong lead for his Christian Demo-cratic Party to the popularity of his peace initiative. He expressed the belief that voter approval of the dialogue had been "deci-sive" in giving his party a clear majority of thirty-three seats in the National Assembly and more than 200 of the mayoralties, and he pledged to renew the peace talks in the near future.

While the prospect of a renewal of peace talks produced a glimmer of hope for war-weary Salvadorans, the immediate reality was a continually escalating war. The ranks of guerrillas had grown to some 10,000, while the government's regular forces had swelled to about 42,000. Training by U.S. officers at the school established for that purpose in Honduras had enhanced the technical skills of the Salvadoran government forces, and perhaps of the guerrillas as well, since about one-quarter of the Salvadorans trained there defected.

Although death squad activity had diminished, the civilian casualty rate remained high as a consequence of aerial bom-bardment of villages in rebel-held territory and sweeps of au-tomatic fire from helicopter gunships. Death squad murders re-ported dropped from 1,090 during the first nine months of 1983 to 185 during the same period in 1984. However, San Salva-dor's archdiocese reported that 1,331 civilians had been killed by the regular armed forces during the first six months of 1984.[8] Moreover, the bombings and strafings, together with the mas-sacres of previous years, had driven more than a million Sal-vadorans, one-fifth of the population, from their homes.

Within the one-third of the country they control, the rebels have established a rudimentary civilian government to attend to such matters as agriculture, health, education, and security. Local functionaries are approved by village assemblies or town meetings. With the development of such infrastructure in rebel-held territory, the so-called civil war has increasingly taken on the characteristics of an international war. Even "civilians" carry arms when they can get them, but the guerrillas, or *muchachos*, attempt to protect the villagers within their territory. In the event of a raid or invasion, combatants surround the villages while civilians seek shelter. Despite bombardment and invasion by government troops, many villagers claim that they feel safer in rebel territory than they would in areas under government control.

With diminishing control on the ground, government forces have taken increasingly to the air. United States military assistance ($196 million in FY84, an increase of 140 percent over FY83) is now manifest in highly modern and sophisticated weaponry, and the strategies pursued in rebel-held areas are suggestive of "total" war rather than counterinsurgency. Government military commanders still speak of winning hearts and minds, but "civic action" projects—the distribution of food, medicine, and such—are undertaken only in areas government forces think they control. Strategy with regard to rebel-held territory appears to be to depopulate and make the area uninhabitable. A "scorched earth" policy has virtually denuded the land in some areas, leaving residents to survive, if they can, on root crops.

At the beginning of 1985, the Salvadoran armed forces had six A-37 Dragonfly jet bombers, equipped with machine-guns and 500-pound bombs. It also had about forty-five helicopters and at least two C-47 gunships. The gunships, noted for their "success" in Vietnam, were equipped with special sights and night vision equipment and with three specially mounted .50-caliber machine-guns capable of firing 1,500 rounds per minute.[9] With these and with UHIH Special Communications helicopters, could the Salvadoran military and its U.S. patrons be said to have turned a corner? Hardly. General Paul Gorman, retiring commander of the U.S. Southern Command in Panama, predicted that, given enough weapons and advisers, the Salvadoran armed forces might be able to establish control, within two years, over 80 to 90 percent of Salvadoran territory, but even Salvadoran military and civilian leaders viewed that prediction as overly optimistic.

Nicaragua: The Not-So-Secret War

To those war-weary but jubilant Nicaraguans who began in July 1979 to rebuild from the rubble of their shattered country, it would have been inconceivable that in a few short years the Sandinistas would be branded as the oppressors of their own people and as stooges of a foreign power. Yet the Reagan Administration has staked its credibility on convincing the American public and the world that that is the case.

The prospects for democracy in postrevolutionary Nicaragua have taken on a significance far greater than the potential power of that small country would suggest. The enemies of revolution in general, and of certain contemporary revolutionary movements elsewhere in particular, would like to cite the case of Nicaragua as evidence that revolution can lead only to "totalitarianism." Social Democrats and democratic socialists, on the other hand, would like to build the case that revolution may lead to open and effective democracy.

The prospect favored by the Carter Administration in the waning days of the Somoza dynasty, that the Sandinistas, having taken the risks and borne the brunt of the fighting, might simply fade into the background, leaving the fruits of victory and the direction of the country to the remnants of bourgeois parties, was never a realistic one. Nor was there the prospect that any combination of middle- and upper-class parties might pose a serious challenge—with or without elections—to the highly mobilized, popular, and populist Sandinistas.

There was, however, a very promising prospect that the New Nicaragua's essentially one-party system might evolve along the lines of the relatively open and tolerant Mexican one rather than in the direction of the Cuban model. That prospect remains a live one for the long term, although in the short term it has been severely damaged by the actuality of "covert" aggression and the threat of overt aggression by the United States.

There was still room for hope when Reagan assumed the U.S. presidency in January 1981 that Nicaragua's new government might abide by the standards it had set for itself. Long before they came to power, the leaders of the Sandinista National Liberation Front had pledged to carry out a genuine social revolution and to do so, if possible, within the framework of Western pluralist democracy. The beginnings of Sandinista rule were auspicious. Leadership was to be collective and broadly representative. While martyrs of the revolution were to be revered, it was declared illegal to pay homage to any living Sandinista leader.

Despite the brutality and genocidal tactics to which Nicaraguans had been subjected by Somoza's National Guard, the new government outlawed capital punishment. The maximum term to which former guardsmen were sentenced for war crimes was thirty years. Among the first acts of the governing junta was adoption of a bill of rights, guaranteeing not only basic human rights but civil liberties as well. During the first two years of Sandinista rule, freedom of the press, freedom of political organization, and freedom of assembly were generally respected. With the exception of the holdings of the Somozas and their loyalists, and such basic economic sectors as exportation, banking, and insurance, most private property was undisturbed.

Since, in the end, opposition to Somoza had been almost universal, it was inevitable that when power was consolidated in a new leadership many who had supported the revolution would find themselves on the outside looking in. Realistically, however, there was never any question as to whether or not the Sandinistas would be in charge. The pertinent question was whether or not opponents of the Sandinista leadership would operate freely.

Several aspects of the Nicaraguan situation after the decisive defeat of the Somocistas suggested that the next phase of the revolution, the redistributive one, might be carried out without circumscription of civil liberties. Sandinista leaders enjoyed very broad popular support. The military arm of the old regime had been dismantled, and the high level of popular mobilization should have served to discourage any flirtation with counterrevolution. The grass-roots mobilization and cooperation demanded by the prolonged conflict against Somoza and the enormous tasks of reconstruction also augured well for popular participation in government. The extensive holdings of Somoza and his relatives and cronies provided the initial fruits of victory for purposes of redistribution, and the devastation of war was such that the initial tasks to be undertaken were hardly controversial.

The sectoral breadth of the revolutionary coalition and the emphasis that representatives of all sectors initially placed on unity were also promising. The Catholic Church, which was later to serve as a pole of conservative resistance, had been in the forefront of the revolutionary movement. The new government also initially enjoyed the goodwill of most other governments, of North and South, East and West, with the prominent exception, however, of some of its Central American neighbors. In the United States, the Carter Administration, far from happy about the outcome of the revolution, nevertheless concluded that extending economic assistance, in hopes of gaining leverage, was preferable to attempting economic strangulation, thus forcing the Nicaraguans to seek other benefactors.

The suspension of all U.S. assistance, however, adopted by the Reagan Administration as one if its first official acts, narrowed the options available to the Sandinista government and rendered decisions on the acquisition and use of resources more conflictual. Furthermore, U.S. destabilization schemes, including the freely acknowledged support for anti-Sandinista groups within Nicaragua, have made it exceedingly difficult for the Nicaraguan government to distinguish between legitimate opposition and subversion. The lessons of the destabilization of Salvador Allende's democratic government in Chile in 1973 remain very fresh in the minds of Latin Americans. Thus it is not surprising that to the beleaguered Nicaraguan government an open society came to appear intolerably vulnerable.

By early 1981, Nicaragua's private sector had been able to make its displeasure with its exclusion from direct political power felt by withholding investment and production. This left the government, under pressure from its own lower income constituency to ease shortages, create jobs, and raise wages, with few alternatives to further expropriation of private property.

The alternative that had been most heavily relied upon in the previous two years, that of seeking foreign grants and loans, was threatened by the suspension of loans and credits from the United States and the signals that such action transmitted to private banks and international lending agencies. Modest amounts of assistance from other governments continued to be available, but acceptance of assistance from socialist countries only deepened the hostility of the Reagan Administration toward the revolutionary government.

Meanwhile, the government had found it necessary to devote much of its time and energy and human resources to dealing with the consequences of U.S. "destabilization" and with threats of invasion. Pockets of insurrection had appeared in various parts of the country, particularly on the Atlantic Coast, where the Miskitos, Sumos, and Ramas, led by a former agent of Somoza's National Security Office, expressed separatist sentiments. Former National Guardsmen and wealthy landowners and businessmen had been implicated in subversive plots spawned on the Atlantic Coast and elsewhere in Nicaragua as well as across the border in Honduras.

In response to such provocation, the government had forcibly relocated a large number of Miskito Indians from villages along the Honduran border to camps in the interior. In September 1981, it enacted the Measures of Economic and Social Emergency, arrogating to itself greater powers to deal with such problems as capital flight and labor strikes. It also expanded and mobilized its popular militias and placed its charge of U.S. aggression before the United Nations. On March 15, 1982, immediately after two bridges in the northern part of the country were blown up, the governing junta declared a state of national emergency, suspending most constitutionally guaranteed civil liberties. The state of emergency has been reflected, in particular, in prior censorship of the media and in selective prohibition of public rallies. Elections were postponed until 1985, but they were subsequently rescheduled for November 4, 1984.

These measures were interpreted by the Reagan Administration as indicating that the Sandinista government had lost most of its support and was now facing an increasingly hostile population. At the same time, however, the Sandinistas were arming the civilian population village by village, something that a government that fears its own citizens would not dare to do.

The Revolution had not proved to be an unmixed blessing. The U.S. trade embargo and the credit freeze had resulted in a scarcity of many commodities, scarcities particularly frustrating to the urban middle class. The attacks of the CIA-backed *contras*, or counterrevolutionary guerrillas, had also taken their toll, and the mobilization required to resist their advances represented an enormous drain of resources from the urgent tasks of reconstruction and production. Nevertheless, in the first two years after the consolidation of the Revolution, Nicaraguans had seen unemployment drop from 40 percent to 16 percent and inflation from 84 to 30 percent. They had seen wages raised, working conditions improved, rents reduced, housing construction accelerated, and public credit extended. They had seen public health programs extended to reach about 70 percent of the population, as opposed to previous coverage of about 30 percent, and they had seen illiteracy shrink from about 52 percent to 12 percent.[10]

The attacks of the *contras* increased in frequency and audacity in 1982. In addition to the several thousand guerrillas, largely former Somocista Guardsmen operating out of Honduran bases and now calling themselves the Nicaraguan Democratic Force (FDN), a few hundred guerrillas, under the leadership of former Sandinista hero Edén Pastora, better known as "Comandante Cero," began to launch attacks in the south from bases in Costa Rica. The latter group dubbed itself the Democratic Revolutionary Alliance (ARDE).

Beginning in 1982, U.S. journalists were in almost constant contact with the *contras*, and the "covert" U.S. war against Nicaragua came to be covert in quotes only. The Boland Amendment, passed by the U.S. Congress in December 1982, banning expenditures "for the purpose of overthrowing the government of Nicaragua or provoking a military exchange between Nicaragua and Honduras," had no apparent effect on the administration's pursuit of its objectives. Despite the *contras'* open assertion that they intended to overthrow the Sandinista government, administration spokesmen alleged that U.S. aid to the *contras* was extended only for the purpose of interdicting arms supplied by Nicaragua to the Salvadoran guerrillas. Evidence of such a supply link was skimpy. The major source of arms for Salvadoran guerrillas was hardly a mystery; U.S. Undersec. of State Fred Iklé conceded in March 1984 that roughly half of the guerrillas' weapons were U.S. arms captured from Salvadoran troops.[11]

In early 1983, the United States began a sequence of massive maneuvers in Honduras near the Nicaraguan border. Later in the year a naval carrier task force was assigned to skirt Nicaraguan territorial waters. (A substantial U.S. Navy flotilla has since become a more or less permanent feature of the coastal waters.) The U.S. invasion of Grenada in the fall of 1983 also gave encouragement to the *contras* and caused the Nicaraguans to wonder if an invasion of their country was imminent.

By 1984, the numerical strength of the *contras* was estimated at from 12,000 to 18,000. The largest group was the Honduran-based FDN. The Costa Rican-based ARDE was believed to consist of 3,000 to 5,500 guerrillas, while the Miskito Indians also based in Honduras claimed about 1,500. The CIA was assisting all three groups, though most of its aid had gone to the Somocista FDN.

Congressional oversight committees that claimed to have been left in the dark were incensed in early 1984, when it became public knowledge that in addition to financing and supervising mercenary operations, the CIA had become directly involved in various acts of aggression, including the bombing of port facilities at Puerto Sandino and Corinto and the mining of Nicaraguan harbors. When Nicaragua brought charges on these and other matters before the World Court, the Reagan Administration declared that for the ensuing two years its activities in Central America would be beyond the jurisdiction of that court.

Twice in 1983 the House voted to terminate all funding for covert operations in Nicaragua. The Republican-controlled Senate, however, continued to appropriate funds for those operations. Through a compromise reached in November 1983, $24 million was appropriated to fund operations until mid-1984. The House, however, appeared disinclined to go along with any further compromises on the matter. In the fall of 1984, the Senate itself finally balked, and all aid to the *contras* was suspended pending reconsideration in 1985.

The *contras* continued to be funded, however, through a variety of mechanisms, some of questionable legality and others that constituted transparent defiance of the congressional ban. Funds, arms, and services were contributed to the *contras*, for example, by the governments most dependent on the United States for military assistance, particularly El Salvador, Honduras, and Israel. Contributions ranging from "humanitarian" aid to *contra* families to the supplying of U.S. mercenaries to participate in combat were arranged by "private" groups, in some cases led by retired U.S. military officers and coordinated from the highest levels in the Pentagon.[12] Top secret missions, involving U.S. planes and crews, continued to be flown by the 160th Task Force of the 101st Airborne Division, based at Fort Campbell, Kentucky, in support of *contra* operations. By early 1985, sixteen members of the Task Force had been reported by relatives to have been killed in action. As the ultimate insult to the Congress, CIA funds were used by the *contras*, according to FDN leader Edgar Chamorro, to lobby members of Congress to support more CIA funds for the *contras*.[13]

A mini-scandal erupted in the United States in the fall of 1984, when it was revealed that the CIA had supplied the *contras* with a manual on guerrilla warfare. The manual included instruction in such matters as the kidnapping and assassination of government officials. Upper-echelon CIA officers denied responsibility in the affair, and it soon disappeared from the headlines, having had little apparent effect on the U.S. presidential campaign.

The atrocities being perpetrated by the *contras* were no secret to the Nicaraguans, of course, and the Nicaraguans knew all too well that former National Guardsmen needed no special schooling in terrorism. By November 1984, the Nicaraguan government reported, the *contras* had murdered some 8,000 civilians, including 910 government officials.[14] The alleged *contra* campaign of terrorism against civilians, including rape, torture, murder, and horrible mutilation of bodies, was investigated and confirmed in early 1985 by several U.S. human rights organizations, including Americas Watch and the International Human Rights Law Group.

Meanwhile, the Nicaraguan election took place, as scheduled, on November 4, 1984. The Sandinistas refused to postpone it, as demanded by the United States and by their domestic opposition, or to allow the *contras* to run their own candidates, but restraints on civil liberties were lifted and opposition parties were given free air time on radio and television. The Coordinadora, a coalition of the three largest opposition parties, two labor unions, and the private sector organization, COSEP, claiming that its demands for fairness had not been met, withdrew just before the election. (The *New York Times* reported that one of its would-be candidates admitted to having taken a bribe from the United States to withdraw.) Six smaller opposition parties participated. Voter turn-out was 75 percent. Sandinista presidential candidate Daniel Ortega Saavedra won by 67 percent, about the same percentage claimed by Reagan two days later. The Reagan Administration declared the Nicaraguan election a sham, but several bodies of foreign observers, including representatives of the U.S.-based Latin American Studies Association, found it to have been remarkably fair and open, given the context of mobilization against invaders.

Immediately after his own reelection, President Reagan initiated another great flap over the threat from Nicaragua. The story this time, complete with satellite photos of Soviet ports and ships, was that Soviet MIG fighter planes were en route to Nicaragua. Congress and the media fell into line in sounding the alarm, and even the most consistent congressional critics of the administration's Central American policies joined the chorus declaring that such a delivery would be unacceptable. The monitored ships carried no such cargo, but the incident served to remind the Nicaraguans of their own Catch-22—that on any pretext, whether well grounded or utterly groundless—the United States might invade in full force, but that arming against such a contingency might well provide the pretext.

For more than two years the Reagan Administration had cited the military mobilization and arms buildup in Nicaragua, made necessary by U.S. aggression, as evidence that Nicaragua harbored offensive intentions with regard to its neighbors and posed a threat to the vital interests of the United States. However, a retired U.S. colonel who visited Nicaragua in mid-1984 reported that administration spokesmen had overestimated the strength of the Sandinista Army and had mistakenly attributed offensive capabilities to forces that were defensive in organization and positioning. The total strength of the armed forces, including the militia, was reported to be less than 85,000, and Cuban and Soviet advisers were fewer than 350, rather than 10,000 as claimed by U.S. officials.[15]

In February 1985, after almost four years of escalating aggression, President Reagan finally made clear his objectives vis-a-vis Nicaragua's Sandinista leaders. Asked in a press conference what the Sandinistas might do to mitigate U.S. hostility, he said they might say "uncle." To children in a wrestling match, "uncle" means surrender. Having seen one of their conciliatory moves after another rebuffed or treated as a "propaganda offensive," the Sandinistas must assume that what the Reagan administration seeks is *unconditional* surrender—of their government, their Revolution, and their newly won modicum of sovereignty.

On the Op-Ed page of the *New York Times*, on March 13, 1985, Nicaraguan President Daniel Ortega Saavedra responded to President Reagan's call for surrender. He laid out four reasons why the American people and their Congress should put an end to the administration's aggression against his government. In the first place, he said, the "covert" war is illegal—contrary to international law, as interpreted by the World Court, and to the Charters of the United Nations and the Organization of American States. It is immoral—contrary to American values; it has resulted in atrocities, well documented by U.S. human rights organizations, committed against unarmed civilians. It is futile and unnecessary—the *contras*, representing the hated vestige of Somoza's National Guard, cannot succeed because they cannot win popular support. At any rate, Nicaragua represents no threat to its neighbors, much less to the United States, and it is fully committed to a political solution that addresses U.S. concerns. Finally, the covert war is counterproductive, as it forces Nicaragua to restrict civil liberties, to seek arms from socialist states, and to divert resources from social and economic development. "As for trying to make us cry 'Uncle,' " he said, "this only stiffens our resistance."

Both the escalation of bellicose rhetoric on the part of Reagan and his spokesmen in the spring of 1985 and the elaboration of peace initiatives by the Sandinista leaders were undertaken with a view toward influencing the decision of the U.S. Congress on the issue of renewing aid to the *contras*. The days of reckoning came on April 23 and 24.

Facing predicted defeat, the administration had come up with what it called a peace plan. The proposed $14 million would be spent only on "humanitarian" aid until and unless at the end of six months the Sandinistas and the *contras* had reached no satisfactory settlement. That ploy failed, and at the eleventh hour, Reagan tried another—assuring the Congress that the $14 million would be used only for "humanitarian" purposes until the end of the fiscal year (the same six months, more or less). Ultimately that one also failed. It passed narrowly in the Senate, but the House first passed a substitute bill allocating the $14 million to refugee programs and to the Contadora process, then reversed itself and killed the aid entirely. Reagan, undaunted, proceeded to ask for $28 million in aid to the *contras* for fiscal 1986, and to make it clear that he would ensure that the *contras* continued to be funded regardless of the decisions of Congress. He followed up that pledge with the declaration of a trade embargo against Nicaragua.

The Democratic victory in the House of Representatives was not long to be savored. Nicaraguan President Ortega unwisely chose the week after the vote against aid to the *contras* to travel to Moscow, giving some members of the U.S. Congress, who had opposed the president with trepidation, an opportunity to posture on both sides of the issue. Reagan, taking full advantage of such vacillation, raised the issue again in June. Following a Senate vote approving $38 million in "humanitarian aid" to the *contras*, the House, on June 12, approved $27 million in "humanitarian aid" and lifted the two-year-old ban on aid for military or paramilitary purposes in Nicaragua.

Honduras: The New U.S. Outpost

Honduras, a mestizo country, has long had the distinction of being the prototypical "banana republic"—totally dominated during the first half of the twentieth century by the United Fruit Company—and of being ranked second only to Haiti in the usual ordering of the poorest and least developed countries in Latin America. In the early 1980s, three-fifths of the population was rural and three-fifths of that peasant population was found to be living beneath the locally established poverty line—the equivalent of U.S.$25 a month. More than three-fourths of the country's children were suffering from malnutrition. A safety valve for social unrest had existed, however, in the country's relative abundance of arable land.

The military establishment that had ruled the country since the 1950s had occasionally instituted meager reforms but had been for the most part conservative and corrupt like its counterparts elsewhere in Central America. After a brief spurt of interest in modernizing reform on the part of the Kennedy Administration, Honduras' backwardness had been a matter of no great concern to subsequent U.S. administrations until the success of the Nicaraguan Revolution. At that time a decision was made in the councils of the Carter Administration that, for geopolitical reasons, Honduras would have to become the new linchpin of the U.S. military's anticommunist alliance in the area. To assume this role it would need the legitimacy that could be enjoyed only by an elected civilian government. At the same time the military was to be bolstered by a major infusion of U.S. aid and was to retain autonomy in matters of personnel and in military and paramilitary operations.

The smoothness of the transition was due in no small measure to the efforts of an extraordinarily competent U.S. ambassador, Mari-Luci Jaramillo. A Constituent Assembly was elected in April 1980. Presidential and congressional elections followed in late 1981, giving victories to Roberto Suazo Córdoba and his Liberal Party. A new constitution adopted at the same time proposed to guarantee both civilian supremacy and military autonomy. United States military loans and grants increased from $2.7 million in FY 1979 to $13.3 million in 1980 and $44.9 million in 1981.

The Carter Administration also promoted the signing of a peace treaty between Honduras and El Salvador—technically at war since 1969—that left disputed border territory to El Salvador. (These pockets, or *bolsones*, of disputed territory had become strongholds of the Salvadoran guerrillas.) Resolution of the border disputes facilitated pincer operations in the area. On May 14, 1980, for example, some 600 peasants were massacred by Salvadoran troops while Honduran troops prevented them from crossing the border.

By late 1981 Honduras had become the base of operations for Reagan's "secret" war against Nicaragua, and the military buildup began in earnest. United States military loans and grants jumped to $120 million in 1982 and $130 million in 1983. Since 1984 total aid, most of which serves military purposes, has been running at $200 million or more.

In November of 1981, Jack Binns was replaced as U.S. ambassador in Tegucigalpa by John Dimitri Negroponte. Like Assistant Secretary of State for Inter-American Affairs Thomas O. Enders, with whom he had served in Cambodia, Negroponte had no training or experience in Latin American affairs, but he was well versed in the conduct of guerrilla warfare. In the meantime, Gen. Gustavo Alvarez Martínez was assuming control of the Honduran armed forces. Alvarez had achieved notoriety through commanding a military operation in 1977 that brutally destroyed the Las Isletas banana cooperative. He had achieved power through the command of the Public Security Forces (FUSEP), which included the secret police and a new urban counterinsurgency unit known as the Cobras. By 1982, Hondurans were speaking of the "triumvirate" of power, consisting of Negroponte, Alvarez, and Suazo Córdoba—in that order. The legislature had become a rubber stamp and the paraphernalia of civilian government a fig leaf.

Historically, neither insurgencies nor human rights abuses had occurred in Honduras on a scale comparable to those in Guatemala or El Salvador. That remained true in the early 1980s. However, death squad murders, disappearances, torture, and other abuses were occurring on a scale unprecedented in Honduras. As elsewhere in Central America, the victims included priests and religious workers. In October 1982, the traditionally conservative Honduran bishops issued a pastoral letter denouncing "terrorism, disappearances, mysterious discoveries of cadavers, assaults, robberies, abductions, and individual and collective insecurity."[16]

Though incipient still, insurgency has also increased. Three small revolutionary organizations have formed a unified politico-military directorate, and U.S. troops have become directly involved in counterinsurgency operations with their Honduran counterparts.

By 1984, Honduras, as the nerve center of U.S. military operations, had the appearance of an occupied country. United

States troops were sidestepping beggars on the narrow streets of Tegucigalpa and worrying about the upsurge in the city's rate of venereal disease. United States military personnel were training thousands of Salvadoran and Honduran soldiers at the new Regional Military Training Center (CREM). Joint military exercises involving Honduran and sometimes Salvadoran troops were taking place almost continuously. There had been more than 2,000 American soldiers in Honduras since August of 1983 on average, and several thousand more at the peaks of the various maneuvers.

The military exercises were being used not only for training in marine landings, parachute jumps, and the like, but also as a guise for the construction of a network of airfields, radar sites, weapon and fuel storage depots, and other facilities that might be used in wartime. Bases consisting of permanent wooden buildings had been constructed at Palmerola, Trujillo, and San Lorenzo, and airport runways in five Honduran communities had been extended. Three of those runways had been improved sufficiently to accommodate massive U.S. C-130 military cargo planes. It was generally believed that such facilities were intended to serve as replacements for the SOUTHCOM regional training facilities being phased out in Panama as well as to serve as a forward base support infrastructure in the event of the commitment of U.S. troops in Central America. Most of this buildup had been conducted without the direct approval either of the U.S. Congress or of the Honduran legislature. The U.S. comptroller general ruled, in June 1984, that Pentagon funding for its Honduran projects violated federal law.

Meanwhile, tension was beginning to build between the Pentagon and the Honduran military's forty-two officer Supreme Council; the latter had become irritated by its lack of control over and, in some cases, of information about, U.S. military activities in Honduran territory. One manifestation of unease among Honduran officers was the ouster, in March 1984, of General Alvarez, who had served as a "point man" for U.S. military operations and, in the process, had arrogated too much power to himself. Alvarez was replaced by the more independent-minded Brig. Gen. Walter López Reyes.

Honduran officers had also begun to suggest that the aid they were receiving might not be enough to justify the risks they were incurring. United States military activities appeared to be drawing them ever closer to engagement with Nicaragua. In an exercise in June known as Granadero, 1,750 parachutists were dropped just sixteen miles from the Nicaraguan border. Furthermore, even the Honduran military was beginning to feel threatened by the presence of some 12,000 armed and trained Nicaraguans with no place to call home. It was revealed in January 1985 that *contras*, acting in the manner of death squads, had killed about 200 people in Honduras and Guatemala in the past year. Even if a satisfactory settlement could be reached with Nicaragua, it was not clear to Honduran leaders how they would rid themselves of the *contras*. In early 1985, after deporting *contra* leader Steadman Fagoth, Honduran Foreign Minister Edgardo Paz Bárnica said, "All *contras* who have compromised our sovereignty will immediately be booted out of Honduras."[17]

Honduran officers were also unhappy about the training of Salvadoran troops at the U.S.-run CREM. Salvadorans were, after all, the traditional enemies of the Hondurans. The "Soccer War" of 1969 had left a bitter legacy, including border issues that from the Honduran perspective remained unresolved. In mid-1984 a Honduran officer told a visiting retired U.S. colonel, "We now have four armies (Honduran, Salvadoran, U.S. and Contra) within our national territory. We want only the Honduran Army here."[18]

Finally, Honduran leaders, military and civilian alike, had grown increasingly humiliated by their inability to affect basic decisions regarding national security and the use of their territory. United States usurpation of Honduran territory in the pursuit of interests that diverged from their own had come to be seen as an affront to personal and national dignity. One Honduran officer commented to a U.S. journalist that the country had become "a whore who doesn't know how to sell herself."[19]

Honduran demands for more information on and control over U.S. military operations, for a special security treaty, and, particularly, for more money finally led to high level negotiations beginning in late 1984. It was announced in March 1985 that the CREM would be closed and that Salvadorans would henceforth be trained elsewhere. Meanwhile, the maneuvers known as Big Pine II wound down at the end of 1984 to be replaced in early 1985 by Big Pine III and other manuevers. The early 1985 agenda called for classic infantry exercises, urban and rural counterinsurgency and antiterrorism drills, tank and armored vehicle maneuvers, and naval and air exercises involving some 3,000 Honduran troops and up to 10,000 North American ones. Some of the exercises were to take place within three miles of the Nicaraguan border.

The fragility of the country's democratic facade was highlighted in 1985, when a dispute between President Suazo Córdoba and his congressional opponents over presidential succession brought troops into the streets and the country into a constitutional crisis. The dispute was played out in the Supreme Court, most of whose original nine members were loyal to the president. In late March, fifty of the legislature's eighty-two members voted to remove five justices for alleged corruption and to elect five new ones. The constitution empowers the legislature to elect the nine justices, but they are not to be removed before the end of their four-year terms; the justices in this case had one more year to serve, and the armed forces backed the president and the sitting justices.

Costa Rica: Fragile Democracy Threatened

Costa Rica has been the exception to most generalizations about Central America. Its tradition of one-term elected presidents was begun in the 1880s. After that tradition was interrupted by civil war in 1948, the army was dissolved and the keys to its fortress, Bella Vista, were ceremonially turned over to the Ministry of Education. Responsibility for national defense, as well as for law and order, has rested with a 4,000-member Civil Guard, a 3,000-member Rural Guard, and a 2,000-member Judicial Police. These bodies have no professional officer corps, and, at least until 1981, they were only lightly armed and trained.

Costa Rica's current problems are traceable to the economic shocks of the 1970s. When oil prices rose and the prices of coffee and bananas dropped, the country's economy entered a downward spiral that has yet to bottom out. Under pressure from the middle and working classes to maintain social programs, and unable seriously to tax the oligarchy of coffee growers, successive governments saw no alternative to sharply increasing foreign borrowing. By 1981 the public external debt was in the vicinity of 100 percent of the gross national product, a far greater proportion of GNP than was represented, for example, by the staggering debts of Brazil or Mexico. Such economic prostration left the country extraordinarily vulnerable to U.S. pressures.

Costa Rican officials reported that in 1981 U.S. Ambassador to the UN Jeane Kirkpatrick informed them that further U.S. economic aid would be predicated upon the creation of an army. The country has yet to create an army, but Pres. Luis Alberto Monge, of the Party of National Liberation (PLN), elected in 1982, has had to walk a tightrope. On some occasions he has appeared to give strong support to U.S. policies, while on others he has resisted and stressed instead the country's tradition of pacifism and neutrality. Nevertheless, while the Costa Rican government had not given the United States a free hand, it had increasingly been drawn into the regional strife, particularly by the cross-border operations of Pastora's ARDE.

On the eve of President Reagan's visit to Costa Rica in December 1982, the Ministry of Public Security announced the formation of a 10,000-member reserve paramilitary force. It was also reported that the PLN had established paramilitary units. In the fall of 1983 Monge bowed to Reagan Administration pressure to accept 900 U.S. "combat engineers." It was alleged that they were to work on roads and bridges, but Costa Ricans were incensed to learn that they were to be deployed along the border with Nicaragua and were to be equipped as if for combat. The agreement was subsequently vetoed by the Costa Rican legislature.[20]

Costa Rica has resisted U.S. pressure to rejoin CONDECA, but it has accepted increasing amounts of U.S. military assistance since 1981. In that year the United States initiated a grant training program focused on air and sea rescue, communications, logistics, and border control. Outlays for the program have grown from $31,000 in FY 1981 to $49,000 in 1982; $125,000 in

1983; and $150,000 in 1984. Costa Rica also accepted $2 million in military equipment in 1982, $2.5 million in 1983, and $9 million in 1984 and again in 1985.[21]

For a time, in 1984, Costa Rican authorities appeared to be dealing with their own Catch-22. The use of the country's northern frontier by ARDE guerrillas as a staging area for attacks against Sandinista installations across the border posed a threat to peace and to national sovereignty. Without an army of its own, Costa Rica was poorly equipped to deal with the threat, but the professionalization of its own security forces would constitute a threat to civilian rule and would amount to playing into the hands of U.S. authorities who were, in fact, supporting the ARDE. In June, Costa Rica issued an official protest to the U.S. government against the use, presumably by the CIA, of U.S. DC-3 planes to supply ARDE guerrillas inside Costa Rican territory. The United States was told, according to one Costa Rican official, that Costa Rica reserved the right to shoot down any aircraft violating its airspace, "albeit with bows and arrows."[22]

Subsequent events served to diminish the threat posed by the ARDE. Edén Pastora, who was strongly resisting pressure from the CIA, the FDN, and others within his own organization, including Alfonso Robelo, to unite with the FDN in its campaign against the Sandinistas, was seriously wounded in an assassination attempt during a press conference. Blame for the attempt has yet to be established, but the ARDE became irreconcilably split. Brooklyn Rivera, representing the Misurasata Indian organization that had fought alongside the ARDE, has since entered into negotiations and reached an accord with the Sandinistas, and the Nicaraguan-Costa Rican Joint Border Commission has served to limit border incidents and reduce tensions.

Costa Rican authorities continue to pursue a strategy of trying to avoid direct confrontation either with the United States or with Nicaragua. They respond to U.S. pressures to militarize with evasions and unending delays, and they continue publicly to declare their neutrality. Meanwhile, President Monge has sought economic and political backing from Western European governments in order to bulwark the country against U.S. pressure and to distance it from U.S. policy.

In the spring of 1985, President Monge allowed himself to be used by the Reagan Administration in its lobbying effort for more aid to the *contras*. At the same time, however, the Costa Rican Civil Guard raided a *contra* camp near its northern border and arrested the combatants encountered there, including U.S. "mercenaries."

Guatemala: The Interchangeable Generals

During the past five years of crisis in Central America, El Salvador and Nicaragua have generally been the foci of official and media attention. In time, however, reverberations from the conflict in Guatemala are likely to be even greater.

In the 1970s, Guatemala had been one of several Latin American countries in which governmental abuse of power became so flagrant as to punish not only the inarticulate poor but also legislators, academicians, clergymen, and others having ties to politically articulate groups in the United States. This brought the U.S. Congress, and subsequently the Carter Administration, under intense pressure to terminate certain activities and programs, such as the arming and training of Latin American military establishments and police forces.

The response of the Guatemalan government and its Rightist constituency to U.S. pronouncements on human rights had been one of scorn. The success of the Sandinista revolution in Nicaragua in 1979, however, caused deep consternation in official and elite circles in Guatemala. Ironically, the responses of the Lucas García government (1978–1982) and of its military and vigilante backers to this perceived threat were akin to the tactics that had been employed unsuccessfully by Nicaragua's deposed dictator, Anastasio Somoza Debayle. Assassination and other means of eliminating potential opponents were intensified in both rural and urban areas. Leaders of moderate opposition groups that might have been embraced by the Carter Administration as acceptable alternatives to incumbent leaders were particularly likely targets.

Also like Somoza, Lucas García and his military cohorts took advantage of their official positions and their preponderant control of the use of force to amass personal fortunes and to establish military officers as an economic as well as political elite. This accumulation of capital and perquisites took place at the expense not only of workers and peasants but also of the traditional landholding and commercial elite. By the early 1980s the private sector was complaining that the government—and the military in particular—was overstepping the bounds of its authority and invading spheres of economic activity previously left to the private sector.

Since early 1982 the country has seen one fraud-ridden presidential election and two military coups—both at least welcomed, if not promoted, by the Reagan Administration. General Efraín Ríos Montt, the "born-again" Christian pentecostal who replaced Lucas García after the coup of March 1982, checked Right-wing terrorism in the capital while escalating the counterinsurgency war in the highlands against some 5,000 to 6,000 guerrillas and pursuing a scorched-earth policy against the Indian peasants assumed to constitute the guerrilla's political base.

Reagan failed in his attempts to persuade the U.S. Congress that the Guatemalan government, under Ríos Montt, had turned over a new leaf. In August 1983 Ríos Montt was overthrown and replaced by Gen. Oscar Mejía Victores; two days before the coup, Mejía, as Defense Minister, had met with Salvadoran and Honduran counterparts aboard the U.S. aircraft carrier *Ranger*.[23]

Mejía promised an *abertura*, or democratic opening, but he also promised "police vigilance on every block." Since his assumption of power, kidnapping and assassinations have been on the rise again in the capital. Professional killers are so plentiful that it is said to be cheaper to have one's spouse murdered than to get a divorce.

Elections have been scheduled for late 1985, but at least fifteen politicians taking part in preelection preparations have been kidnapped or murdered. According to a poll conducted by a Guatemalan radio station, only 10 percent of the population expected the election to be free of fraud.[24]

Whatever the mix of greed, racial prejudice, and fear of revolution in the motivations of Guatemala's military government, the escalation of the war against the Indians in the 1980s is further accelerating the decimation of the Indian population and the alienation of Indian land. Some 50,000 persons—mostly Indian peasants—have been killed since 1979. More than a million Indian peasants have been displaced, leaving their land up for grabs by military and civilian speculators. The displaced peasants live in militarized camps, doing construction work in exchange for food, or roam the mountains looking for food or for the Mexican border or for the guerrillas.

Since its inception the Reagan Administration has sought congressional approval for reinstatement of the program of military assistance to Guatemala. Reagan has consistently been rebuffed by Congress, but Guatemala, nevertheless, has received considerable amounts of U.S. arms. Military loans and grants have been banned, but cash sales by private companies, requiring a State Department license, have continued. In 1981, the Commerce Department removed trucks and jeeps from a list of items forbidden to gross human rights violators and added them to a new list for "Control for Regional Stability," to facilitate a $3.2 million sale to the Guatemalan military. The United States sold Guatemala more than twenty Bell "civilian" helicopters, to be fitted later with machine-guns and other weapons. A $2 million cash sale finalized between the governments in early 1984 provided A-37 counterinsurgency aircraft, C-47 transport planes, helicopter spare parts, and vehicles.

The United States has also continued to maintain a Military Advisory Assistance Group of some twenty members in Guatemala. Both the spirit and, apparently, the letter of the law banning training have been defied. Guatemalan Air Force pilots have been trained by Bell employees. Furthermore, in 1982 investigative journalists found a U.S. Army Green Beret captain teaching counterinsurgency tactics at a military school and a U.S. Air Force colonel instructing Guatemalan pilots.

The Reagan Administration managed to slip $300,000 in military training assistance to Guatemala into its foreign aid budget for fiscal 1985. For fiscal 1986 it is proposing a leap to $35.3 million. Meanwhile, the Guatemalan government has made its own priorities clear. As a consequence of pressures from the IMF, the overall budget for 1985 was reduced slightly from the

1984 level, but military expenditures were increased by 10 percent.[25]

The Contadora Challenge

Reagan Administration officials have charged Nicaragua with exporting revolution to neighboring states, with being a Soviet-Cuban puppet, with engaging in a massive and unwarranted arms buildup, and with repressing domestic critics. Reagan himself even declared that the Sandinistas had turned Nicaragua into a "totalitarian dungeon." But none of Nicaragua's actual or alleged actions have appeared to be more irritating to the Reagan Administration than the country's unhesitating acceptance, in September 1984, of the Contadora group's draft treaty. With that display of peaceful intent and of commitment to regional conflict resolution, the Nicaraguan leaders called the Reagan Administration's bluff and exposed its hypocrisy. By pulling back its own Central American clients, who had been on the verge of signing, the administration managed once again to sabotage the regional peacemaking process, but not without severe damage to its own credibility.

The Contadora countries sought, in particular, to remove the Central American crisis from the rhetorical context of the Cold War and to establish a precedent for regional resolution of regional conflict. This intent placed them on a collision course with U.S. policy, underpinned as it has been by the phantom of superpower confrontation. Furthermore, as has surely been recognized at some levels of consciousness and of bureaucracy in the Reagan Administration, the regional collaboration in itself stems from and advances one of the major motives of rebellion in Central America—that of diluting the hegemony of the United States in the Western Hemisphere.

Nevertheless, the administration has been unable, for reasons of domestic and intra-alliance politics, to oppose directly such a peace initiative. Thus it has sought on the one hand to shape the content of peace proposals to its own advantage, and on the other, while paying lip service to Contadora goals, to slow the process and to sabotage prospective settlements that contravene its own objectives. It has sought, for example, through Contadora-sponsored negotiations, to impose mea-

sures of political openness and restraint in military prepared-
ness on Nicaragua only, leaving to its own clients greater latitude for autocratic rule and expansion of military capabilities and
operations.

The Contadora countries, however, have been neither easily
discouraged nor easily outsmarted, nor have they been utterly
lacking in resources. The conditions and restraints that the
United States would impose on Nicaragua, the Contadora
countries have insisted upon multilateralizing. In that manner,
the United States has been placed in the position of running
the risk of being trapped by its own rhetoric and bound by its
own proposals. In fact, the Contadora group has turned its indirect engagement with the United States into a sort of jujitsu,
whereby at regular intervals the United States must either re-
veal its hand or accept certain aspects of the peace proposals.

Moreover, the Contadora process has provided a handle, or
a meeting ground, for the many domestic and foreign opponents of the Reagan Administration's belligerent stance in Central America. It has been particularly useful for those categories
of opponents, such as members of the U.S. Congress and diplomats of allied countries, who do not feel free to comment
openly on the mental health of U.S. officials.

The Contadora countries did not presume to impose a solution but rather to promote fruitful negotiations. In that, their
achievements have been considerable. On September 9, 1983,
the governments of Costa Rica, El Salvador, Guatemala, Honduras, and Nicaragua, meeting under the auspices of the Contadora group, approved a twenty-one-point program, or Document of Objectives.[26] The signatories pledged, among other
things, to eliminate the traffic in arms from one country to another within the region, or in arms from beyond the region, intended for use against a government of the region; to negotiate
a reduction, and eventually the elimination, of foreign military
advisers; and to prevent the installation on their territories of
foreign military bases. The original ten points proposed by the
Contadora group dealt only with security concerns and included no reference to domestic political arrangements. Before
the September meeting, at the insistence of the United States,
a pledge was added to adopt measures conducive to the establishment—or improvement—of "democratic, representative, and

pluralistic systems." As this was proposed as a stumbling block for Nicaragua, the group added, for balance, a pledge to promote social and economic reform.

On January 8, 1984, the first anniversary of the meeting on Contadora Island, at the twelfth meeting of the Contadora group and the group's fifth meeting with Central American foreign ministers, the five Central American countries reaffirmed their commitments in a document entitled Principles for the Implementation of the Commitments Undertaken in the Document of Objectives. The principles were then incorporated into a draft treaty.

The launching of the Contadora group's peace initiative came at a time when the Reagan Administration was feeling particularly vulnerable in Central America. Pressure on Nicaragua was producing defiance rather than humility. Weaknesses and corruption in the Salvadoran armed forces had been highlighted by rebel victories, and Congress was balking at the prospect of steadily increasing military aid. An administration more firmly grounded in reality might have welcomed a friendly third-party initiative that offered a face-saving way out; but the Reagan Administration could scarcely conceal its resentment of the Contadora interlopers.

Constantine Menges, of the National Security Council staff, speaking for the administration on November 28, 1983, implied that the Contadora countries that proposed to monitor compliance with a regional accord were the same countries that earlier failed to hold the Sandinistas to their pledge of establishing a democracy. United States Special Envoy Richard Stone conveyed the administration's reservations about Contadora proposals to Colombian Foreign Minister Rodrigo Lloreda Caicedo in January 1984. Lloreda commented after the meeting that the United States was not yet prepared to discard the possibility of a military solution.[27]

Indeed, the Reagan Administration appeared to have interpreted Nicaragua's many concessions over the previous year and its adherence to the Contadora peace plan as indications of the utility of military pressure, and it continued to escalate. With the revelation in early 1984 of direct CIA involvement in the mining of Nicaragua's harbors, however, the administration found that it had gone too far. Expressions of indignation from

European allies and subsequently from previously quiescent members of Congress were such as to raise doubts about the fate of future funding for the *contras*.

It was only at that juncture of enlightenment that the administration discovered its own most important use for the Contadora process. From this time on, Reagan reassured national allies, members of Congress and the U.S. public of his peaceful intent by paying homage to Contadora initiatives, even as he sought to undermine those initiatives and to press on toward a military solution. The U.S. strategy then became one of fuller "participation" in the process, that participation taking the form of the introduction, through its Central American clients, of new issues and obstacles each time the Sandinistas came to terms on issues previously raised.

In April 1984, for example, Costa Rica, El Salvador, and Honduras had raised the issue of verification of compliance with security accords. They proposed that the Inter-American Defense Board, formally an arm of the OAS but in fact a vehicle of U.S. military policy in the hemisphere, assume the role of inventorying each country's weapons systems and combat units. Nicaragua branded the proposal an attempt to sabotage progress in the negotiations.

Meanwhile, however, domestic critics of Reagan's policies had also "signed on" to the Contadora process and had begun to use it as a means of keeping pressure on the administration and of highlighting its hypocrisy. On May 1, 1984, the House of Representatives voted unanimously for a resolution urging support for Contadora efforts.

A first draft of the Contadora Act on Peace and Cooperation in Central America was presented to the Central American governments in June 1984, and a second draft reflecting the observations of those governments was presented at the seventh meeting of the Contadora group and the Central American ministers in September. The position of the Contadora countries was strengthened at that meeting, which took place in San José, by the participation of all of the members of the European Community, plus the two candidates for membership, Spain and Portugal. The European countries offered their assistance in the implementation of the provisions of the treaty, and several of them said they were prepared to sign binding protocols attached to the Contadora treaty. The European Community also established a link between progress achieved in the Contadora process and a fruitful followup in talks on economic assistance to Central America.[28]

Much to the surprise of the U.S. government, which had not been invited to the San José meeting, the draft treaty presented there was quickly accepted by Nicaragua. The other Central American countries had already indicated their intentions of signing, but, under heavy pressure from the United States, they backed off and, at a meeting in October in Tegucigalpa, drew up a new set of proposed amendments. The amendments proposed by Costa Rica, El Salvador, and Honduras in October, in the so-called Tegucigalpa Draft Agreement, would have the effect of slowing and weakening the implementation of military deescalation and peaceful resolution. Whereas the September draft, which Nicaragua had signed without reservation, called for an arms freeze of indefinite duration, the Tegucigalpa proposals would limit the freeze to sixty days, leaving open the prospect of a renewed arms race. Firm timetables set forth in the September draft for the departure of foreign military advisers engaged in training and operations and for the elimination of foreign bases and schools were missing from the Tegucigalpa proposals. Foreign military exercises, proscribed in the September draft, would be permitted under the terms of the October agreement.

Some of the amendments proposed in October appeared to be designed to dilute the influence of the Contadora group. According to the September draft, disputes that could not be resolved by the foreign ministers of the five Central American countries would be referred, for good offices, to the foreign ministers of the Contadora group. The proposed amendments would call for appeal of disputes from the five foreign ministers to an enlarged group including the original five plus four ministers representing the Contadora countries. Finally, some roles assigned by the September draft to the Contadora-sponsored Commission on Verification and Control would be assumed by an ad hoc disarmament group.[29]

The amendments proposed by the three Central American governments appeared to be designed to assure either that there should be no treaty or that any treaty that might emerge would be toothless. An internal assessment by the U.S. National Security Council (NSC), leaked to the media, said, "We have trumped the latest Nicaraguan-Mexican efforts to rush signature of an unsatisfactory Contadora agreement." The NSC notes added "the situation remains fluid and requires careful management."[30]

The prospects for peaceful settlement can hardly be good at a time when the Reagan Administration is escalating its air war over rebel-held territories in El Salvador, mounting ever more massive maneuvers in Honduras and elsewhere and pledging to settle for nothing less than surrender from Nicaragua. Nevertheless, reports of the death of Contadora have been exaggerated. In August 1985, the governments of Brazil, Argentina, Uruguay and Peru formally offered their support to the efforts of the original four Contadora countries. For the many unrelenting opponents of Reagan's Central American policies, the Contadora peace process remains the only game in town.

THE CHANGING OF THE GUARD IN THE CARIBBEAN

Since the mid-1960s, and with increasing fervor since the late 1970s, the U.S. government has sought to absorb the Caribbean mini-states, newly emerging from European colonial rule, into its sphere of influence. A considerable investment in the Jamaican election of 1980, which replaced the socialist government of Michael Manley with the unequivocally procapitalist and proAmerican one of Edward Seaga, demonstrated this thrust, as did Reagan's unveiling in 1981 of the Caribbean Basin Initiative (a development program based primarily on incentives to U.S. investors). But the "rescue mission" staged on October 25, 1983, in Grenada was the first outright, overt U.S. military invasion in the area since the invasion of the Dominican Republic in 1965.

Grenada, southernmost of the Windward Islands, has an area of 120 square miles and a population of some 110,000. The United States had withheld economic assistance from the former British colony and had subjected it to hostile rhetoric ever since Maurice Bishop, a London-trained barrister, and his socialist New Jewel Movement took power, replacing a bizarre dictator, in 1979.

Following a schism in the ruling party's central committee, Bishop and many of his supporters were slain by the armed forces in a street confrontation on October 19, 1983. The chaos following the killing of the popular prime minister provided the Reagan Administration the opportunity it had been waiting for.

As in the Dominican case, the first and most persuasive rationale for the invasion was the need to "rescue" Americans—in the Grenadian case some 1,000—most of them students at St. George's Medical School. It appears, however, that the invasion served more to endanger American lives than to protect them. Despite urgent prompting by the U.S. ambassador to Barbados, Charles Modica, chancellor of the school, initially refused to suggest that the students were in danger. It was only after the invasion and after a meeting at the State Department that he was persuaded to change his story. In fact, the Grenadian government had assured the Reagan Administration that the students were safe and free to leave if they so chose. Parents of more than 500 of the students, meeting in New York on October 23, sent a telegram to Reagan assuring him that their children were safe and urging him not to take "precipitous or provocative actions." On the night before, Vice-Chancellor Bourne of the medical school had convened a meeting of the student body and had taken a vote as to whether the students wished to stay or leave. Only about ten percent expressed a desire to leave. Some left on Monday, October 24, on chartered planes. Contrary to what the Reagan Administration claimed, the airport was not closed that day, but regular passenger service from Barbados had been cancelled in preparation for the invasion.

The second rationale, presented along with the first, was that the United States had intervened at the behest of the seven-member Organization of Eastern Caribbean States (OECS). Resort to the smaller organization, of which Grenada is a member and the United States is not, was taken after a similar proposal was rejected by the more inclusive Caribbean Community (CARICOM). (The OAS, which was not consulted in advance, subsequently condemned the invasion by an overwhelming margin, as did the United Nations.) In fact, however, a U.S.

armada of two aircraft carriers and ten warships had been diverted toward Grenada on October 20, and Naval Commando units had already landed before the formal OECS proposal, drafted in the United States and presented by U.S. emissaries, was sent back from Barbados on October 23.[31]

Later reports that the United States and the OECS were acting on behalf of Sir Paul Scoon, the governor-general of Grenada, were contradicted by reports that the governor-general was in the custody of the Grenadian junta until after the invasion. A letter from Scoon, presented as evidence of his solicitation, was not signed until after the invasion. In any case, the British government, to which the governor-general is responsible, was sharply critical of U.S. actions.

A third rationale, related to the first two, was that the invasion had been prompted by the military coup on the island the previous week that had left power in the hands of "leftist thugs" said to be more closely linked with Cuba. While the incivility of the new government was self-evident, Cuban inspiration for its actions was not. Minutes of the meetings of the New Jewel Movement's Central Committee, seized by the invading U.S. forces and later released by the Department of State, make clear that the relationship between Castro and Bishop had been a warm one. The Cuban government had condemned the overthrow of Bishop and criticized the new government for heightening the threat of U.S. invasion.

Nor was the Reagan Administration's belated regard for the slain prime minister convincing. It was no secret that Reagan had been seeking some means of toppling Bishop's government for the previous two years, although the CIA's proposal for destabilizing the Grenadian government had been laughed out of the Senate Intelligence Committee's hearing room.

In his televised address on Thursday, October 27, Reagan presented the fourth rationale—his all-purpose strategic one. Grenada, he said, was a "Soviet-Cuban colony" being readied to export terrorism. This assessment was said to have been confirmed by great stockpiles of Soviet and Cuban arms and by reams of secret documents. The documents, we now know, confirm Cuban displeasure with the new regime rather than sponsorhip of it. The arms aid accords with the Soviet Union and North Korea, antedating Grenada's regime change, hardly suggested a scheme for "exporting terrorism." Each of the accords contained a prohibition against the transfer of arms to third parties.[32]

Pentagon sources reported that the stockpiles of weapons filled three warehouses from floor to ceiling. Journalists later found that one of the warehouses was filled with truck engines and another with sacks of rice. The third, while not filled "floor to ceiling," did contain a lot of arms, but some of them, it turned out, dated from the 1870s.

As to the Cuban presence, the Administration first estimated that there were 500 to 600 Cubans on the island. A few days after the invasion the estimate was raised to 1,000; then to 1,100; and it was claimed that most of them were combat forces. By the end of the first week, with most of the Cubans in captivity and journalists roaming the island, the administration had to admit that the number of Cubans was between seven and eight hundred, as the Cuban government had said, and that fewer than fifty of them were soldiers, the remainder being construction workers.

The Pentagon initially reported encountering greater resistance than had been expected, but General Vessey, chairman of the Joint Chiefs of Staff, subsequently said that the level of force employed by the U.S. forces was greater than necessary. At any rate, whatever the extent of local and foreign weapons and troops, the evidence was soon utterly conclusive that it was not enough to defend the island mini-state against its most obvious threat—invasion by the United States.

The fifth and most dramatic rationale was paraded out just in time to make headlines on Friday, October 28. It was that missile bunkers had been sighted in intelligence photographs of the island, prompting the joint chiefs to urge an immediate invasion. That one must have bombed right away because it vanished as quickly as it had appeared. The only subsequent reference to it was a negative. Among the things the U.S. troops *did not* find in combing the wooded hills were missile bunkers.

It was not until day five of the invasion that a fully credible rationale made its appearance. Rationale number six was floated on Saturday, October 29, by unnamed "administration officials." They said that the administration's overriding reason for invading Grenada was to keep the United States from being perceived as a "paper tiger." The government of the most powerful nation on earth felt that it had to conquer a nation with a population about 1/2,000 of its own, one of the tiniest on earth, in order to prove its prowess? Embarrassing, but credible.

We are not yet in a position to weigh fully the outcome of Reagan's "splendid little war." The administration promised to establish a democratic government, of course; but a few weeks after the invasion Governor-General Scoon banned public meetings, authorized arrests without warrants, and threatened to impose formal press censorship. The U.S. combat troops that were to be withdrawn within a few days were finally withdrawn after more than a month, but it appeared that preparations were being made for an indefinite period of occupation by military police and other specialized forces. Meanwhile, more than 600 Grenadian civilians had been detained at some point by U.S. forces, some of them in crude wooden crates.

United States casualties of the invasion—nineteen killed and more than one hundred wounded, according to official reports—were called "minimal" by Pentagon spokesmen. Media reports a year later, based on the testimony of Pentagon insiders, that there had been twenty-one additional, unreported casualties—six killed and sixteen wounded—were officially denied. The additional casualties were said to have resulted from faulty execution of a mission by the top secret Delta force.[33] At any rate, it could not be denied that many of the U.S. troops had been killed by accidents and by "friendly fire" rather than by "enemy" assault. Many of the civilian casualties in Grenada were also accidental; a mental hospital, for example, was bombed by mistake.

The promised elections in Grenada finally took place at the end of 1984. To no one's surprise the victorious presidential candidate was the one who had been favored by the United States. By that time some $45 million in U.S. assistance had been expended, much of it for the completion of the airport project begun with Cuban assistance. Nevertheless, unemployment remained at one-third of the work force, about where it had been before the invasion.

The medical student population, down from 631 at the time

of the invasion to about 430, lived in cramped quarters on the Grand Anse campus, next door to the government-owned Grenada Beach Hotel, which still housed some 270 U.S. military personnel. United States forces were engaged in training Grenadian police officers and an eighty-man counterinsurgency unit. British law-and-order experts were also on hand, building a 500-man police force, along with the 300-member multinational Caribbean Peacekeeping Force, which continued to establish surprise late-night checkpoints to search for guns.

The final phase-out of U.S. military police and support personnel began in April 1985 and ended in June, but about twenty-five special forces troops were to remain as military trainers until September. Also remaining, as a legacy of U.S. intervention, was a new militarization, not only of Grenada itself, but also of St. Vincent, St. Lucia, St. Kitts, and Dominica. The police forces of each of the Eastern Caribbean Islands included Special Services units, paramilitary units of some eighty members each, specially trained by U.S. forces in counterinsurgency. The islands had become fully incorporated into the U.S. sphere of influence and the seeds of the next insurrectionary upheaval had been planted.

NEW CHALLENGES IN SOUTH AMERICA

Since the inception of the Reagan Administration in early 1981, some of Latin America's most offensive military regimes have fallen—victims of their own poor judgment and economic management. Bolivia's drug-dealing generals finally withdrew to the barracks in 1982, as the economy collapsed at their feet; they left the reins of government to Hernán Siles Suazo, who had been elected but denied power in 1980. But economic prostration and the demands of creditors and the IMF on one hand and of long-deprived workers on the other made it all but impossible for him to govern. In May 1984, Siles sent shock waves through the international financial community by announcing that Bolivia was suspending for two years all payments on its foreign debts. Since then, foreign credit has been scarce and the economy has deteriorated further. In mid-1985 inflation was exceeding 10,000 percent. Siles was no doubt relieved to pass the chaos on to another civilian government after elections in July returned the aged and moderated MNR leader, Victor Paz Estenssoro, to the presidency.

The Argentine junta of General Galtieri was hounded out of the Casa Rosada after foolishly provoking an unwinnable war with Great Britain over the Malvinas/Falkland Islands. The generals had gambled that in a surge of patriotic fervor the population would forget about the approximately 30,000 "disappeared" persons and cope passively with an inflation rate of more than 200 percent. But military defeat coupled with a scandalous disregard for the welfare of their own troops finally rendered their position untenable.

Elections in October 1983, the first since the coup of 1976, gave the presidency to Raúl Alfonsín of the Radical Civic Union and appeared to launch a new era of civic peace and reconciliation. The generals, however, were not to escape retribution. Every officer who had served on the junta since 1976 was indicted; most were charged with such major crimes as kidnapping, torture, and murder. Meanwhile, by 1985 inflation had soared to more than 1,000 percent and the foreign debt had become unmanageable. Difficulties in meeting the conditions of the IMF and creditor banks had left the country in a chronic credit crisis.

In late 1984, Uruguay celebrated the end of an eleven-year period of brutalizing military rule. After suffering humiliating defeat in a constitutional referendum in 1980, the military government, headed by Gen. Gregorio Alvarez, promised to schedule elections. The country's two most popular political figures, Ret. Gen. Liber Seregni of the Frente Amplio (Broad Front) and Wilson Ferreira of the Blanco (White) Party, were barred, however, from seeking the presidency. The elections, which took place in November, were to choose a president, vice-president, 130 members of the national legislature, nineteen mayors, and hundreds of city councillors. The victor in the presidential election, Julio Sanguinetti of the Colorado (Red) Party, which had held power during most of the twentieth century, was inaugurated on March 1.

The regime of Chile's General Pinochet, an international pariah since its bloody inception in 1973, finds itself beginning its

second decade in power under multiclass assault, as unemployment and inflation climb, economic "growth" plummets,
and bankruptcy becomes epidemic. Massive demonstrations have
been taking place almost monthly since May of 1983. Pinochet's characteristic response to open opposition makes it clear that
his demise would not come without great cost. Arbitrary detention and torture have escalated sharply since late 1982.

Brazil's situation in 1985 is enviable by comparison, as the
abertura fulfills its promise. The elections of November 1982
produced stunning victories for the opposition, and in 1984, for
the first time in more than twenty years, the country elected a
civilian president. Moreover, the choice of the Electoral College, Tancredo Neves of the Brazilian Democratic Movement
Party (PMDB), was the opposition candidate. (The government's Social Democratic Party had supported Paulo Maluf.)
Undergoing surgery, however, Neves missed his scheduled inauguration in March 1985; he died on April 21. Vice-President
José Sarney, who then assumed the presidency, had been a late
defector from the Social Democratic Party. Thus he assumed
office with a twofold problem: colleagues of the party he left
looked upon him as a traitor, and those of the party he joined
looked upon him as an opportunist.

Even with its obvious strengths, Brazil has not escaped the
economic crisis plaguing the hemisphere. With inflation exceeding 200 percent and a foreign debt in excess of U.S.$100
billion, Brazil, since 1983, has subjected itself to IMFization, with
its consequent deprivation of the lower and middle classes.
Nevertheless, compliance with IMF terms remained problem-
atic and credit was periodically suspended.

In Colombia a vicious cycle of insurgency and selective military repression appeared to have been broken by President Belisario Betancur, elected in 1981. In 1982 he ended a state of siege
that had been in effect for several years. He also offered amnesty to political prisoners and to guerrillas who would lay down
their arms. By 1984 a truce had been arranged with the largest
group, known as FARC, and promising negotiations were under way with the next largest, the so-called M-19 movement.
The Betancur government had also launched investigations into
the fate of the "disappeared" and into the activities of Right-

wing death squads and, in general, had shown extraordinary respect for human rights.

Narco-dollars had provided for a narrowly distributed prosperity of sorts, but the mushrooming drug trade had also contributed to the general climate of violence. Betancur imposed a new state of siege to combat drug dealers after the interior minister was assassinated in mid-1984. The crackdown in Colombia has driven many of the drug traffickers into Peru and Ecuador, causing new headaches for the besieged civilian governments of those countries.

Peru has yet to emerge from its economic crisis of the 1970s. Furthermore, in the early 1980s it had experienced a growing insurgency among Indians, particularly in the area of Ayacucho, under the leadership of a movement known as Sendero Luminoso (Shining Path). In 1984 a spate of strikes by teachers and civil servants compounded the turmoil and prompted Belaúnde periodically to declare a nationwide state of emergency. Belaúnde's party was almost buried in the elections of April 1985, which resulted in a strong plurality for the APRA and its youthful presidential candidate, Alan García Pérez.

REAGAN'S WARS: UNOBTAINABLE VICTORY, OBTAINABLE PEACE

The Reagan Administration, like Great Britian's Churchill a few decades back, seems now to be presiding, probably unwittingly and certainly unwillingly, over the liquidation of an empire. The vehicles of access, leverage, or control that served in the past to bend even the more developed and more distant Latin American countries to the will of the United States are no longer available or adequate for that purpose.

The U.S. banks and international financial institutions that once held Latin American countries hostage have themselves become the hostages. With U.S. banks so dramatically overextended, leverage now belongs, to a large and increasing degree, to the debtor countries that by merely threatening to default can bring financial institutions to their knees. Nor can the United States so readily turn the tables by conspiring against uncooperative governments. Having played the military card so heavy-handedly in the 1960s and 1970s, the United States now finds itself short on trumps as angry civilian populations turn on their uniformed oppressors.

Meanwhile, in the spreading conflict in Central America, the Reagan Administration, fighting a phantom (Soviet-Cuban aggression), has nothing to win but much to lose. The Soviet Union has shown little enthusiasm for supporting revolutionary movements or governments in Central America and great reluctance to engage the United States in the area. It cannot be taken for granted, however, that the insistence of the Republican leadership on casting the Central American conflict as a Cold War confrontation will not become a self-fulfilling prophecy.

United States military sales and aid to all of Central America totaled $372.7 million for the years 1980 through 1983, more than twice the total for the previous thirty years. The figure for 1984 alone was $320 million, with another $520 million extended as "security" assistance. Those figures do not include expenditures for the "covert" war against Nicaragua, which by early 1984 already exceeded $80 million.

Thus, the United States is now spending well over a billion dollars annually in Central America, more than a million a day in El Salvador alone. From what began as the extension of military training, arms, and advisers to the Salvadoran government, we now find U.S. pilots flying U.S. reconnaissance planes on daily missions over rebel-held territory, selecting targets for bombing and strafing by the Salvadoran military. The number of U.S. military "advisers" in El Salvador has increased from the initial "ceiling" figure of fifty-five to more than 100, not counting the training teams rotated in and out or the very substantial CIA presence. Now armed with machine-guns, U.S. "advisers" accompany Salvadoran soldiers on "training" patrols that sometimes find themselves in combat.

From what began as a covert war waged by surrogates drawn from remnants of Somoza's National Guard, the United States, through the CIA, moved to direct involvement in the bombing of strategic targets and the mining of harbors. The CIA's surrogate army, no longer covert, has grown to at least 12,000. Nevertheless, even the CIA has concluded, in a National Intelligence Estimate provided to Congress in late 1983, that there are no circumstances under which the U.S.-backed *contras* can achieve their goal of a military or political victory over the San-dinistas. The *contras*, they reported, lacked both the military ca-pability and indigenous political support.[34] Retiring SOUTH-COM Commander Paul Gorman offered a similar assessment in February 1985.

Unable to destabilize the Sandinista government, the Reagan Administration is destabilizing instead the governments of Honduras and Costa Rica. As the decade of the 1980s opened, Honduras and Costa Rica, despite severe economic problems, had managed to avoid domestic strife and to remain aloof from the fighting elsewhere in the region. No more. Honduras, se-lected as a staging area for the wars against Nicaragua and against Salvadoran rebels, has been virtually occupied by the U.S. armed forces. A number of U.S. troops ranging from sev-eral hundred to several thousand is on duty or on maneuvers at all times now in Honduras, and permanent U.S. military in-stallations are cropping up all over the country. Border inci-dents between Honduras and Nicaragua become ever more fre-quent and menacing. Moreover, organized insurgency has been growing in Honduras in response to the U.S. occupation.

Nor has Costa Rica, until recently seen by Latin American standards as a model of democracy and social progress, es-caped involvement in Reagan's wars. The northern part of the country is being used as a staging area for assaults against Nic-aragua. Meanwhile, recognizing that the absence of a profes-sional military establishment has helped to preserve their de-mocracy, Costa Rica's civilian leaders have nevertheless succumbed to U.S. pressure to expand and professionalize some units of their armed forces.

Guatemala continues to be ruled by a succession of murder-ous generals. With each change at the pinnacle of power Rea-gan attempts to convince the U.S. Congress that human rights abuses have diminished and a formal renewal of military assis-tance is in order.

More than 100,000 people have died in Central America's wars since 1979. An overwhelming majority of them have been non-combatants, murdered by government forces or government-sponsored death squads. While the military solution sought by the Reagan Administration—reimposition of U.S. hegemony on traditional terms by traditional means—is not obtainable at any price, political and diplomatic solutions have always been readily available. Both Nicaragua's Sandinista government and El Salvador's opposition coalition have always been prepared to come to reasonable terms for peaceful coexistence with the United States, including the signing of treaties guaranteeing that no foreign bases would be established on their territories. The Sandinistas have also agreed to all the terms proposed by the peace-seeking Latin American Contadora countries. Only the refusal of the United States to withdraw its own military forces and terminate its military aid stands in the way of a general settlement.

NOTES

1. Hedrick Smith, "Reagan: What Kind of World Leader?" *New York Times Magazine*, November 16, 1980: pp. 47, 161–177.

2. "CIA Cleared to Act Against Nicaragua," *Washington Post*, reprinted in the *Manchester Guardian Weekly*, March 21, 1982.

3. William M. LeoGrande, "Washington's Wars: Slouching Toward the Quagmire," *Nation*, vol. 238, no. 3, January 28, 1984, pp. 72–76.

4. "The Boiling Caldron," *The Defense Monitor*, vol. XIII, no. 3, 1984, p. 3.

5. Consultation with Barry Sklar, minority staff director, U.S. Senate Committee on Foreign Relations, February 1982.

6. It was subsequently revealed that the informant was Col. Roberto Santivañez, who had directed El Salvador's central intelligence agency, ANSESAL, in 1978–1979.

7. *New York Times*, March 3 and 22, 1984.

8. James Chace, "In Search of a Central American Policy," *New York Times Magazine*, November 15, 1984, pp. 48–51, 60–70.

9. Washington Office on Latin America, *Latin America Update*, vol. X, no. 1, January–February, 1985, pp. 1, 5.

10. Thomas Walker, ed., *Nicaragua in Revolution* (New York: Praeger, 1981); also Managua newspapers *La Prensa* and *Barricada*, 1981, and conversations with Reynaldo Tefel Vélez, director of social security, Managua, January 1980, and with Celina U. Peñalba, Nicaraguan ministry of housing, Albuquerque, May 1981.

11. "Soviet and Cuban Military Involvement," *The Defense Monitor*, vol. XIII, no. 3, 1984, p. 9.

12. Fred Hiatt, "Retired Military Officers Lead Groups Aiding the Contras," *Washington Post Weekly*, December 24, 1984, p. 17.

13. "CNSS Requests Investigations of CIA Domestic Operation," *First Principles*, September–October, 1984, p. 13.

14. Jonathan Steele and Tony Jenkins, "The Contras' Litany of Destruction," *Manchester Guardian*, November 25, 1984.

15. Lieutenant Col. Edward L. King (Ret.), "Out of Step, Out of Line: U.S. Military Policy in Central America," Unitarian Universalist Service Committee, September 11, 1984, pp. 17–29. Colonel King reported that the Sandinista Army was organized into approximately twelve multiobjective motorized infantry battalions; two or three armored brigades equipped with some fifty aged and worn T-54 and T-55 Soviet medium tanks, thirty to sixty used PT-76 Soviet light amphibious tanks and armored personnel carriers; and several field artillery and antiaircraft battalions, generally armed with older model Soviet 85, 122, and 152 MM guns supported by rocket launcher and heavy mortar companies.

16. Leyda Barbieri, "Claiming Honduras as Our Own: The Rise and Fall of a Democracy," *Worldview*, vol. 27, no. 4, April 1984, pp. 5–13.

17. *Central America Report*, vol. XII, no. 1, January 11, 1985.

18. Lieutenant Col. Edward L. King (Ret.), "Out of Step, Out of Line," p. 38.

19. Dan Williams, "Honduras Reportedly Wants Change in U.S. Ties," *Los Angeles Times*, July 5, 1984.

20. Joseph Eldridge, "Lay Off Costa Rica," *New York Times*, May 14, 1984.

21. U.S. Department of State, "Sustaining a Consistent Policy in Central America One Year After the Bipartisan Commission Report," Special Report No. 124, April 1985, p. 20.

22. Dennis Volman, "U.S. Anti-Sandinista Efforts Begin to Strain Ties with Costa Rica," *Christian Science Monitor*, July 3, 1984.

23. "Guatemala," *The Defense Monitor*, vol. XIII, no. 3, 1984, p. 13.

24. Victor Perea, "Guatemala Under Siege: Chaos in the Scorched Earth," *The Nation*, vol. 238, no. 3, January 28, 1984, pp. 92–94.

25. *Central America Report*, vol. XII, no. 1, January 11, 1985.

26. *International Legal Materials*, vol. XXIV, no. 1, January 1985, pp. 219–232.

27. Roy Gutman, "America's Diplomatic Charade," *Foreign Policy*, no. 56, Fall 1984, pp. 3-23.

28. Marc Pierini, "The Role of the European Community in Central America," paper presented at the Conference on Prospects for Peace in Central America: The International Dimension, Las Cruces, New Mexico, March 25, 1985.

29. United States Information Service, American Republic File 317, February 14, 1985, pp. 10–13.

30. Robert Borosage and Peter Kornbluh, "The Smear-Nicaragua Campaign: Behind Reagan's Propaganda Blitz," *Nation*, vol. 240, no. 14, April 13, 1985, pp. 423–426.

31. Reports on events in Grenada and on the Reagan Administration's misrepresentations of those events were taken from a number of newspapers and magazines, including in particular, the *New York Times*, the *Washington Post*, and the *Manchester Guardian Weekly*.

32. Copies of the arms accords were released to the public by the Department of State, along with minutes of the meetings of the Central Committee of the New Jewel Movement and other kinds of documents.

33. On October 21, 1984, NBC News reported that there had been at least twenty-two additional casualties among U.S. servicemen, six killed and sixteen wounded, that had not been reported at the time of the invasion. The Pentagon denied it.

34. "Nicaragua," *The Defense Monitor*, vol. XIII, no. 3, 1984, p. 12.

9

Conclusion: The Limits of Hegemony

STABILITY AND INFLUENCE, IRONY AND HYPOCRISY

Destabilization is an awkward business for a country that has made stability the major professed goal of its foreign policy. All U.S. administrations in the period since World War II, from the most liberal to the most conservative, have maintained that stability in friendly countries is in the long-term national interest of the United States. Foreign affairs spokesmen have stressed, in particular, the necessity of promoting stability in areas, such as Latin America, considered strategically important to the United States.

That being the case, it is at once ironic and tragic that the United States can always be expected to frustrate or, if necessary, to crush revolutionary movements in client states. Countries that have undergone successful revolution tend to be far more stable than those in which progressive movements have been thwarted. And countries in which revolutions have been aborted are the least stable of all.

The redistribution that generally takes place within the first few years following the consolidation of a revolution gives most citizens a stake in the new government. That loyalty is likely to last at least for a couple of decades, until the passing of the revolutionary generation and may, in fact, last long after the redistributional phase has given way to the reconcentration of wealth and power in a "new class." On the other hand, where reform has been thwarted or revolution aborted a vicious cycle of insurgency and repression generally sets in, a cycle which likewise may last for several decades.

Mexico, which underwent revolution early in the twentieth century, and China, which consolidated its revolution in the wake of World War II, are now among the most stable countries in the world. They are also among the "best friends" and most reliable trading partners of the United States.

Among the least stable countries in the world now are those in which the United States, the Soviet Union, or other hegemonic powers are helping unpopular governments to suppress popular movements. In fact, the neglect of majority needs and the frustration of popular political and economic goals appear to be the most common roots of instability. As violent revolution is caused, in part, by the violent arrest of the nonviolent pursuit of change, it might be argued that it is the status quo powers themselves, like the United States and the Soviet Union in recent decades, that cause revolution.

In Guatemala in 1954 a more or less peaceful movement that promised to free the descendants of the proud Mayan empire from the conditions of serfdom they had suffered since the Spanish conquest was crushed through a CIA-sponsored coup d'etat. Violence has been endemic ever since.

In El Salvador, since the 1940s, the United States has supplied arms to the military governments that have kept the peasants in wretched poverty. For the last couple of decades the maintenance of that system of inequality has required ever more official brutality and ever larger tranfusions of U.S. weapons and advisers.

A transformation of that untenable system might have been initiated as recently as late 1979 without full-scale armed revolution. The government that came to power immediately after the fall of the dictatorship of Gen. Carlos Humberto Romero in

October 1979 included individuals who were serious advocates of reform and who enjoyed popular support. It was precisely because of those individuals who were serious and popular and therefore less malleable that U.S. officials urged senior Salvadoran military officers to maintain control and to keep civilian leaders on a short leash. American officials refused to see what was so very clear to Salvadorans—that, with the fall of that government, there was "no way out."

It may be that the Reagan Administration will choose to employ sufficient force to stop the spread of revolution in Central America for the time being, but it will not thereby purchase stability; it will only ensure the continuation of insurgency and repression. If the administration were genuinely interested in stability, it would step back and allow those revolutions to succeed.

United States government spokesmen would claim, of course, that revolutions, particularly those within the U.S. sphere of influence, must be blocked because they are inspired by communism. (The Soviet Union, maintaining the symmetry, charged that the abortive Polish revolution was inspired by capitalism.) But communism, in itself, is not the problem. Since the Nixon Administration's rapprochement with China, there have been more communists in the U.S. camp than in the Soviet bloc.

Some might say that the problem is simply the Soviet Union. The Soviet Union, however, has shown more interest in doing business with Right-wing dictatorships, like that of Argentina from 1976 to 1983, than in giving alms to struggling guerrillas. Moreover, Western Hemisphere revolutionaries are not drawn to the Soviet Union; they are thrust toward it by the unrelieved hostility of the United States.

Fidel Castro, pursuing the tradition of José Martí, was on record as an advocate of political, social, and economic reform long before his band of rural guerrillas marched triumphantly into Havana. Like Martí, he viewed the United States with suspicion and resented its domination of his island nation. It is not at all unlikely that he had envisioned from the start a thorough-going social revolution for Cuba. However, even CIA Director Alan Dulles expressed doubts in 1959 that Castro had any Communist leanings.

A considerable degree of socialization of the economy would surely have been undertaken regardless of the stance of the U.S. government. But Castro was (and still is) a nationalist. It is most unlikely that he would have freely chosen, in the absence of hostile actions by the United States, a path of subservience to the Soviet Union.

It was only after the United States had discontinued trade with Cuba, the CIA had entered into a contract with the Mafia for the assassination of Castro, and CIA-led Cuban exiles had invaded the island at the Bay of Pigs that Castro declared himself to be a Marxist-Leninist. After the United States succeeded in 1964 in coaxing all of the Western Hemisphere states except Mexico to join in a trade embargo against Cuba, trade with and aid from the Soviet bloc became an indispensable lifeline, and Soviet military backing stood as a major barrier to overt U.S. military aggression. Despite repeated incidents of covert invasion, economic sabotage, and assassination attempts extending at least through 1972, the Castro government has consistently responded favorably to friendly overtures from the United States. For that matter, the Soviet Union, anxious to be relieved of the burden of supporting Cuba, has also responded favorably to such overtures.

Now the Reagan Administration would have us believe that Castro has methodically guided the leaders of Nicaragua's revolution into the Soviet camp. Nothing could be farther from the truth. Just a week after the departure of Somoza and the cessation of hostilities in Nicaragua, a jubilant twenty-six member delegation of Sandinistas arrived in Cuba to join in Cuba's 26th of July celebration. On that occasion, a seasoned Castro urged the victorious young rebels to observe caution and moderation in the pursuit of revolutionary goals. Above all, he warned them not to engage in unnecessary provocation of the United States. Castro's message was addressed also to the United States. This latest revolution, he said, need not and should not produce a "New Cuba"; rather, it should produce a "New Nicaragua."[1]

While proclaiming the philosophical pillars of their foreign policy to be self-determination and nonalignment, the leaders of the New Nicaragua went out of their way to try to establish good relations with the United States. They even agreed to repay the staggering foreign debt contracted by Somoza for the purpose of feathering his own nest and bombing his own cities. But the Reagan Administration, in terminating aid to Nicaragua and imposing a credit freeze, left the revolutionary government with a vexing dilemma. In the absence of U.S. assistance, Nicaragua had little choice but to seek aid from every feasible source, even though acceptance of aid from countries the United States considered unfriendly was sure to intensify U.S. hostility.

When the United States, in the spring of 1981, cancelled a $9.6 million credit to Nicaragua for the purchase of wheat, the Soviet Union came to the rescue with a donation of more than 20,000 tons of wheat. This transaction was made possible, paradoxically, by the Reagan Administration's decision to lift the grain embargo that had been imposed by the Carter Administration on the Soviet Union.

That the United States, always proclaiming stability and influence to be its goals, would, by its own actions, perpetuate instability and systematically drive potentially friendly governments into dependence upon the Soviet Union seems ironic indeed. The usual liberal explanation for the "failures" and absurdities of U.S. foreign policy is bungling bureaucratic inefficiency and outright ignorance. Evidence to support explanations of that sort is plentiful. But the selective ignorance and ideological blinders that are characteristic of individuals and institutions in the U.S. foreign policymaking apparatus are not subject to correction because they are self-serving.[2]

The better explanation, then, lies not in irony but in hypocrisy. Stability, as such, is not and never has been a major goal of U.S. foreign policy. The last thing U.S. policymakers want to see is a revolution, or for that matter an election, that brings to power a truly independent, democratic, socialist government in "our own" hemisphere. Such a model might prove irresistible to the repressed and exploited elsewhere.

THE ECONOMICS OF REPRESSION

Optimists will surely be tempted to see the U.S. posture at the Cancun North-South Summit of 1981 as the last vulgar gasp of an approach to "development" that should have been buried long ago—buried not by its supposed benefactors but by its supposed beneficiaries. The Reagan Administration's for-profit-only formula for feeding the Third World's hungry masses is crude but not so very different, in essence, from previous U.S. approaches. It flows from the same basic assumptions that have underpinned development theory and the same ultimate objectives that have guided U.S. development policy for more than two decades.

Convinced that exotic peoples, especially if they were barefoot and illiterate, suffered from attitudinal weaknesses, U.S. officials and academicians firmly asserted and probably believed that the imposition of foreign models on their societies was for their own good. An AID director in Northeast Brazil in 1963–1964, justifying the agency's effort to undermine the Superintendency for the Development of the Northeast, said, "They didn't see their problems as clearly as we felt we did."[3]

United States officials structured events in the Third World on the assumption that the problems in Africa, Asia, and Latin America lay in the quality of the Africans, Asians, and Latin Americans. The blame for poverty and powerlessness was placed squarely on the poor and powerless.

Even the most overeducated of the U.S. advocates and planners of development programs have professed to believe that the interests of multinational corporations and of Third World democrats and reformers could be served simultaneously, and even the most generous-minded have found it necessary to plead that development was being promoted as a means to "security." Thus, democracy could be welcomed—within limits—and reform could be promoted—as an antidote to revolution. But Latin American nationalists have chafed at the limits, and U.S. liberals, feeling betrayed, have beaten a fast retreat, setting the stage for confrontation between mobilized and hopeful Latin Americans and surly U.S. chauvinists.

Reagan's warning, at the beginning of 1980, "We now enter one of the most dangerous decades of Western civilization," may well turn out to be self-fulfilling prophecy.[4] But the Reagan presidency is not the only reason Third World prospects for the 1980s are grim.

Latin America now faces its worst economic and financial crisis since the Great Depression of the 1930s. In the region as a whole, production was declining by 3 to 4 percent annually in the early 1980s. Per capita productivity declined by 10 percent between 1980 and 1984. Meanwhile, inflation was rising sharply; by 1985 the region's average annual inflation was running at more than 100 percent.[5]

Most of the Latin American countries have fallen into an international version of debt peonage from which they could never hope to emerge without a revolution of sorts in the international financial system. The total external debt of Latin American countries rose from $75.4 billion in 1975 to some $360 billion in 1984. More than one-third of the region's total export income was devoted to meeting interest payments alone, not to mention amortization.

Increases in oil prices in the 1970s only partially explain the soaring debts. Unproductive use of capital and the debt treadmill itself—especially in light of sharp increases in nominal and real interest rates—share responsibility.

Moreover, Latin American debt in general is increasingly owed to private transnational banks rather than to governmental or intergovernmental institutions. Credit from commercial banks tends to be both high interest and short term. Obligations with maturation of less than one year increased from 15 percent of the region's total foreign debt in 1965 to 23 percent in 1981.[6]

Not surprisingly, with public as well as private financial institutions, Latin America's few democracies tend to suffer from a lower credit rating than do the dictatorships. The International Monetary Fund has always claimed that its loan decisions were apolitical except for a general hesitancy to extend loans to unstable governments. Nevertheless, in the fall of 1980, while Jamaica's democratic socialist government of Michael Manley suffered from a virtually complete banker's boycott, the IMF approved loans to the shaky juntas of El Salvador and Bolivia. The loan to Bolivia was approved despite the fact that a member of the IMF's own team was detained by the drug-dealing generals. The loan to El Salvador had to be approved without on-site inspection because the level of civil strife was such that the government could not guarantee the IMF envoy's personal safety.[7]

Most Latin American countries are also plagued by high rates of unemployment, not to mention underemployment. It has not been uncommon for more than one-third of the labor force to be unemployed. Furthermore, the currently favored formula for economic growth, stressing capital-intensive industry and agribusiness and production primarily for export, secondarily for a cosmopolitan elite, simply writes off large portions of national populations who are needed neither as workers nor as consumers.

Those who are written off by the economic planners cannot be entirely ignored, however. The poverty-striken are presumed to be inclined to insurrection, or at least susceptible to Marxist teachings. Well-trained and well-funded intelligence agencies, police forces, and military establishments are thought to be needed to teach them to appreciate the "free world."

PRAETORIANISM AND THE ARMS RACE

By 1985, the dictatorial regimes of Bolivia, Argentina, and Uruguay had given way to democratic governments. The gradual *abertura*, or opening, of Brazil's two-decade-old military regime had finally produced a civilian president. Chile's ruling tyrant remained unyielding but was clearly on the defensive. One may hope that South America in the years ahead will enjoy an interlude of freedom and democracy; but praetorianism is also resilient. The attractions of the presidential palace, of power and its perquisites, are not easily forgotten by the men in uniform. Furthermore, a return to free-wheeling democracy, particularly if it means increasing participation by the lower classes, would surely appear threatening to their sense of order as well as to their institutional interests. In Latin America, as Bolivia can attest, even revolution has offered no long-term guarantee against praetorianism.

The organizational and technological modernization of the Latin American military, undertaken in the 1950s and 1960s primarily under the impetus of the United States, was premised on the need for a global strategy in the face of a permanent global war. That premise was shattered by U.S. detente with both the Soviet Union and the Peoples Republic of China during the Republican administrations of 1968–1977. Nevertheless, Latin America's arms imports tripled during those years. By 1980, U.S.-Soviet relations were once again strained but hardly by Soviet support for insurrection in Latin America. Both the Soviet Union and China had been highly supportive of some of the most counterrevolutionary regimes in the area. Far from dampening the arms race, however, such convergence of great power interests fueled it all the more, as the communist states joined the capitalist ones in competing for the hearts and mines of military dictators. The arms race, like the praetorianism that accelerates it, has its own momentum, independent of the supposed ideological struggles of the great powers.

THE PASSING OF PAX AMERICANA

Latin America's greatest tragedy of the "dangerous decade" continues to be the spreading conflict in Central America. Reagan has shunned all overtures—from Latin American and European allies, from the FDR, the Salvadoran political opposition in exile, from Nicaragua's Sandinista government, and from the U.S. Congress—for peace through negotiation. Instead, in El Salvador he has steadily increased U.S. military assistance and increased pressure on the corrupt and demoralized Salvadoran armed forces to seize the initiative. He cannot hope to win, however; he can only hope to postpone defeat.

In Nicaragua, the Reagan Administration has no prospect of driving the Sandinistas from power or reversing the changes in social structure achieved at the cost of some 50,000 lives. It will continue, however, to cause widespread death and destruction. It is likely to snuff out Nicaragua's prospects for democracy. And it is likely to push the country toward a relationship of dependency on the Soviet Union desired neither by Nicaragua nor by the Soviet Union. It also threatens to submerge the entire Central American region in a chaotic mélange of internal and external wars from which would emerge no winners—only losers.

Reagan's wars in Central America are not proxy wars between the superpowers, as his administration has claimed. There are indeed foreigners on both sides of the issues; but the foreigners who matter most, on both sides, are U.S. citizens—

hawks and doves whose still unresolved conflict is being played
out this time in Central America. Nor are they civil wars in the
usual sense attached to that phrase. They are no longer revolutionary wars: the Nicaraguans won theirs in 1979; even El
Salvador's defeated oligarchy fled to Miami long ago. These wars
are, rather, colonial wars. Only the massive involvement of the
United States sustains them. At issue is not the identity of individual policymakers or the precise nature of policy but, rather,
whether or not the United States will retain a veto power over
policy and the selection of policymakers.

United States strategy, in keeping with the general late-
twentieth-century approach to hegemony, has been to maintain in Latin America all the advantages and all the controls implied by colonialism without assuming any of its responsibilities. United States policy makers have been able to insist that
client states offer incentives and protection to foreign agribusiness, for example, and when those businesses swallow up the
land, leaving the peasants hungry and desperate, to dismiss the
plight of those peasants as none of our affair. The United States,
through its military advisers and intelligence agencies, has been
able to pass out arms and money to the vilest thugs in Central
America and then, when they went on a murderous rampage,
to stand back and protest its inability to intervene in the internal affairs of a sovereign nation. But massive insurrection is proof
sufficient that that strategy has run its course.

For a brief period in the 1960s, the United States was generally able to work its will with minimal bloodshed, using a combination of carrots and sticks. Since then, however, the Japa-
nese and European economies destroyed by World War II have
recovered and modernized and have ended the near monopoly
of the United States on aid to, investment in, and trade with
Latin America. Obsessed with the military aspects of its presumed global mission, the United States has weakened its own
economy, leaving it with more sticks but fewer carrots with
which to pursue its goals. Meanwhile, even as previously
promising Latin American economies slumped, Latin American
populations have become better educated and better organized
and less susceptible to facile control from the top.

As Johan Galtung has observed, "only imperfect imperialism needs direct violence."[8] Reagan's desperate and futile wars in Central America show very clearly that Pax Americana has passed its peak. But the fact that the United States has lost its ability to dominate the Western Hemisphere is not to be mourned. What *is* to be mourned is the refusal of the U.S. government to face that reality.

Fortunately, the United States does not *need* to dominate its neighbors. The balance of nuclear terror has rendered previous calculations of geopolitical significance obsolete with reference to a superpower confrontation. As for conventional wars within the area, the cold war has been our only permissible excuse for fighting them. At any rate, the most reliable means of preventing the establishment of new Soviet bases in the area would be allowing neighboring countries to feel confident that their independence was not threatened by the United States.

United States economic interests in the area have diminished greatly in relative terms in the last two or three decades. Whereas in the 1950s, the United States supplied fifty percent of Latin America's imports and purchased 50 percent of its exports, those figures are now about 25 percent and 30 percent, respectively. Latin America is also of decreasing interest to U.S. private investors, having attracted less than 10 percent of new U.S. foreign investment since the 1960s.[9] Moreover, such economic interests as do exist would be better served by noncoercive diplomacy and reliable trading relationships than by a pattern of threats and intrigues.

While the importance of traditional state-to-state ties—generally frustrating at best to Latin Americans—diminishes, other kinds of ties—people-to-people ones based on common interest—come to the fore. The last two decades have seen a remarkable quickening of the two-way flow of information, ideas, and influence among scholars, artists, clergymen, development specialists, and many other categories of Americans, north and south of the Rio Grande. If the U.S. government would only lower its own menacing profile, perhaps the best of what the country has to offer would enter more freely into the exchanges among the Americas.

NOTES

1. The author was in Cuba at the time, July 26, 1979, and heard the speech as it was delivered.

2. The author spoke with Deputy Chief of Mission and Acting Amb. James Cheek in July 1983 in Kathmandu, where he had been "exiled" by the Reagan Administration. Cheek, deputy assistant secretary of state for Latin American Affairs under the Carter Administration, was more fortunate than many other foreign service officers trained or experienced in Central American affairs. Most of them were "exiled" to less pleasant places or forced into resignation or retirement in 1981.

3. Joseph A. Page, *The Revolution that Never Was: Northeast Brazil, 1955–1964* (Grossman, 1972), p. 138.

4. Hedrick Smith, "Reagan: What Kind of World Leader?", *New York Times Magazine*, November 16, 1980:47, 161–177.

5. Conversations with Osvaldo Hurtado, president of Ecuador, 1981–1984, Albuquerque, April 7 and 8, 1985.

6. *IDB News*, May 1984, pp. 8–11.

7. *Latin America Weekly Report*, October 10 and 24, 1980; *Central American Report*, November 8, 1980.

8. Johan Galtung, "A Structural Theory of Imperialism," *Journal of Peace Research*, vol. 8, no. 2, 1972, pp. 81–117.

9. Jerome Slater, "United States Policy in Latin America," in Jan K. Black, ed., *Latin America: Its Problems and Its Promise* (Boulder, Colo.: Westview Press, 1984), p. 237.

Bibliography

BOOKS

Aguilar, Alonso (1968). *Pan Americanism from Monroe to the Present: A View from the Other Side*. New York: Monthly Review Press.

Anderson, Thomas P. (1971). *Matanza*. Lincoln, Neb.: University of Nebraska.

——— (1982). *Politics in Central America*. New York: Praeger.

Arnson, Cynthia (1982). *El Savador: A Revolution Confronts the United States*. Washington, D.C.: Institute of Policy Studies.

Baker, Ross K. (1967). *A Study of Military Status and Status Deprivation in Three Latin American Armies*. Washington, D.C.: Center for Research in Social Systems.

Barber, Willard F., and C. Neale Ronning (1966). *Internal Security and Military Power: Counterinsurgency and Civic Action in Latin America*. Columbus, Ohio: Ohio State University Press.

Black, Jan Knippers (1977). *United States Penetration of Brazil*. Philadelphia: University of Pennsylvania Press.

Black, Jan Knippers, ed. (1984).*Latin America:Its Problems and Its Promise*. Boulder, Colo.: Westview Press.

Blasier, Cole (1976). *The Hovering Giant: U.S. Responses to Revolutionary Change in Latin America*. Pittsburgh: University of Pittsburgh Press.

Booth, John A. (1981). *The End and the Beginning: The Nicaraguan Revolution*. Boulder, Colo.: Westview Press.

Campos Coelho, Edmundo (1976). *En Busca de Identidade: O Exército e a Política na Sociedade Brasileira*. Rio de Janeiro: Forenze-Universitaria.

Chomsky, Noam, and Edward S. Herman (1979). *The Washington Connection and Third World Fascism*. Volume I of *The Political Economy of Human Rights*. Boston: South End Press.

Connell-Smith, Gordon (1966). *The Inter-American System*. London: Oxford University Press.

Corbett, Charles D. (1972). *The Latin American Military as a Socio-Political Force: Case Studies of Bolivia and Argentina*. Coral Gables, Fla.: Center for Advanced International Studies, University of Miami.

Dinges, John and Saul Landau (1980). *Assassination on Embassy Row*. New York: Pantheon Books.

Ferreira, Oliveiros (1966). *O Fim do poder civil*. São Paulo: Editôra Convivio.

Finer, Samuel E. (1975). *The Man on Horseback*. Hammondsworth, England: Penguin Books.

Green, David (1971). *The Containment of Latin America: A History of the Myths and Realities of the Good Neighbor Policy*. Chicago: Triangle Books.

Huntington, Samuel (1968). *Political Order in Changing Societies*. New Haven, Conn.: Yale University Press.

Ianni, Octavia (1970). *Crisis in Brazil*. Trans. Phyllis B. Eveleth. New York: Columbia University Press.

Kommers, Donald P., and Gilbert D. Loescher, eds. (1979). *Human Rights and American Foreign Policy*. Notre Dame: University of Notre Dame Press.

LaFeber, Walter (1978). *The Panama Canal: The Crisis in Historical Perspective*. New York: Oxford University Press.

Langguth, A. J. (1978). *Hidden Terrors*. New York: Pantheon Books.

Lieuwen, Edwin (1964). *Generals Versus Presidents: Neo-Militarism in Latin America*. New York: Frederick A. Praeger.

MacEoin, Gary (1974). *No Peaceful Way: The Chilean Struggle for Dignity*. New York: Sheed and Ward, Inc.

Malloy, James M., and Richard S. Thorn, eds. (1971). *Beyond the Revolution: Bolivia Since 1952*. Pittsburgh: University of Pittsburgh Press.

Millett, Richard (1977). *Guardians of the Dynasty*. Maryknoll, N.Y.: Orbis Books.

Millett, Richard, and W. Marvin Will, eds. (1979). *The Restless Caribbean: Changing Patterns of International Relations*. New York: Praeger Publishers, Praeger Special Studies.

Moniz Bandeira, Luiz Alberto (1973). *Presença dos Estados Unidos no Brasil*. Rio de Janeiro: Editôra Civilização Brasileira.

Montgomery, Tommie Sue (1984). *Revolution in El Salvador: Origins and Evolution*. Boulder, Colo.: Westview Press.

Nef, Jorge, ed. (1978). *Canada and the Latin American Challenge*. The University of Guelph. Ontario Cooperative Programme in Caribbean and Latin American Studies.

Nordlinger, Eric A. (1977). *Soldiers in Politics: Military Coups and Governments*. Englewood Cliffs, N.J.: Prentice-Hall, Inc.

Nun, José (1969). *Latin America: The Hegemonic Crisis and the Military Coup*. Politics of Modernization Series, No. 7. Berkeley, Calif.: University of California Press.

Pérez, Louis A., Jr. (1976). *Army Politics in Cuba, 1898–1958*. Pittsburgh, Penn.: University of Pittsburgh Press.

Rosenbaum, H. Jon, and William G. Tyler, eds. (1972). *Contemporary Brazil: Issues in Economic and Political Development*. New York: Frederick A. Praeger.

Sampson, Anthony (1975). *The Seven Sisters*. New York: The Viking Press and Bantam Books, Inc.

Schlesinger, Stephen, and Stephen Kinzer (1982). *Bitter Fruit: The Untold Story of the American Coup in Guatemala*. New York: Doubleday.

Schmitter, Philippe C., ed. (1973). *Military Rule in Latin America: Function, Consequences and Perspectives*. Beverly Hills, Calif.: Sage Publications.

Solaun, Mauricio, and Michael A. Quinn (1973). *Sinners and Heretics: The Politics of Military Intervention in Latin America*. Urbana, Ill.: University of Illinois Press.

Stepan, Alfred (1973). *Authoritarian Brazil: Origins, Policies and Future*. New Haven, Conn.: Yale University Press.

——— (1971). *The Military in Politics: Changing Patterns in Brazil*. Princeton, N.J.: Princeton University Press.

Tanzer, Michael (1969). *The Political Economy of International Oil and the Underdeveloped Countries*. Boston, Mass.: Beacon Press.

Villanueva, Victor (1969). *Nueva mentalidad militar in el Peru?* Lima: Editorial Juan Mejía Baca.

Walker, Thomas W. (1981). *Nicaragua: The Land of Sandino*. Boulder, Colo.: Westview Press.

Walker, Thomas, ed. (1981). *Nicaragua in Revolution*. Boulder, Colo.: Westview Press.

Wolpin, Miles D. (1977). *Military Aid and Counterrevolution in the Third World*. Lexington, Mass.: D.C. Heath and Company.

ARTICLES AND CHAPTERS

Alba, Victor (1962). "The Stages of Militarism in Latin America." In John J. Johnson, ed., *The Role of the Military in Underdeveloped Countries*. Princeton: Princeton University Press.

Baines, John M. (1972). "U.S. Military Assistance to Latin America: An Assessment." *Journal of Inter-American Studies and World Affairs* 14, 2:469–487.

Barbieri, Leyda (1984). "Claiming Honduras as Our Own: The Rise and Fall of a Democracy." *Worldview*, vol. 27, no. 4, (April):5–13.

Bobrow, Davis B. (1966). "The Civic Role of the Military: Some Critical Hypotheses." *The Western Political Quarterly* XIX, 1:101–111.

"Brazil: The Escola Superior de Guerra" (1971). *Bolsa Review* (London) 5, 49:2–7.

Brown, Cynthia (1980). "Feeling the Pinochet in Chile." *Nation*, 231, 9 (September 27):271–275.

Camarinha Nascimento, Prof. J. (1973). "Conflictos Contestatorios," *Revista do Clube Militar* (Rio de Janeiro) Ano 48, Edição 202 (Nov–Dec):35.

Farer, Tom J. (1984). "The Inter-American Commission: A Personal Assessment." *Center Magazine*, vol. XVII, no. 3, (May/June):38–60.

Ferreira, Oliveiros S. (1969). "La Geopolítica y el ejército brasileño." *Aportes* (Paris) 12:112–132.

Fitch, John Samuel E. (1979). "The Political Impact of U.S. Military Aid to Latin America: Institutional and Individual Effects." *Armed Forces and Society* 5, 3 (Spring):360–386.

Fragoso, Augusto (1970). "A Escola Superior de Guerra." *Problemas Brasileiras* (São Paulo) 8, 88:19–34.

Francis, Michael J. (1964). "Military Aid to Latin America in the U.S. Congress." *Journal of Inter-American Studies* VI, 3:389–404.

Galeano, Eduardo (1969). "The De-Nationalization of Brazilian Industry." *Monthly Review* 21, 7:11–30.

Galtung, Johan (1972). "A Structural Theory of Imperialism." *Journal of Peace Research*, vol. 8, no. 2, 81–117.

García, José Z. (1978). "Military Factions and Military Intervention in Latin America." Pages 47–75 in Sheldon W. Simon, ed., *The Military and Security in the Third World: Domestic and International Impact*. Boulder, Colo.: Westview Press.

Gutman, Roy (1984). "America's Diplomatic Charade." *Foreign Policy*, no. 56, (Fall):3–23.

Hammond, Paul Y., David J. Louscher, and Michael D. Salomon (1979).

"Growing Dilemmas for the Management of Arms Sales." *Armed Forces and Society* 6, 1 (Fall).

Horowitz, Irving Louis (1977). "Castrology Revisited: Further Observations on the Militarization of Cuba." *Armed Forces and Society* 3, 4 (Summer).

Hyman, Elizabeth H. (1972). "Soldiers in Politics: New Insights on Latin American Armed Forces." *Political Quarterly* LXXXVII, 3:401–418.

Jaguaribe, Helio (1969). "Political Strategies of National Development in Brazil." Pages 390–439 in Irving L. Horowitz, Josué de Castro, and John Gerassi, eds., *Latin American Radicalism: A Documentary Report on Left and Nationalist Movements.* New York: Random House.

Jonas, Susanne (1974). "Guatemala: Land of Eternal Struggles." Chapter One in Ronald H. Chilcote and Joel C. Edelstein, eds. *Latin America: The Struggle with Dependency and Beyond.* New York: John Wiley and Sons.

Kennan, George F. (originally published anonymously) (1947). "The Sources of Soviet Conduct." *Foreign Affairs,* July. Reprinted in Needler, Martin C., ed. (1966). *Dimensions of American Foreign Policy: Readings and Documents.* Princeton, N.J.: D. Van Nostrand Company, Inc., pp. 69–77.

Kossock, Manfred (1972). "The Armed Forces in Latin America: Potential for Changes in Political and Social Functions." *Journal of Inter-American Studies and World Affairs* 14, 4:375–398.

Lang, Kurt (1973). "Trends in Military Occupational Structure and Their Political Implications." *Journal of Political and Military Sociology* 1, 1:1–18.

LeoGrande, William M. (1984). "Through the Looking Glass: The Kissinger Report on Central America" *World Policy,* vol. I, no. 2 (Winter):251–284.

Lernoux, Penny (1980). "Monetarist Repression: Brazil Spends Its Way to the Guardhouse." *Nation* 230, 25 (June 28).

Lieuwen, Edwin (1973). "Neo-Militarism in Latin America: The Kennedy Administration's Inadequate Response." *Inter-American Economic Affairs* XVI (Spring):11–19.

Lowenthal, Abraham F. (1974). "Peru's Revolutionary Government of the Armed Forces: Background and Context." In Catherine McArdle Kelleher, ed. *Political-Military Systems: Comparative Perspectives.* Sage Research Series on War, Revolution and Peacekeeping, vol. IV, Beverly Hills, Calif.: Sage Publications.

Maldonado Solari, Gral Dr. Jorge Fernandez (1975). "Fuerza Armada,

Cristianismo y Revolución en el Peru." *Actualidad Militar* no. 216 (Lima) Diciembre.

Manwaring, Max G. (1978). "Career Patterns and Attitudes of Military-Political Elites in Brazil: Similarity and Continuity, 1964–1965." *International Journal of Comparative Sociology* XIX, 3–4 (Sept.–Dec.):235–250.

Military Review (1970) L, 4. 25th anniversary issue of publication in Spanish and Portuguese.

Millett, Allan R. (1974). "Arms Control and Research on Military Institutions." *Armed Forces and Society* 1, 1 (November):61–75.

Moffitt, Michael (1980). "The Third World: Deeper in Debt." *Nation*, 231, 1 (July 5):18–20.

Nash, June (1979). "Bolivia: The Consolidation (and Breakdown?) of a Militaristic Regime." *Latin American Studies Association Newsletter* X, 3 (September):37–42.

Needler, Martin C. (1969). "The Latin American Military: Predatory Reactionaries or Modernizing Patriots?" *Journal of Inter-American Studies* XI, 2:237–244.

——— (1975). "Military Motivations in the Seizure of Power." *Latin American Research Review* 10, 3:63–79.

——— (1966). "Political Development and Military Intervention in Latin America." *The American Political Science Review* 60:616–626.

——— (1980). "The Military Withdrawal from Power in South America." *Armed Forces and Society* 6, 4 (Summer):614–624.

Nef, Jorge (1974). "The Politics of Repression: The Social Pathology of the Chilean Military." *Latin American Perspectives* 1, 2 (Summer).

Nordlinger, Eric A. (1970). "Soldiers in Mufti: The Impact of Military Rule upon Economic and Social Change in the Non-Western States." *American Political Science Review* LXIX, 64:1131–1148.

Nunn, Frederick, M. (1972). "Military Professionalism and Professional Militarism in Brazil, 1870–1970: Historical Perspectives and Political Implications." *Journal of Latin American Studies* (London) 4, 1:29–54.

O'Donnell, Guillermo (1978). "Reflections on the Patterns of Change in the Bureaucratic-Authoritarian State." *Latin American Research Review* XIII, 1.

Petras, James (1980). "Terrorism in El Salvador: The Junta's War Against the People." *Nation* 231, 21 (December 20):1, 673–676.

Philip, George (1976). "The Soldier as Radical: The Peruvian Military Government, 1968–1975." *Journal of Latin American Studies* 8, 1 (May):29–51.

Powell, John Duncan (1965). "Military Assistance and Militarism in Latin America." Part I. *The Western Political Quarterly* XVIII, 2:382–392.

Redick, John R. (1975). "Prospects for Arms Control in Latin America." *Arms Control Today* 5, 9 (September):1–3.

Remmer, Karen L. (1978). "Evaluating the Policy Impact of Military Regimes in Latin America." *Latin American Research Review* XII, 2.

Russett, Bruce, and Alfred Stepan (1972). "New Jobs for the Brass: The Military in Public Affairs." *Nation* 215, 21 (December):655–657.

Schaeffer, Ronald (1972). "The 1940 Small Wars Manual and the 'Lessons of History.' " *Military Affairs* XXXVI, 2 (April):46–51.

Slater, Jerome (1984). "United States Policy in Latin America." Chapter 14 in Jan K. Black, ed. *Latin America: Its Problems and Its Promise*. Boulder, Colo.: Westview Press.

Smith, Hedrick (1980). "Reagan: What Kind of World Leader?" *New York Times Magazine*, November 16:47, 161–177.

Smith, Peter Seaborn (1971). "Bolivian Oil and Brazilian Economic Nationalism." *Journal of Inter-American Studies and World Affairs* XIII, 2:166–181.

Stein, Jeff (1980). "Reagan's Plans for Intelligence." *Nation*, 231, 2 (July 12):40–41.

Tannahil, R. Neal (1976). "The Performance of Military Governments in South America." *Journal of Political and Military Sociology* 4 (Fall):233–244.

Tyson, Brady (1973). "Brazil: Nine Years of Military Tutelage." *Worldview* 16, 7:29–34.

——— (1973). "The Emerging Role of the Military as National Modernizers and Managers in Latin America: The Cases of Brazil and Peru." Pages 107–130 in David H. Pollack and Arch R. M. Ritter, eds. *Latin American Prospects for the 1970s, What Kinds of Revolutions?* New York: Frederick A. Praeger.

Whitehead, Laurence (1977). "Politics and the Military in Bolivia." *Bulletin of the Society for Latin American Studies* 26 (London, March):24–43.

PUBLIC DOCUMENTS

Heare, Gertrude, E. (1971). *Trends in Latin American Military Expenditures, 1940–1970*. Department of State, Inter-American Series 99. Washington, D.C.: Government Printing Office.

McNamara, Robert S. (1968). "Government Documents: Assessment of the Latin American Situation (January 1968) as It Bears on Military Policy." *Inter-American Economic Affairs* XXI, 4:89–92.

Porter, Gen. Robert W. (1968). "Latin America: The Military Assistance Program: *Vital Speeches of the Day* 34, 18:573–576.

Rockefeller, Nelson A. (1969). *The Rockefeller Report on the Americas: The Official Report of a United States Presidential Mission for the Western Hemisphere.* New York Times Edition with an introduction by Tad Szulc. Chicago: Quadrangle Books.

U.S. Arms Control and Disarmament Agency (1980). *Arms Control 1979,* Publication 104. Washington, D.C.: Government Printing Office, June.

—— (1979). *World Military Expenditures and Arms Transfers, 1968–1977.* Washington, D.C., October.

U.S. Army Command and General Staff College (1971). *Internal Defense.* Vol. I. RB 31–100. Fort Leavenworth, Kans.: August 1.

U.S. Congress, House Committee on Foreign Affairs, Subcommittee on National Security Policy and Scientific Developments (1970). *Military Assistance Training.* Hearings, 91st Cong. 2d sess., October 6, 7, 8, and December 15. Washington, D.C.: Government Printing Office.

U.S. Congress, Senate, Committee on Foreign Relations, Subcommittee on Western Hemisphere Affairs (1969). *United States Military Policies and Programs in Latin America.* Hearings, 91st Cong., 1st sess., June 24 and July 8. Washington, D.C.: Government Printing Office.

U.S. Congress, Senate, Select Committee to Study Governmental Operations with Respect to Intelligence Activities (1975). *Alleged Assassination Plots Involving Foreign Leaders.* Report No. 94–465. 94th Cong., 1st sess., November 20.

—— (1975). "Covert Action in Chile: 1963–1973," vol. 7. *Covert Action.* Hearings, 94th Cong., 1st sess., December 4 and 5.

U.S. Department of the Army (1968). Headquarters. *Psychological Operations: U.S. Army Doctrine.* FM 33–1. June.

U.S. Department of Defense (1970). Office of the Assistant Secretary, Internal Security Affairs. *Military Assistance and Foreign Military Sales Facts.* Washington, D.C.: Government Printing Office.

U.S. Department of State (1973). Bureau of Public Affairs. Office of Media Services. *Arms Sales to Latin America.* News release. Washington, D.C.: Government Printing Office.

—— (1973). Bureau of Public Affairs. Office of Media Services, Public Inquiries Division. *Historical Chronology: U.S. Policy Toward Governments of Brazil, 1821–Present.* Washington, D.C.: Government Printing Office. August.

U.S. Department of State, Historical Office, Bureau of Public Affairs (1972). *Foreign Relations of the United States: Volume VIII: The American Republics.* Washington: Government Printing Office.

"Visit of President Médici of the Federative Republic of Brazil" (1971).

Weekly Compilations of Presidential Documents 7, 50 (December 13):1625–1626.

OTHER SOURCES

Brill, William H. (1967). *Military Intervention in Bolivia: The Overthrow of Paz Estenssoro and the MNR*. Washington, D.C.: Institute for the Comparative Study of Political Systems.

Cochrane, James D. (1970). "Changes During the Past Decade in U.S. Policy Toward the Military and Military Regimes in Latin America." Prepared for the annual conference of the Midwest Association for Latin American Studies. University of Nebraska, October 1–3. Department of State Foreign Affairs Research Series 12248.

Commission on United States-Latin American Relations, Sol. M. Linowitz, Chairman (1974). *The Americas in a Changing World*. New York: Center for Inter-American Relations.

Council of the Americas (1980). "Toward Realism in Western Hemisphere Relations—A U.S. Policy for Latin America and the Caribbean." Washington, D.C.: Council of the Americas.

Estep, Raymond (1966). "United States Military Aid to Latin America." Maxwell Air Force Base, Air University, Aerospace Studies Institute, Documentary Research Division, September.

Finegold, Edmund S. (1972). "Comments on Professor Kemp's Paper, 'Strategy and Arms Control in Latin America: A Framework for Analyzing the Military Dimension.' " Prepared for the Conference on Arms Control, Military Aid, and Military Rule in Latin America, University of Chicago, May 26–27.

Fitch, John Samuel (1980). "A Latin American Perspective on Human Rights and the U.S. Military Training Program." University of Colorado at Boulder. In manuscript.

Frank, André Gunder (1979). "The Arms Economy and Warfare in the Third World." Presented at the annual meeting of the American Political Science Association, Washington, D.C., August 31–September 3.

García Robles, Alfonso (1979). "The Latin American Nuclear-Weapon-Free Zone." The Stanley Foundation, Muscatine, Iowa, Occasional Paper 19. May.

Kaplan, Stephen S. (1972). "U.S. Military Aid to Brazil and the Dominican Republic: Its Nature, Objectives and Impact." Department of State Foreign Affairs Research Series 16217 (September).

King, Edward L., Lt. Col. (1984). "Out of Step, Out of Line: U.S. Military Policy in Central America." Prepared for the Unitarian Universalist Service Committee, September 11.

Kossock, Manfred (1970). "Potentialities and Limitations of the Change of the Political and Social Function of the Armed Forces in the Developing Countries: The Case of Latin America." Presented at the meeting of the Seventh World Congress of Sociology, Varna, Bulgaria (September). Department of State Foreign Affairs Research Series 13872.

Nef, Jorge (1980). "Re-Institutionalization and the Prospects for Military Withdrawal in Contemporary Chile." Presented to the Western Social Science Association Meeting, Albuquerque, New Mexico, April 24–26.

—— (1980). "Stalemate and Repression in the Southern Cone: An Interpretive Synopsis." Presented to the Joint Seminar of the Latin American Studies Committee and the Department of Political Economy, University of Toronto, May 14.

Pierini, Marc (1985). "The Role of the European Community in Central America." Paper presented at the Conference on Prospects for Peace in Central America: The International Dimension, Las Cruces, New Mexico, March 25.

Ronfeldt, D. F., and Luigi R. Einaudi (1971). *Internal Security and Military Assistance to Latin America in the 1970s.* Santa Monica, Calif: The Rand Corporation, December. R-294-ISA.

Rosenbaum, H. Jon, with Glenn M. Cooper (1971). *Arms and Security in Latin America: Recent Developments.* International Affairs Series 101. Washington, D.C.: Woodrow Wilson International Center for Scholars.

Stepan, Alfred, and Luigi Einaudi (1971). *Changing Military Perspectives in Peru and Brazil.* Santa Monica, Calif.: Rand Corporation.

U.S. Department of State (1985). "Sustaining a Consistent Policy in Central America One Year After the Bipartisan Commission Report." Special Report No. 124. April.

Wall, James Thomas (1974). "American Intervention in Nicaragua, 1848–1861." Ph.D. dissertation, University of Tennessee, Knoxville, August.

Wolpin, Miles D. (1977). "Socialism and Civilian Supremacy vs. Militarism in the Third World: A Comparison of Development Costs and Benefits." Prepared for the Annual Meeting of the Canadian Political Science Association, University of New Brunswick, Fredericton, N.B., June 9–11.

INTERVIEWS AND CONVERSATIONS

Bahia, Luiz Alberto, columnist for O Estado de São Paulo. Rio de Janeiro, July 1978.

Beauduy, Guy, former minister of trade and commerce, Haiti. Port-au-Prince, September 1976.

Belaúnde Terry, Fernando, twice president of Peru. Washington, D.C., May 1975.

Bloomfield, Richard, former U.S. ambassador to Ecuador. Quito, January 1977, and Lisbon, June 1981.

Borja, Rodrigo, leader of Ecuador's Party of the Democratic Left (ID) and candidate for the presidency in 1984. Quito, June 1982.

Caamaño, Claudio, first lieutenant, nephew of Colonel Francisco Caamaño Deño and survivor of guerrilla invasion of the Dominican Republic in February 1973. Santo Domingo, January 1985.

Calderon Berti, Humberto, minister of mines and hydrocarbons, Venezuela, and former secretary general of OPEC. Caracas, June 1977.

Calvani, Aristides, secretary-general of the World Union of Christian Democrats and former foreign minister, Venezuela. Caracas, June 1977.

Castillo, Jaime, former secretary-general of Chilean Christian Democratic Party and former minister of justice in Chile. Caracas, June 1977.

Cheek, James, deputy chief of mission, Nepal; deputy assistant secretary of state for Latin American Affairs under the Carter Administration. Kathmandu, July 1983.

Chonchol, Jacques, Chilean scholar and political leader in exile; author of the late President Salvador Allende's agrarian reform program. Rio de Janeiro, August 1982.

Dean, Robert, U.S. ambassador to Peru. Lima, January 1977.

D'Escoto, Miguel, minister of foreign affairs, Nicaragua. Pittsburgh, April 1979, and Bloomington, October 1980.

Enríquez, Magda, member of the Nicaraguan Council of State and a founding member of the Nicaraguan women's organization, AMNLAE. Albuquerque, February 1984.

Fernández, Eduardo, speaker, Venezuelan Chamber of Deputies. Caracas, June 1977.

Gil, Elena, central committee member, Communist Party of Cuba. Havana, June 1979.

Gutiérrez, Carlos José, member of national legislature; since 1982, minister of foreign affairs, Costa Rica. San José, January 1980.

Haya de la Torre, Victor Raúl (deceased), founder and life-long leader of the APRA, Peru. Lima, January 1977.

Hurtado, Osvaldo, president of Ecuador, 1981–1984, Quito, January 1977, and Albuquerque, April 1985.

Jaguaribe, Helio, political scientist, Brazil. Rio de Janeiro, July 1978.

Lema, Narciso, Otavalan Indian leader, Ecuador. Peguche, January 1977.

Letelier, Orlando (deceased), former minister of foreign affairs and of defense, Chile. Washington, D.C., May 1975.

Maciel, Marcos, speaker, Chamber of Deputies, Brazil. Brasilia, August 1978.

McAuliffe, Gen. Dennis, administrator of the Panama Canal. Balboa, January 1980.

Mendes de Almeida, Candido, political scientist and director, Sociedade Brasileira de Instrução. Rio de Janeiro, July 1978.

Moniz Bandeira, Luiz Alberto, political scientist, Brazil. Rio de Janiero, August 1982.

Morales Erlich, José Antonio, member of the governing junta, El Salvador. San Salvador, January 1980.

Moreira Alves, Marcio, journalist and former member of Brazil's National Chamber of Deputies. Rio de Janeiro, August 1982.

Moreno Martínez, Alfonso, founding member and former presidential candidate of the Dominican Republic's Social Christian Revolutionary Party (PRSC). Santo Domingo, November 1982, and January 1985.

Orrego Vicuña, Francisco, director, Institute of International Relations, University of Chile, and prominent Christian Democrat. Viña del Mar, January 1977.

Pastor, Robert, Latin American specialist on the staff of the Carter Administration's National Security Council. Various occasions, 1976–1980.

Paz Estenssoro, Victor, thrice president of Bolivia and leader of the MNR revolution. Albuquerque, Spring 1978.

Peña Gómez, José Francisco, mayor of Santo Domingo and secretary-general of the Dominican Revolutionary Party (PRD). Santo Domingo, January 1985.

Peñalba, Celina U., an administrator in the Nicaraguan Ministry of Housing. Albuquerque, May 26, 1981.

Pérez Olivares, Enrique, mayor of Caracas and former minister of education, Venezuela. Caracas, June 1977.

Pezzullo, Lawrence, U.S. ambassador to Nicaragua. Managua, January 1980.

Poblete, Renato, S. J., Chilean sociologist and religious leader. Santiago, January 1977.

Popper, David R., former U.S. ambassador to Chile. Santiago, January 1977.

Ramírez, Sergio, member of the governing junta, Nicaragua. Pittsburgh, April 1979, and Bloomington, October 1980.

Ramírez Peres, Jorge, counselor, department of the interior, Mexico. Albuquerque, May 1985.

Rey Prendes, Adolfo, mayor of San Salvador. San Salvador, January 1980.

Ricardo, Joaquin A., nephew of Joaquin Balaguer and secretary-general of the Dominican Republic's Reformist Social Christian Party (PRSC). Santo Domingo, January 1985.

Rivas Leiva, Luis, secretary-general, Social Democratic Party, Nicaragua. Albuquerque, May 1985.

Roca, Carlos, member of the chamber of deputies, Peru. Albuquerque, November 1980.

Rogers, William, former undersecretary and assistant secretary of state for Inter-American affairs. Washington, D.C., December 1974, and April 1976.

Smith, Wayne, chief of U.S. interests section, Cuba. Havana, July 1979.

Solaun, Mauricio, former U.S. Ambassador to Nicaragua. Miami, May 1979.

Tefel Vélez, Reynaldo, director of social security, Nicaragua. Managua, January 1980.

Terraza, Pinot, Colonel Mario Rolando, second commander of Huehuetenango Military Zone, Guatemala. Albuquerque, May 1985.

Ungo, Guillermo Manuel, president of the Revolutionary Democratic Front (FDR) and former member of the governing junta, El Salvador. San José and Managua, January 1980.

Uriosti, Monsignor Roberto, auxiliary archbishop of San Salvador. San Salvador, January 1980.

Velasco Ibarra, José María (deceased), five times president of Ecuador. Buenos Aires, January 1977.

Villanueva, Victor, Peruvian social scientist and former military officer. Miraflores, January 1977.

Volman, Sacha Z., consultant to the Dominican government on labor affairs; former adviser to Dominican Pres. Juan Bosch and to Pres. John F. Kennedy. Santo Domingo, January 1985.

Walker, Jerry, U.S. military attaché, El Salvador. San Salvador, January 1980.

Wetter, Raquel, Uruguayan social scientist in exile. Merida, Vene-
    zuela, June 1977.
Wheeler, Wayne, Colonel, U.S. military attaché, U.S. Embassy, Do-
    minican Republic. Santo Domingo, January 1985.
Wilson, Arlen, former El Salvador desk officer, U.S. Department of
    State. Las Cruces, New Mexico, February 1981.
Zamora, Rubén, Salvadoran Christian Democrat in exile and vice-
    president of the Revolutionary Democratic Front (FDR). Mexico
    City, September 1983.

Index

About the Author

JAN KNIPPERS BLACK is Research Associate Professor, Division of Public Administration, at the University of New Mexico. Among her many publications are *Latin America: Its Problems and Its Promise: A Multidisciplinary Introduction* (1984), *United States Penetration of Brazil*, (1977), and *The Dominican Republic: Politics and Development in an Unsovereign State* (1986). Her articles have appeared in scholarly journals as well as in newspapers and magazines, including *The New Republic, The Nation, Ms.,* and *The Washington Monthly.*